Just Be a Dad

Things My Father Never
Told Me

George Cave, Ph.D.

Tignor Publishing, CA

JUST BE A DAD

Tignor Publishing
1230-5 Madera Road #211
Simi Valley, CA 93065
805-501-9429
Fax: 805-624-7956

First Tignor Publishing hardcover edition September 2013
Just Be a Dad is a registered trademark of George Cave, Ph.D.

For information about special discounts for bulk purchases, please contact Tignor Publishing
Special Sales at 1-805-501-9429 or business@TignorPublishing.com.

The author can appear at your live event. For more information or to book an event, contact
the Tignor Publishing Speakers Department at 1-805-501-9429
or visit our website at www.TignorPublishing.com.

Manufactured in the United States of America

Library of Congress Cataloging-in-Publication Number
20139023968

ISBN
978-0-9889575-1-0

For my wife, Carla,
who truly understands what
it means to love someone

For my children,
Thomas, Gilbert,
Joseph, Jarrod,
Aaron, Colin,
Nicole, and Sammy

Author's Note

The anecdotes and dialogue in this book are based on Dr. George Cave's years of experience studying and counseling individuals, couples, and families. All names and identifying information have been changed except where permission has been obtained. Although those examples are from real-life situations, permission has been obtained by these persons to use them. Any similarities between further examples contained herein and other people are completely coincidental.

About the Author

Dr. George Cave graduated from California State University, Northridge with a Bachelor of Arts degree in Psychology. Subsequently he obtained his Master of Arts degree and his Doctorate in Psychology at Fielding Graduate University in Santa Barbara, California.

Being a psychologist is Dr. Cave's second career. His first career was that of an airborne system integration and test engineer and project manager. Dr. Cave made a career change after participating in psychotherapy for himself. After seeing and feeling the effects of research-based treatment, he decided to dedicate his life to helping others.

Dr. Cave has worked with a diverse population of patients during his training and practice at a psychiatric hospital, substance abuse treatment center, adolescent mental health treatment center, the children's crisis team and private practice. Dr. Cave has worked with thousands of individuals, couples and families over the course of his career. His observations and research has indicated that the influence of a father is paramount for the psychological well-being of children.

Just Be a Dad

Contents

Contents

Introduction

This book was written in an attempt to help men come to understand the importance of being a father and a husband. It is not meant to make men feel warm and fuzzy and that everything is going okay or even well enough. It is not meant to make men feel that being a father is all about throwing balls and playing games with their children. This book will demonstrate the significant influence that a man has with his children and his wife. I will show that the way a man treats his wife has significant influence as to the way his children behave. It is nearly impossible to be a good father if a man is not a good husband.

The techniques contained herein are, for the most part, equally important for being a father to sons and daughters. The book, therefore, alternates between male and female from chapter to chapter. The book was also written with the understanding that the father (or father figure) lives with his family. This may not always be the case and, as we will see, a father's influence drops significantly if the father leaves the family home. A man can still be a good father in this case but it will be much harder to have influence on his children's lives. I will also go over the necessary skills and strategies for a man to become a good stepfather and things that will help being a non-custodial father more effective and beneficial to his children.

This book was written for men. The majority of the concepts and behaviors would naturally apply to a mother as well. However, since this book was written for men. I have gone to extremes not to offer advice to mothers. It is assumed, within this book, that a husband and wife will be raising their children together and that when I suggest that Dad make a decision, the decision-making process will include Mom. Additionally, when I recommend that a father engage in psychotherapy when his child is seeing a psychotherapist, this would include the mother as well. When a parent's child is in psychotherapy and only one parent is able to attend, it would be better for the father to attend. As you read through this book, you will understand why that makes sense.

Included within this book are explanations of why children and adults do the things they do and ways to effect change over one's own behavior and the behaviors of others. Also included is the distinction between teaching a child and punishing a child as well as behaviors that are inappropriate for a father and the effects those behaviors have on one's children.

I encourage married couples to work things out and stay married. I believe that, under most circumstances, women are very caring and loving and will do whatever they can to work together with their husband to make a relationship work (there are always exceptions, of course). I am also aware that there are times when a husband does everything he can, and the marriage still ends. As you read through this book, you will probably notice that I too have been divorced. I was single for about eleven years between being divorced and getting remarried. During that time, I went to psychotherapy and learned what I needed to know to feel better about myself and became more emotionally functional.

After six months of psychotherapy, I had never felt so good in my life, physically and emotionally. It was at that point that I decided to change my occupation from electronic engineer to psychologist. It was during this eleven-year period after my divorce that I learned what it takes to be in a successful relationship and applied what I had learned to my own life and the relationship I enjoy with my own children. I also returned to college and received my Ph.D. in psychology with the focus of my study on the influence that a father has in his household.

During the time I was attending psychotherapy, I was able to mend the relationship with my former wife who was about to remarry. Our custody agreement was such that my children and their mother lived in the family home and I would live in an apartment. During my visitation periods, the children's mother would stay at my apartment and I would stay at the house. This was done in an effort to disrupt the children's life as little as possible. Eventually, I talked with my children's mother about buying the house next door. There was some getting used to the idea but by this time she was remarried and pregnant with their first child.

It was decided that this change would benefit, not only the kids, but everyone in that my children could spend significant time at my house giving their mother and new stepfather more privacy and a built-in babysitter. This arrangement turned out to work very well but it was necessary that all of the adults got along well. The children's mother and new stepfather had two children who also became very close to me, and they too spent a great deal of time at my house as well. They are both adults now and I love them as if they were my own children.

This arrangement certainly would not work for everyone but it is important to do what is best for the children. Our children seem to have flourished from the arrangement. It is important for children to see that their parents' love for them is more important than their petty differences. Being a father is the most important thing a man will ever do, too important for it to be done poorly. Anyone can sire a child, but it takes something special to be a dad.

Just Be a Dad

1

A Father's Influence

Being a good father can be the most challenging thing a man will ever do. His actions and reactions can have life-altering consequences for himself and those around him. His influences over those who love him are far-reaching and everlasting. The influence of a father can determine whether a child will become an engineer or be homeless, a doctor or a drug addict, an attorney or a criminal. His influence could determine whether a child grows up to be a caring, loving, polite, and law-abiding adult or remains a self-centered, impulsive, and immature child for the rest of his life.

We, as men, want to use our influence appropriately. If we do, we will find that life can be much more enjoyable, beneficial, and satisfying, not only for those we love but for ourselves as well. We will find that it is much more satisfying to make ourselves the means to our family's needs, rather than focusing primarily on our own needs. When we do this, we realize that our needs are not such a priority. In short, it is better to give love than to receive love.

WHAT IS INFLUENCE?

For our purposes, influence is defined as the capacity to have an effect on those around him, positive or negative. A father's influence will also have an effect on the way that other family members treat each other. As you will see in upcoming chapters, everyone in a family has influence over other family members. However, under most usual circumstances, the father has *more* influence, often *significantly more*, than any other family member. This influence can be by direct contact and interaction, or indirect, that is by the way a father treats others. This will all be discussed in more detail, and become more evident, in subsequent chapters.

The early part of my career as a psychologist was spent working in a psychiatric hospital, primarily with adolescent children and their families. There are a multitude of reasons why an adolescent child might be admitted to a psychiatric hospital. However, the predominant solution to the child's problem was usually wrapped around and within the *family dynamic*. By this I mean the way in which the family members interacted with each other (more on this in Chapter 4). Central to the family dynamic was the father. This was the case regardless of the status of the psychological or emotional well-being of the child, the education of the parents, or the income of the family.

As I worked with thousands of adolescent children and their families, there was in fact a continuous and repeating dialogue, one centering on the important role and the influence that a father has on his children – either directly or by the way he interacts with his wife. This is not to say that the father is solely responsible for the emotional well-being of his children but that the father has *significant influence* within a family.

When a father uses his influence to foster good relationships within his family, the father/child relationship will most likely flourish. On the other hand, when the relationship between a father and his children is poor or contentious, the relationship with him often causes more damage to a child than it does the child good.

Many of the fathers I counseled during their child's treatment were surprised to hear that their influence had any significant effect on the child's psychological well-being. I would go on to explain the significance of a father's behaviors on his child's psychological and emotional development and on the child's subsequent behaviors. I would then continue to explain that when a child is having problems, behaviorally and emotionally, it is Dad who has more influence to produce change than does any other single person in that child's life.

Unfortunately, in too many cases, the father (like most of those dads I counseled at the psychiatric hospital) is unaware of his influence. Therefore, he does not exercise it, nor does he know how to go about exercising it.

Most often, as I explained the influence that a dad holds, the child's father would ask me, "But what do I do? How can I help?" My response would inevitably be "Just be a dad." That might sound like an easy thing to do, but as I already pointed out it is actually very difficult. It's difficult in the sense that the attributes (qualities and characteristics) and skills that make a man a "dad" must be continually developed over the lifetime of his children. These attributes include being patient and kind, being a good listener, and being physically and emotionally available. If a man does not learn how to be a dad early on, the task gets even harder over time if not impossible. Often we just do what we think is right and pray for the best. However, all the best intentions in the world will not make a man a good father if he does not come to understand how to do this.

When done properly, being a dad will be the most rewarding endeavor a man can ever do. Yet it means putting the family's needs, all they hold true and cling to, ahead of one's own needs. It means sacrificing one's own desires for the benefit of the people he loves, and those who rely on him for their very life. This, of course, is not really a sacrifice, though it may sound that way for now. In truth, it is very emotionally satisfying for the father.

Bear in mind that men are naturally selfish and self-centered (egocentric). We want what we want when we want it and oftentimes we want our needs to come first. In men, these are generally innate traits; we are born with them. Even so, as a man's emotional development matures, he comes to realize that his ego strength is derived from the way *he* loves *others*. Nothing is more important than the way a man loves his wife and children. Through this expression of love, positive influence is increased.

DAD'S DEVELOPMENT OF INFLUENCE

Like his fatherly qualities and skills, a man's influence as a parent develops over the life of a child. Dad's primary role in the early years of a child's life is that of providing security, as well as various other types of support for the child and the mother. This security includes emotional, physical, and financial. A father can certainly be instrumental in the caring, loving, nurturing, and teaching of the child, starting at the newborn stage and continuing throughout the child's life. Keep in mind that when I discuss loving, nurturing, and caring of a child, it is not the actual mechanics of the caregiving that I am emphasizing here – which involves feeding, bathing, changing diapers, etc. All that is important, but primarily what is crucial is *the quality of the interaction* during the caregiving.

When a baby is born and continuing throughout his development, the central question of caring and nurturing of the child does not revolve around who changes the diapers, who feeds him, etc. The central question is *Who loves him?* An infant is cognitively incapable of understanding what love is or even who his parents are. Yet a child needs to *feel* loved by those who care for him.

MEN WILL USUALLY DO WHAT THEY ARE SUPPOSED TO DO

I believe that most men will do what they are supposed to do, given the assumption that they know what that is. For example, most men, when instructed how to be a good father, will do whatever is needed to accomplish this. The majority of the time, men learn how to be a father from the behaviors of their own father (or a father figure). They mimic the parenting skills that their father used. This could be good or bad, depending upon the father whose behaviors are being copied. If a man's father modeled good parenting skills, in all probability he will turn out to be a good father himself.

However, let's say that a father is not present in the life of a particular male child – emotionally and/or physically. As this individual develops into a man, he will need to *learn* the necessary parenting skills to be a good father. For example, my mother and father divorced when I was quite young, and my father was absent for my entire life. This meant that when I became a father, I'd had no role model from which to learn how to father my own children. I only knew how to be a "man" by what my mother had told me, and I surmised how that equated to being a father. Of course, I also learned about being a dad from watching the way other men acted.

There is a monumental difference between being a good man and being a good father. A good father must be a good man, however a good man may not be a good father – especially if he does not know how. Both processes, becoming a good man and becoming a good father, are learned. Men are not born with the knowledge of how to be a good father, they must *learn* how.

In addition, in cases where a boy grows up with a father who is absent or abusive, he may learn what *not to do* as a father. However, this does not teach a man what *to do* to be an effective father. To be a good father, a man has to take the time to actively learn how to be a dad. Any adult male can sire offspring but it takes something special to be a dad.

IS CHILD REARING A MOTHER'S JOB?

More often than not, people in our society today, including many fathers, believe that rearing children is the sole responsibility of the child's mother. Interestingly, in times past, the father was intimately involved in the rearing of his children. It has not been until the last fifty or so years that the father's role diminished and became minimized to the point where it seems that he is inconsequential to a child's emotional well-being. This is certainly not the case, nor could it be further from the truth based on recent research in this area.

In a country, and in a world, where men and women often seem to compete for their place in the home, at work, in the community, at church, in political office, and for equal rights, just who has the most influence within the home seems to become more convoluted. In reality, we are discovering that it is quite clear. As you have been learning in this chapter, fathers most assuredly have the most influence within a family, or at least *should* be the most influential, if they elect to use their influence. As you continue to read through this book, you will come to understand why that is.

At the same time, others in the household also play a part. For instance, anyone who has had the pleasure of raising a child knows that when that child is an infant, the infant pretty much runs the household.

The entire life of the infant's parents revolves around the infant. Every need of the child is dependent upon his parents. Still, the father retains a significant amount of influence.

In our household, my wife is clearly the one in charge, however I still retain significant influence. If my wife gets upset, or is in need of comfort, or needs to talk (which is how women exchange intimacy), I am the one who mediates these issues, by use of my influence. In this way, she feels loved, heard, and validated. Without such exercising of my influence, our household would be very chaotic, and subsequently, very uncomfortable for everyone. I want my wife to be happy, to feel loved, to feel that she is cared for and cared about. I do what is best for her to make her feel this way, and I do the same for our children. The way to do this is to "just be a dad."

CHANGES OVER THE YEARS

There is little doubt that the most important person in the life of a newborn child is the mother. Even though fathers are quite capable of caring for an infant, mothers are more so. This is not to say that Dad cannot change a diaper, feed and clean up the baby just as well as Mom. However, mothers are more comforting, nurturing, and loving by nature than are men, and especially more so toward infants and toddlers at a time when those attributes are critical for development.

These are the attributes that create an *attachment*, also referred to as a *bond*, between the mother and child, and they have a lasting effect on the psychological well-being of the child. This attachment/bond with the mother is effectual for the entire life of the child, and it is critical for the healthy development of *every* child. Some researchers go so far as to say that the bond between a mother and child is all that is required for a child to grow into a productive adult. This, of course, is not true. Still, it is quite common for mothers to be the children's *primary caregiver*, with the father taking more of a supportive role to the mother of a baby and later being more of a playmate to younger children. Regardless, fathers also are a *necessity* for the healthy development of children.

The older a child becomes, the more necessary and influential Dad becomes. This develops in a distinctly different, more direct, and separate manner from the child's connection to his mother. It happens through *developing a relationship* with the child. If a relationship is not established between a young child and his father, then that relationship must still be established later in the child's life. That is, if the father expects to have a *positive* influence on the child. Interestingly, a negative influence can be established at any time in a child's life and with surprisingly little effort. However, this negative influence can be reversed at almost any point during a child's life with a few simple changes in the way a father interacts with his wife and his children.

Mothers are critical to the development and well-being of their infant children, and as the children develop, the importance and subsequent influence of a father becomes more and more salient. Somewhere around the age of eight years, a significant shift occurs in children. It is a time when the absence of a father, or having a father who has a poor or contentious relationship with his children (and his wife), starts to become more critical. The consequences become more obvious in the behavior of his children.

That is not to say that all fatherless children grow up with behavioral problems; there are always exceptions. However, there will always be a void where the love and guidance of a good father should have been. Being a *good* father is key to the development of children. Then again, a father who lives in the home and has a poor or contentious relationship with his children, and his wife, will have more of a negative impact on the children than having no father at all. So the central questions are then "What makes a man a *good* father?" and "How does a father 'just be a dad'?" These questions will be explored as the book continues.

TIME TO PUT ASIDE CHILDISH BEHAVIOR

For now, I need to stress that people who care about each other have empathy for each other, that is, they feel the other person's emotions – good and bad. When we interact with our wife and children, we want to behave as if there is nothing more important in this world than the relationship we have with them. There are no excuses for bad behavior. Being the man, husband, and father of the house means that we are capable of not overreacting to things that someone might say or do. We do not need to yell, be verbally assaultive, or be physically aggressive. We are men, and men should not act like children. It is hard to teach our children to act in mature ways and to become healthy adults if Dad continues to act like a child.

WHAT'S NEXT

In the next chapter, we will look more closely at ways to be a good dad.

Key Chapter Points

1. A father's actions and reactions can have life-altering consequences for himself and those around him.
2. The father is the most influential member of the family, and his influence increases as the children grow older should he elect to use his influence.
3. When the relationship between a child and his father is good, the child is likely to flourish.
4. When the relationship between a father and his children is poor or contentious, the relationship with him can cause more damage to a child than it does the child good.
5. Men are naturally selfish and self-centered (egocentric); these are generally traits that they are born with.
6. Even so, "being a dad" means putting the family's needs ahead of one's own, which becomes very emotionally satisfying for the father.
7. Dad's primary role in the early years of a child's life is that of providing security and support for his child and the child's mother.
8. Most men will do what they are supposed to do given the assumption that they know what that is.
9. Being a good man does not automatically mean that the man will be a good father.
10. Fathers are not born good dads but must *learn* how to be a dad.
11. The older a child becomes the more important a father's influence becomes.

2

What Makes a Man a Good Father?

The attributes (qualities and characteristics) that make a man a good father are the same ones that make a man a good husband. Therefore, a good father is, first and foremost, a good husband. This is extremely important to understand. A man who can love, cherish, respect, adore, and honor his wife has no problem being a good father. When the mother/father relationship is filled with mutual respect, consideration, and understanding, the father/child relationship will in turn flourish under most circumstances. When the husband has a deep emotional connection with his wife, it is easy to establish an emotional connection with his child. On the other hand, it is very difficult for a man to be a good father if he is not a good husband. When a husband does not love, cherish, respect, adore, and honor his wife, how could he expect to be able to convey those feelings to his child?

GOOD HUSBAND / GOOD FATHER 101

When a husband has a deep emotional connection with his wife, it is easy to establish an emotional connection with his children. In order for a husband to make an emotional connection with his wife, and subsequently with his children, he must be a good listener. He must be understanding and slow to anger. A good husband is not someone who blames other family members, calls them names, or makes berating comments; he is not a keeper of wrongs. A good husband does not argue but discusses issues without getting upset. A good husband is the person that his wife can always come to with problems, concerns, or worries, and she can do this without fear that he will overreact or blame her. Instead, he practices *the 4 Cs* (calm, consistent, caring, and concerned). Though she may be at fault, it does no good to emphasize that. A good husband listens when all that his wife needs is to be heard, and he lifts up his wife regardless of how bad the situation may seem. A good husband validates his wife's feelings so that she feels that she is loved, cherished, and important to him.

A good father does these exact same things with and for his children. Throughout this book, it will be suggested that a father practice the attributes that will make him a good husband with his wife and then apply many of those same behaviors and feelings to his children. It is also important to understand that there are times when a man does all of the right things yet the parental relationship still does not flourish.

It takes two to make a relationship successful, and some even say it also takes two to mess it up. This latter statement is just not true; one person can mess up a relationship all on their own, regardless of what the other person does. Still, a good father does all the things that will make him a good father, regardless of how the other occupants of the house behave. Even in relationships that end in divorce, a good father acts civil toward his children's mother as one would if he were in a successful relationship. (This will be discussed in more detail in Chapter 13, "Broken Families.")

The health of the marriage relationship may not be fully the result of a father's behavior toward his wife. He may be doing everything within his realm of influence to be a good husband. However, there are times when other factors are involved on his wife's part. This can include inappropriate behaviors, such as substance abuse/dependency, or other psychiatric issues, like a personality disorder or a mental illness. These challenges can make being a model husband very difficult. I would urge a father under such circumstances to continue to practice the teachings contained herein in order to model behavior to his children that they will need as they grow older. All of these attributes will be discussed in greater detail in subsequent chapters.

GOOD ENOUGH IS NOT ENOUGH

Why does this book stress a husband having a good relationship with his wife in order to be a good father? The reason is that even before a child is born, there is an emotional connection between the child and the child's mother. Whatever feelings the mother feels, so feels the child. Also, if a husband is not sensitive to the needs of his wife, how could he possibly be sensitive to the needs of his child? Mothers naturally love the child as it develops within her, and fathers learn to love the child if for no other reason than he loves the child's mother.

A mother's emotional connection between herself and her child is innate. This same type of emotional connection *can* also develop between the father and his child, over time, but it is *not* innate. Since the mother/child connection *is* innate a mother would have to go out of her way and intentionally severe that connection. On the other hand, a father needs to make an effort to make the emotional connection with his children, just as he has to consciously and intentionally make an emotional connection with his wife.

When the marital relationship exhibits anything less than the goals stated above, the best a father can hope for is to be a *good enough* father, but not a good father, and a good father is synonymous with "just being a dad." If a man is content with being *good enough,* he will probably never truly understand what love is and how phenomenal life can be. Good enough is never what a man should strive for, and there is no place on earth where being successful is more important than being successful in the home with the ones we love and those who love us.

Unfortunately, in more than half of families, fathers fall far short of what a child needs from a dad, and damage is done to the developmental well-being of the child. This damage can begin to manifest itself in the form of undesirable behaviors at any age, but can become more evident when the child is about eight years old or may not become obvious until adolescence. A child who has been seemingly very well behaved can become quite a problem as a teenager. There are very specific reasons for this, and it will be discussed in more detail in later chapters.

IS A FATHER'S LOVE EARNED?

Children are wonderfully loving and generally very forgiving of their parents' shortcomings. Even in cases of severe child abuse and neglect, children still often desire a close relationship with their parents, each parent individually and both together. This desire might even be to the detriment of the child.

Most people do not contemplate the details or subconscious motivations of a relationship, especially the relationships children have with their parents. Still a mother's love is generally considered to be *unconditional*. By this I mean the children understand, often subconsciously, that their mother loves them and always will regardless of the children's behaviors. That is not to say that a mother will not be upset with a child's behavior but she will generally continue to love the child.

On the other hand, a father's love may be *perceived* to be conditional, based on performance and behavior. This is not meant to be taken too literally. Instead, it is mentioned to explain that there is a difference in the way in which a child's mind works, and the dynamics of family relationships. Keep in mind that the love a husband has for his wife should be unconditional, just as a father's love for his children should be unconditional. It is just that, very often, children do not perceive it that way as it pertains to them.

Most children who are having problems, behaviorally and/or emotionally, are not consciously contemplating the thought of losing the love of their mother; they do not generally think about it in those terms. On the other hand, those same children may believe that in order to gain acceptance from their father, certain performance and/or behavioral requirements must be met. Unfortunately, if the relationship between the father and child is not well formed, the child can become disillusioned or feel hopeless about ever being able to please her father. Subsequently, she may stop trying to please her dad. This is true especially in the teenage years, when there is a poor relationship between the father and a child. In this scenario, the child may come to care very little about what her father thinks of her and therefore any influence a father has is minimal or negative.

This type of scenario is the root of all kinds of problems within the family dynamic. Meanwhile, kids do not think these types of family dynamics through thoroughly and often merely act in a manner that, based on experience and parental modeling, seems to "work" for them.

MODEL THE DESIRED BEHAVIOR

In order for the father to be effective in parenting, he must first and foremost *model* behaviors that he wants his children to emulate. In order to do this, he needs to have some experience in this area and learn the best way to be a good husband. The relationship a husband has with his wife is the cornerstone of the family.

It is important to understand that all behaviors that children emulate are *learned*. That does not mean that they are necessarily learned from the parents, or even inside the home. Television, for instance, is a major source of *vicarious learning* as will be discussed further in Chapter 3.

But getting back to the father for the moment, part of Dad's job as a parent is to always model the desired behavior. If you do not want your child to yell and call people names, then don't do it yourself. A child will not understand that it is okay for you to call someone "a jerk" when that person cuts you off in traffic but it is not all right for her to call her brother or the kid next door a similar name. So remember, a dad is always a dad – there are no breaks, no vacations, no days off. Keep modeling the desired behaviors.

FEELING THE FEELINGS OF OTHERS

For now, it is important to also remember that the mother and child are connected emotionally, just as the husband and wife should be connected emotionally. And when a father makes an intentional effort, he will also be emotionally connected to his children. So when the child is in pain, the mother and father feel the child's pain. And when a man's wife is in pain, he feels that pain when they're emotionally connected.

In fact, it is not unusual that the pain one feels for someone else is greater than the actual pain the other person feels. For example, I recently was standing on a chair in the backyard when the chair broke. As I fell through the chair, I also fell over and hit several other items on the way to the ground. My wife was terrified. In her mind, I was in dire pain and hurt very badly. She ran over and tried to comfort me, however I ended up comforting her because I was not injured at all. Yet, in her mind I was seriously hurt, and she felt the pain that she *perceived* I was experiencing.

Another example is when my youngest son had to have surgery at two years old. After the surgery, the doctor came into his room and redressed the pressure bandage. My son screamed in pain and I know in my mind I felt every bit of his pain. That night, I could not sleep as I remembered what had happened. The next morning as I went to the hospital to visit him, the memory of the pain he experienced remained forefront in my mind. However, when I walked into his hospital room, my son was running around the room playing, acting as if nothing had ever happened to him.

These examples indicate the emotional connection that people have for one another when they love each other. When a husband and wife truly love each other, and they are emotionally connected, they are one. In the case of an infant, the child cannot actively return the love a parent exhibits, but the love that a parent exhibits towards that child will have a life-long effect on that child and those around her.

DOES THE HUSBAND LOVE HIMSELF?

But what happens when a man does not love himself? What happens when he has feelings of worthlessness, inadequacies, anger, and shame? How does one love, nurture, and care for someone else if he does not have the same feeling for himself? Feelings of poor self-esteem may also make a man feel that he is not good enough to be cared for or does not deserved to be loved. In these cases, it is very difficult to truly and honestly care for someone else. In such situations, it is necessary for the man to learn the necessary behaviors and strategies to love himself, to be secure in who he is, and to be able to direct that security and confidence toward his family.

Men *can* learn to love themselves. This can start by learning to love others, especially his wife and children. This will be discussed in more detail throughout the book. For now, understand that something changes when we treat others in a way that we would like to be treated, and that this happens even when we do not feel that we deserve to be treated that well. What happens is that the way we feel about ourselves changes. This step has a powerful effect on the person we become.

A CHILD'S DEVELOPING BRAIN

It is important to know that when a child is born, her brain is not yet fully developed. A child's brain then develops in a manner that prepares the child to survive in the environment in which she lives. Understand that the term "environment" may refer to the physical environment (the home, the neighborhood, and the surroundings) or the environment that is created by the people within the physical environment by the way they treat each other.

If the environment is caring, loving, and nurturing, the child's brain develops to live in that environment. On the other hand, if the environment is not nurturing or is abusive in any way (with yelling, name-calling, physical violence, neglect, etc.), the child's brain develops to live in the stressed environment. There are many stressors and circumstances beyond the control of parents; however, it is the parents who have the most influence over the child's environment. Parents who have a loving, caring, and nurturing relationship with each other, acting in a way that promotes maximum brain development for the child, can overcome living in a bad geographical area. This is true even in homes that are in neighborhoods where hostility, insecurity, and instability are prevalent. A loving, caring, and nurturing home environment can have a strong positive effect on brain development, even for children with a predisposition for behavioral and emotional problems. Love never fails.

It now becomes easy to see that the environment is crucial to the development of a child beginning even while she is still in the womb. The unborn child feels the feelings of her mother and the child's brain, in utero, begins to develop based on the input received by the mother and the way that she is treated.

MODELING THE HUSBAND AND WIFE RELATIONSHIP

One of the main points of this chapter is that the relationship between a husband and his wife is ultimately a model the children learn from. Children learn how to love, how to resolve conflict, how to treat each other, how to socialize, and how to be successful in relationships, all from watching their parents. A person who is successful in relationships has the potential to be successful in every facet of her life. This is true, not only at home, but at school, at work, and in the community as well.

If the parental relationship is contentious, there are probably relational issues for one parent or both outside of the home with non-family members as well. This could be with peers at work, with employers, or with subordinates, or just during the everyday interactions with people like our children's teachers or cashiers at neighborhood stores. Children learn from watching their parents, in the home and outside the home.

The bottom line is that when parents do not get along together and with others, the children will suffer in their own relationships.

A FATHER'S INFLUENCE ON CHILD BEHAVIOR

Parents often wonder why their child is having problems at school, not sharing with other kids, throwing temper tantrums, or hitting others. These are all behaviors learned, for the most part, at home. Parents do not necessarily need to yell and scream for their children to learn how to throw a temper tantrum, though. But once a behavior works for a child, she will continue to use it until it is no longer useful.

Fathers who model the desired behavior for their children, as suggested, have much better results than fathers who do not. If a father throws temper tantrums, there is a fairly good chance the children will throw temper tantrums too. Similarly, if a father overreacts to situations, there is a good chance that the children will also.

All of this does not mean that the mother cannot instill negative behaviors in a child; however, when the father behaves in an acceptable manner, the children are more likely to model his behavior. If the father responds poorly to his wife's actions, the children are going to be inconsistent and confused in their own behaviors and the way they interact with others.

PROBLEM BEHAVIORS AND RELATIONSHIP PROBLEMS

Problems between individuals within a household are generally attributable to failures within relationships and the *expectations* of those relationships. The biggest reason why teenagers stop listening to their parents, for example, is because the parental relationship is not important to them. Teenagers who value the relationship with their parents will have a deep sense of concern about what their parents (both individually and together) think of them, and they will act in a manner that will make the parents happy (most of the time).

As discussed earlier, often the child is fully aware (although not consciously so) that a mother will love them regardless of what they do. This includes how well they do in school, whether or not they follow the house rules, or any of the other things we would like our children to do without being told. A father's love, on the other hand, may appear to be earned, but it should only *seem* that way.

Men generally work on a merit system. Kids learn this very quickly, and it can be used to the child's advantage, In other words, kids will often make great strides in improving behaviors if they believe that Dad cares. However, Dad must show that he cares not only about the child's behaviors, but also about *the child*. As fathers, it is essential that we behave in ways that show our children that we love them, care for them, value their opinion, and respect who they are as they develop towards adulthood. When we do this, children will generally react in a way that will make us, as dads, proud.

Later in the book, I will discuss how parents, especially fathers, need to be able to separate their own feelings of self-worth from the actions of a misbehaving child. This becomes very important when there is an adolescent in the household who is having a difficult time growing up. It will also be helpful for those who want to help a troubled teen and have the ultimate goal of raising the child to become a self-governing adult. That is, an adult who is capable of being respectful and loving to others, makes good decisions, earns a decent wage, follows the rules, knows how to select friends and acquaintances who are good for them, is assertive enough to stand up for themselves, and generally knows how to function in an adult world.

WHAT'S NEXT?

In the next chapter, we will look more closely at children's behavior. It is not unusual for a dad not to understand why his kids act the way they do or how to change the children's behaviors. Keep reading!

KEY CHAPTER POINTS

1. The relationship a husband has with his wife is the cornerstone of the family.
2. The attributes (qualities and characteristics) that make a man a good father are the same ones that make a man a good husband.
3. A good husband is a good listener (more on communication in later chapters); he is understanding and slow to anger.
4. Practice the attributes that make a man a good dad with your wife and then apply the successful behaviors to the kids.
5. If a husband is not sensitive to the needs of his wife, how could he possibly be sensitive to the needs of his child?
6. A child may perceive that a father's love is conditional, based on performance and behavior, but it should only *seem* that way.
7. When there is an emotional connection between a husband and wife, they feel each other's pain and joy.
8. A child's brain develops in a manner that prepares the child to survive in the environment in which she lives.
9. In order for a father to be successful as a dad, he must first and foremost model behaviors that he wants his children to emulate.
10. The relationship between a husband and his wife is ultimately a model the children learn from.
11. Problems within a relationship are often due to one's *expectations* of the other person(s) in the relationship.
12. Adolescent children stop listening to their parents when the parental relationship is not important to them.

3

Understanding Children's Behaviors

The single thing that causes more problems within a home is the way people behave. If everyone did as they were supposed to do, there would be very few reasons for conflict. Unfortunately, that is not the way it generally works. However, the more we understand about behavior and why people do the things they do, the easier it is to make changes to those behaviors. This certainly holds true for a dad who takes the time to understand why kids do what they do. As you read this chapter, you'll see that the way Dad acts and reacts has significant influence on the way others within the home behave.

As noted earlier, being a dad is not an easy undertaking. It requires hard work and dedication to the task at hand. Part of that undertaking is to actively be a part of our children's lives. Understanding why children, as well as adults, do the things that they do helps us to be more involved and influential in the lives of our kids.

Most dads who do not like the behaviors of their child need to look no further than the mirror. Although this might not always be the case, it is true that a father's influence on the behaviors of his children is so great that it has the potential to overcome nearly any other source of influence. That is not to say that a dad is responsible for every behavior that a child develops. However, a father has the influence, should he decide to utilize it, to establish and change a child's behavior, for better or worse, more so than anyone else within the family dynamic.

FEELINGS CAN BE DEMONSTRATED IN BEHAVIOR

Any activity we undertake, including work, play, or raising our family, raises the question of behavior. In the last chapter, I discussed emotional connectedness. Well, the status of our emotional connectedness is reflected in the way we behave. It also contributes to how we feel. At the same time, the way we feel in general can also be demonstrated in how we behave. If a person is angry, and that feeling of anger does not manifest itself in a behavior that appears angry, then others may not see the person's anger as a problem. On the other hand, if a person gets angry and manifests that feeling by yelling, making degrading comments, throwing things, hitting things or people, etc., his anger and subsequent behavior then becomes an issue.

Say, for instance, that an adolescent is depressed, but he continues to do well at school, to do his chores, and acts as if nothing is wrong. In this situation, his depression may very likely go unnoticed. However, once the adolescent makes aggressive acts, starts to fail in school, or harms himself or someone else, then it becomes obvious that something is wrong and an intervention is needed. So we can see the difference between an adolescent's feelings of depression, and his behavior that is driven (or not driven) by that depression.

A CHILD IS BORN WITH A BLANK SLATE (EXCEPT INNATE REFLEXES)

Once again, it is important to emphasize that *all behavior is learned.* That is extremely important to remember when we talk about the development of a child. When a child is born, his brain is like a blank slate. All of the behaviors that a newborn baby has when he is born are *innate reflexes,* such as the sucking reflex or the startle response. All *voluntary behavior,* on the other hand, is learned as we began to explore in the previous chapter. This behavior is learned from the environment in which the infant resides. The primary caregiver of the baby, who is usually the mother, has a great deal of influence as to whether the child feels loved, cared for, and wanted.

The father also has *direct influence* on the child through the way he interacts with him. In addition, the dad also has *indirect influence* over the infant's emotional well-being as it relates to the environment that the father creates and how the child's mother feels. Does the mother feel loved, cared for, and wanted by her husband? The feelings a mother experiences and the related behaviors she is exposed to are significantly influenced by her husband and those feelings are relayed to the infant.

Additionally, the father has other types of influence over the environment in which the child lives. For instance, Dad can make the environment calm, consistent, and caring or he can make it hostile and neglectful. In either case, this can be done with little or no direct interaction with the infant, but a dad's influence will be greatly enhanced through direct interaction with the infant. Direct interaction with Dad is also important as the child grows older.

In addition, children learn how to behave by direct contact with others, by innate behaviors (reflexes) that are reinforced, and by watching others. Innate reflexes, such as crying, can quickly be reinforced. An infant or young child cannot consciously reason that he is hungry and therefore needs to cry to have his needs met. He feels hunger pains, which are uncomfortable, and therefore he cries. To keep a hungry child from crying is simple, just feed him.

As the child grows older and becomes mobile, he learns from everything and anything around him. He learns by direct experience but he also learns vicariously.

VICARIOUS LEARNING

Vicarious learning, which is learning from watching the behaviors of others, is very influential to the development of a child. And it never stops. Vicarious learning begins as soon as a baby can comprehend intentional behaviors, and it continues throughout one's lifetime. Even as adults, we are constantly learning by watching the behaviors of others. This can be through direct observation, with videos or television, or by listening to someone explain a behavior. Any person can learn a behavior from any other person. For example, I came to be a Christian by the example of my son, who at the time was only twelve years old.

23

Of course, children do not only learn the behaviors that parents want them to learn or from those who love them. Practically anyone's behavior can serve as a model. Children learn behaviors from other adults and children when they are on an outing to the zoo, accompanying you to the grocery store, while riding in the car, and by watching television and movies.

As noted in the previous chapter, television is an extremely influential source of behavior modeling, especially in young children. A child younger than about two years old cannot tell the difference between a television show, a movie, and real life. Can you imagine what it would be like to witness a murder, a shootout, or an assault on TV as a child? You can now see how important it is to be very aware of what is being watched in your household, not only by the young children, but also by others who live there. Hearing the sounds of someone being assaulted or being verbally abused is also emotionally damaging to a developing mind.

Very young children also cannot tell the difference between something being done to someone else and something being done to them. When young children witness traumatic experiences in real life or on the media, they may very well develop the same emotional issues as if the trauma happened to them directly.

Understand that what children are watching on television, or other media, does not have to be real, rational, or an actual representation of the truth to be an influence on their behaviors. For example, children may not realize that the pro wrestling they are watching on television is staged, and they might try some of those wrestling moves they saw last night on TV on their little sister or the kid next door.

The older a child gets, the more he understands that a film is not real. He gradually realizes that if someone gets hit by a truck in a TV movie, for instance, they are not actually hurt. He also comes to see that, per the storyline, this character will not stand up and continue to chase the bad guy. But for young children, even cartoons are a source of learning behaviors. If a cartoon character hits another cartoon character, a child may very well learn to hit others. What may seem like humor to an adult may very well be a learning experience to a child.

As children get older, television is a significant source of *social* learning. That is, it becomes a source of information on how to act and react in social situations. When TV characters that kids admire are disrespectful to their TV families, kids might generalize that behavior to their own family. What seems funny on television may not be so funny at home when those behaviors and comments are directed at oneself. So many times, I have paused a movie I was watching with my kids to say, "You know this isn't real, right?" or "You know that's not appropriate, right?" Most of time, this was done with a sense of humor but there was a serious side to it as well. Often, at the end of a movie, we would critique the film and discuss its authenticity and how it pertains to real life.

One recent example is the *Twilight* movie series, where the female star seems to believe that the only two choices she has available to her for a boyfriend on the entire planet are between a blood-sucking vampire or a werewolf. This film series is fun to watch; however, to think that either of those two very limited choices would be a good life choice would be naïve. Just the same, there is now an entire subculture that romanticizes these movies.

LEARNING FROM OTHER CHILDREN

Even before the age of one or two years old, children learn behaviors from the actions of other children of the same or different ages. Children also learn from their peers' parents, including the way these parents interact with their own children, and the way the peers respond to their own parents. When children start school, there are now dozens, if not hundreds, of other students, all of which are inputting behaviors into your child. Whether the child decides to incorporate the new behavior is up to the child and what the child has already been taught. Meanwhile, the most influential figures in a child's life are still his parents and, more specifically, Dad.

Let's say that a child has been taught that using bad language is not allowed. If he hears another child at school use bad language (and he will), the child will have to make a decision whether to copy that child or do as he has been taught. If the relationship between the child and his parents is one of love and respect, the child will be more likely not to adopt a behavior that he already knows is wrong. In terms of language, like any other behavior, it is important to model the desired behavior. If you do not want your child to use a word, then do not use that word yourself.

It would be a mistake to pretend that we can protect our children from being exposed to the barrage of behavioral input from outside sources. We cannot teach at home everything that children will need to know when they are outside the home. It would be equally misguided to try to keep him from being exposed to every child or media outlet that presents a behavior that is not approved by the parents. It would be better to teach him what appropriate behavior is and to praise him for using it. When a new behavior is utilized that is not appropriate, it is best to calmly explain, "That is something we do not do," and of course do not engage in similar behaviors yourself. Again, model the desired behavior.

TYPES OF BEHAVIOR REINFORCERS & EXTINGUISHERS

What causes and then reinforces behaviors has been exhaustively researched. A behavior that is *reinforced* is a behavior that, when utilized, has a positive effect for the person using the behavior. It is a behavior that gets a child what he wants. That does not mean that the behavior will have a positive effect for those around the user of the behavior. For instance, let's say that a young child comes to realize that when he throws a temper tantrum in the grocery store, he will get what he wants (for example, candy, treats, a desired toy, etc.). In such a case, he will probably continue to use that behavior when he wants something.

Behaviors are very easily learned when a child is young. Even before a child can talk, or express a thought verbally, they are learning behaviors and incorporating those behaviors into their daily routines. If an infant has to cry to have his basic needs met, he learns, even before the age of one year old, to cry for his every need. As this child grows older, he learns to cry, or engage in other behaviors that most parents wish he did not engage in, to get his needs met. By the time the child grows to be an adolescent, some very serious problem behaviors may have developed. I will discuss how to handle such serious problem behavior in subsequent chapters.

INCONSISTENT PARENTING

In terms of reinforcing behaviors, it is essential to be *consistent* with what acceptable behavior is and what it is not. If a dad wants a child to behave in a certain way, he must be consistent with reinforcement for that particular behavior. The reinforcement may be something as simple as mentioning that Dad noticed the behavior and telling that child that you appreciate it. Say for example, "Thank you for..." or "I appreciate that you..." Kids will do a great deal to be appreciated by their dad. So get into the habit of reinforcing the appropriate behaviors.

When an unwanted behavior is learned and it is not reinforced, the behavior will usually be extinguished by the child; that is, the behavior will be stopped. The most difficult type of behavior to stop is one that is *intermittently reinforced*; that is, being allowed sometimes and not allowed at other times. This same concept is used with the design of casino slot machines. One never knows when a payout is going to occur, and little payouts will keep a person playing until all of their money is gone. The same is true with behaviors of children. Say a child wants stay up past bedtime and is told no, but cries and then gets his way. In all likelihood, the child will cry the next time that he is told to go to bed earlier than he would like to go to sleep.

When a parent gives in to a child's behavior on some occasions and not on others, the child becomes confused. However, all too often the child realizes, consciously or subconsciously, that if he cries long enough he "might" get his way. Since the child never knows how long he needs to cry, the fit can become quite lengthy. A behavior that has been intermittently reinforced will probably get worse, possibly much worse, before it is extinguished. That's because the child has been conditioned to act out longer and longer in the hope that he will get what he wants.

If inappropriate behaviors, such as crying or lying on the floor and kicking his feet, are not extinguished when a child is young, he may engage in more extreme behaviors as he gets older. These behaviors may include slamming doors, punching walls, hitting others, doing drugs, skipping school, or worse. Some teenagers are fully aware that if they throw a big enough fit, their parents will give in.

A father needs to decide before the child throws a fit whether or not he is going to give in. If you intend to give in, do it soon so that the behavior of throwing the fit is not reinforced. If the decision is not to give in, then do not give in regardless of how bad the behavior gets. It is better to give in to a behavior before it gets out of control if you are going to give in at all. If a dad is willing to go the distance with the bad behavior, it is best to know that ahead of time rather than saying "no" to something only to give in as the outburst gets bigger.

Again, remember that when reinforcement of behaviors is inconsistent, the child gets mixed messages. He becomes anxious and can develop more serious acting out behaviors. Teens and even younger children may engage in self-injurious behaviors like cutting or burning themselves, making suicidal threats, or even go as far as attempting suicide. This problem could have been resolved when the child was quite young; now it is harder to resolve but the solution is the same. Be consistent; if at all possible, know what you are going to do before the behavior occurs. Then follow through with what you have decided.

GENERALIZATION OF BEHAVIORS

Both children and adults generalize behaviors. That is, if a particular behavior is acceptable in one situation, then it must also be acceptable in a different situation. Children have a tendency to generalize behaviors more often and to more extremes than do adults. For example, if a parent yells at the driver of another car while driving, the child may in all likelihood generalize that behavior to think that it is okay to yell at other people.

Children can also be very specific with their understanding of a behavior. Therefore, the words that Dad uses, even in normal everyday discussions, can be taken very literally. So if my young son, who watches me play my guitar every day, gets caught playing with my guitar without permission, and I explain to him, "Don't play with Daddy's things… the guitar's not yours, it's mine," the child, in all likelihood, will not share his toys with other children. After all, they are "his." It would be better if I explained to the child not to play with the guitar because "It is not a toy," rather than telling him not to play with it because it is mine.

As children get older, the generalization of behaviors can be even more pronounced, damaging, and frustrating. For instance, if a parent smokes cigarettes, it becomes very difficult to try to convince an adolescent that it is a bad idea to smoke cigarettes. Taking this line of reasoning a step further, if the adolescent is led to believe by the actions of his parent that smoking cigarettes is acceptable, the adolescent may generalize the behavior. He may think that it is not only acceptable to smoke cigarettes but believe it is acceptable to smoke marijuana as well. After all, smoking is smoking. Another example is that if the parents drink alcohol, research has shown that adolescents will generalize that behavior to believe it is okay to not only drink alcohol but also smoke marijuana and use cocaine.

CORPORAL PUNISHMENT

Another example of generalizing behaviors arises when a parent uses *corporal punishment* as a means to discipline their child. (Corporal punishment means using physical force, like spanking or slapping, as a means of punishment.) In this case, the child may very likely generalize the behavior of being hit to hitting other people. If a child is hit when Dad is mad, the child may hit others when he does not get what he wants or when he is upset.

When using corporal punishment, one may in fact get the child to comply; however, we have just damaged the relationship between the parent and the child. Additionally, the child was just taught behaviors that we would just as soon the child not use, such as hitting others. These behaviors were reinforced as well.

Research supports, and it is generally accepted, that there is no way to predict the behaviors that will be reinforced by hitting a child. It is also generally accepted that the long-term behaviors reinforced by hitting a child will not be good and any short-term benefit derived from striking a child will have no long-term positive effect. More than likely, this type of punishment will have long-term negative effects.

I also want to point out that when Dad uses corporal punishment, he has either consciously or subconsciously admitted to himself that he does not know what else to do. Things have gotten so bad that there is just no other way to deal with the behavior. This is, in fact, a failure in the relationship between the parent and child, as well as in the parenting process. That being said, there may be a point in the disciplining of a child where nothing else has worked and corporal punishment may *seem* to be the only solution. There will be more on this topic in subsequent chapters.

If a dad wants his child to adopt more adaptive behaviors and extinguish maladaptive behaviors, it is best for the dad to model the desired behavior. A dad's influence is far reaching and long lasting if he chooses to use it. When a father models the desired behavior, that child learns to trust his dad and respect his dad, because Dad has earned it.

MORE ON REINFORCING BEHAVIORS

There are a few more things that we need to keep in mind about behaviors and reinforcing them. The younger the child, the more ingrained the behavior will become if it is reinforced – that is, repeated and is effective *for the child*. Very young children, before they can talk and reason, cannot communicate intellectually, nor can they make their needs known by putting together a logical expression of those needs. Crying is a reflex-type behavior, and it is the only way that most infants and young children have to communicate when they have a need that is not being met.

When a young child cries excessively to get his needs met while in public, he can be picked up and taken to the car and then returned home. If a young child misbehaves at home, he can be sent to his room for a timeout. If he refuses to go to his room for a timeout, he can be picked up and taken to his room for the timeout. When a child is a teenager and misbehaves in public, it becomes a bit more difficult. (And the same would be true at home.) If an older child comes to the realization that compliance to his parents' wishes is voluntary, he can be very difficult to control. This is when the value of the dad/child relationship is critical as well as the influence that Dad possesses.

The older a child becomes, the more likely he is to understand the reason as to why or why not a behavior is acceptable. It is important to know that when we try to reason with our children, whether they are two years old or twenty-two years old, we should do our best to have our reasoning make sense as well as being the truth. Let's say a dad is trying to reason with a two-year-old who was throwing a temper tantrum because he wants some candy, and the dad tries to convince him that he really does not want to have any candy. The child will know that is not true (because who does not want candy?), and Dad's comment will have very little positive impact, if any. This is similar to when a child falls down and hurts himself and comes running over to Dad crying. It would be a mistake to tell the child that it does not hurt in an attempt to stop the crying. The child is fully aware of whether or not it hurts. If someone tells him that it does not hurt, he will start to question his own feelings as well as the legitimacy of the person he is going to for comfort.

A good first practice for Dad when a child is crying is to pick him up and give him a hug. When a child is in pain, being picked up, hugged, and spoken to with a calm, caring voice shows him that Dad truly does care about him. This will not create a needy, manipulative, attention-seeking child. In fact, it creates just the opposite, especially if done from an early age and with sincerity. However, it is never too late to show a child affection, and that his father truly loves him and cares about him. This is never more true than when a child is in pain, emotional or physical, or having difficulty with something.

THINK ABOUT A PROBLEM BEFORE IT BECOMES ONE

It is always a good idea to think about what you would do about a problem before it becomes a problem, if at all possible. This is never going to be truer than in the rearing of children. For example, you see someone else's child or teenager do something that you would not allow your child to do or at least you would prefer that your child not do it. Consider what you would do if that were your child.

Are we to believe that our children will never make a mistake? Of course not! Children learn valuable lessons from their mistakes, just as adults do (including dads). There have been many times when I've thought to myself, "I wish I had handled that differently." And that is not unusual. However, as dads, we can minimize the "I wish I had handled that differently" situations if we already know what we are going to do before it happens.

Being prepared ahead of time allows a father a chance to think things through and not come up with ineffective and even foolish ways to resolve problems. Rather, it allows Dad time to reflect and come up with real solutions to problems. For instance, "You're grounded for life" is not a good response to a problem, *ever*. No one is ever grounded for life and kids know this. Additionally, as a dad, I do not want my kids grounded for life, or at all for that matter, because when a child is grounded so is the adult – and I do not want to be grounded.

It is also very important to understand that there are things a parent has little direct control over. It would be illogical or unrealistic to use a behavioral intervention to try to control such behaviors. An example of this is the age-old question about what age is a child allowed to have a boyfriend or girlfriend? There is a big difference between a daughter having a boyfriend and the daughter being allowed to have a boyfriend. Since we cannot be with our children 24/7, it would be impossible for us to dictate something we have little control over.

Be aware that a daughter *can* have a boyfriend at school without Dad's permission, and that is different than her not having one at all. On the other hand, her choice to have a relationship there does not mean that we, as dads, should sanctify it (if we disapprove of her choice or think she's too young) or should make her relationship more accessible by facilitating it. Facilitating the relationship would be done by allowing the boyfriend over to the house, or taking the kids to a movie, etc. Remember this as there will *always* be relationships of which we, as dads, do not approve.

The best that can happen when we are met with a challenge that we were not prepared for is to learn from it. In this way, if it happens again, we should have a better idea of what we will do the next time. An example would be what is a dad going to do the first time he hears his darling little girl use a cuss word? Another example is what will the father do when he finds out that his nineteen-year-old son was drinking beer? Both of these situations are very likely to occur; in fact, it would be unusual if they did not occur. We will discuss in more detail what to do about these types of issues in later chapters. For now, know that it would, of course, be better to head off the problem than to ignore it. At the same time, allow your child to make as many decisions for himself as possible that are appropriate and safe.

Sometime during the rearing of a child, a situation will arise that you were not prepared for, and you will say something that is not appropriate, not realistic, or both. If you come to the decision that your first response was not exactly the best, explain to your child that "Dad overreacted, and after giving this some thought, I have decided…" Try to keep in mind that our objective as a dad is to raise a child into a self-governing adult. We cannot believe that a child is not going to make some mistakes along the way. How we handle those mistakes is what makes Dad a person his child will come to in times of trouble. If the dad does not handle these situations well, there is a good possibility that the child will avoid talking to his father, lie to his father, and otherwise try to deceive his father so that he does not find out what the problem is.

OTHER CONSISTENCY ISSUES

The rationale for whether a behavior is acceptable or not acceptable should also be consistent from day to day and between similar circumstances. A good example might be whether or not a child is allowed to have candy in the checkout line at the grocery store. If the child was allowed to have candy today, why would it not be okay to have candy tomorrow? There may be a very good reason why candy was acceptable yesterday but not today (for instance, it's closer to dinnertime today). Even so, the rationalization for the acceptance or denial of a behavior needs to stay consistent.

Another thing to consider is the age of the child in terms of consistency and rationalizations. A young child may not understand the rationalization of it being "too close to dinnertime" and therefore, in their way of thinking, if candy was acceptable yesterday, it should also be acceptable today. Keep the reasoning simple for younger children, as they will not understand complicated reasoning. It is easier to teach a younger child by using very simple, black and white rationalizations, such as "We don't get candy when we go to the grocery store." That tells the entire story to a young child. An older child (after about five years old) will be able to understand other reasons as to why something may or may not be permissible today when it was yesterday. Sometimes it can be as simple as telling a young child, "We don't do that." It is then important that *you* don't do *that* too. It would be difficult to explain to a four-year-old, or a child of any age, that he cannot have candy when you are eating candy.

An example for older children might be "If drinking alcohol is not acceptable today, it will not be acceptable tomorrow." The rationale would simply be that it is illegal to drink until a person is twenty-one years old. Under most circumstances, it is *never* acceptable for someone under the age of twenty-one to consume alcohol. That does not mean that every child is going to wait until he is twenty-one before he consumes his first drink of alcohol but he needs to know that it is not acceptable. As you will see in later chapters, there is a monumental difference between believing a behavior is appropriate just because one engages in the behavior and the behavior truly being appropriate.

Once again, it is important to model the desired behavior. If you do not want your children to drink alcohol (smoke cigarettes, use drugs, have sex out of wedlock, hit people, swear, etc.), then it would be best not to model such behaviors. If a behavior is not acceptable in front of your children, then it probably should also not be engaged in when the children are not present either. Of course, sex with a spouse would be excluded from this rule.

On the other hand, it is necessary to teach children that some behaviors are acceptable once they get older. This does not merely include drinking and smoking, two behaviors that most people do not ever *have* to participate in. This might include what time a child goes to bed, going over to a friend's house, or being able to come home at a later time.

PUNISHMENT SHOULD BE REALISTIC

Older children can make changes to behaviors just as easily as younger children, sometimes more easily. Older children have a more developed brain and *should* be able to reason better than a younger child. On the other hand, if a behavior has been ingrained for years in the child, he may continue to use the behavior in the slight chance that it might work to get his way. If a dad gives in to this type of manipulation, the behavior will continue until the dad stands his ground. Even then, the child will in all likelihood raise the ante and act out worse before realizing that the behavior (such as a temper tantrum) is no longer effective.

When an occurrence arises that requires punishment, any punishment rendered should be realistic and then be a benefit to the child. For example, as pointed out earlier in this chapter, "You're grounded for life" is not realistic punishment. Another example might be "You can never see that boy again" when they attend the same school, and there is absolutely no way to keep them from seeing each other while there. In addition, discipline should never be handed out while Dad is upset. One needs to calm down before making decisions that may affect their child or others in the house for a very long time to come.

WHAT'S NEXT?

In the next chapter, we will be examining the intricacies of the family dynamic and how each member of the family affects everyone else.

KEY CHAPTER POINTS

1. A father's influence on the behaviors of his children is so great that it has the potential to overcome nearly any other source of influence.
2. The way a person feels can be demonstrated in their behaviors.
3. All behavior is learned.
4. When a child is born, his brain is like a blank slate.
5. Children learn behaviors through direct contact with others, by innate reflexes that are reinforced, and from watching others (*vicarious learning*).
6. What may seem like humor to an adult (such as cartoons) may very well be a learning experience, for better or worse, to a child.
7. Consistency is essential to teaching children appropriate behaviors and extinguishing inappropriate ones.
8. Intermittently reinforced behaviors are the most difficult to extinguish.
9. Children generalize behaviors.
10. Think about a problem before it becomes one.
11. Children learn valuable lessons – good or bad – from their mistakes, just like adults do (including dads).
12. Punishment should be used sparingly, be realistic, and should be somehow tied to the offense if possible. Try to also make it beneficial to the child in some way.

4

Family Dynamics & Dad's Influence

A *family dynamic* is the way in which family members interact with each other. In a family, each member of a family interacts with each of the other members of the family and therefore an overall dynamic is developed. The more individuals there are within a family, the more those individuals increase the dynamics of the family as a whole.

Think about it. The larger the family, the more interactions there are within the dynamic. This increase in interactions increases the effect that each member has on the dynamic as a whole and subsequently on each of the other members individually. For example, a simple family may be comprised of only a husband and wife, where just a two-way interaction occurs. The behavior and communication of each one affects the other. When the husband and wife are getting along and both are happy in the relationship, then the overall family dynamic has the potential to also be happy or *functional*. This occurs when each member of the family is treated with respect, compassion, and understanding; more importantly, it is when each member of the family feels loved.

In a family dynamic where the wife is upset with her husband, her behavior has an effect on her husband. The amount of effect and the significance of the effect that she has over her husband would be defined as *influence*. It would not be good if a wife was upset with her husband

37

and he did not care. This would be an example of a wife having very little, if any, influence over her husband. This would also be defined as a *dysfunctional relationship*. Note that there is much more that contributes to a relationship being dysfunctional or functional than the degree of happiness that a family enjoys as will be discussed further.

The same would hold true if the actions and/or reactions of the husband had no effect on his wife. This would indicate that the husband has little to no influence over his wife. Influence is something that should be respected, used appropriately, and cherished by those who hold it. It would be a mistake to believe that any member of a family has no influence on the other family members. Influence can be beneficial or it could be detrimental to those within the family, but rarely is influence neutral.

CHILDREN IN THE DYNAMIC

When a third family member is added to the family dynamic, often being the addition of a newborn child, there are now three points of interaction. The parents interact with each other and each parent interacts with the child for a total of six possible interactions. Notice how the total possible interactions went from two for a husband and wife to six when a third person is added. The net effect of possible interactions has tripled. When a fourth person is added to the family dynamic, the possible interactions goes to twelve; and with five people in the family dynamic, the number of possible interactions goes to twenty.

Here are the possible interactions in a family of three (to help you follow how the two interactions between the husband and wife increased to six when the baby was added). There are: (1) a direct interaction between the husband and the wife, (2) a direct interaction between the wife and the husband, (3) a direct interaction between the father and the baby, (4) a direct interaction between the baby and the father, (5) a direct interaction between the mother and the baby, and (6) a direct interaction between the baby and the mother.

It may seem in the family-of-three scenario that the newborn possesses no direct influence on her parents. However, since a newborn has no sense of deliberate thought, her only means of communicating her needs is to cry. This limited ability to communicate and use rational thought gives the newborn significant *indirect* (indirect because it is not intentional) *influence* over her parents. So you can see how any member of a family can affect any other member of the family, either by direct or indirect interaction.

Unlike older children, a newborn's existence is entirely dependent upon her parents. However, it is easy to see that an infant has significant influence over her caregivers merely by her own dependence on the caregivers. As a child grows and develops, her dependence upon her parents for the necessities of life diminishes to the point that the child becomes self-governing. Although the influence of the child and of the parents changes as the child develops, it is always present.

A dad can measure the influence he possesses over his children by the influence that he commands when he is not present, such as when the children are at school or the father is on a business trip away from the children. In such cases, when the relationship is such that the child cherishes the relationship with her dad, a father's influence is very high and a child will go out of her way to make Dad happy with her even when he is not physically present.

In a family dynamic where there are multiple children, interactions with each one of those children affects each of the other members of the family. If the mother and father are not getting along, that puts stress on the children who in turn may not get along with each other. When the children are not getting along, it then seems reasonable that the parents may get upset with the children. There are cases where a dad is upset with his spouse but then takes out his anger and frustration on the children. The older children may then take out their frustrations on the younger children. It then becomes easy to see that in a circumstance like this, being the youngest member of the household carries with it a fairly severe disadvantage.

As explained earlier in the book, in a household where the father understands and effectively uses his influence, the entire family dynamic can be more functional and positive. A husband needs to exercise his influence by being calm, consistent, caring, and concerned (*the 4 Cs*). When a husband does this, he exercises significant influence over the way his wife feels and subsequently acts and reacts towards the children. When children see their parents treating each other with patience, kindness, respect, consistency, and nurturing, the children will treat others outside the home in the same manner. As the children grow older, they will continue to treat their parents in such a manner as well as those outside of the home. This will make parenting an adolescent child much more enjoyable. This is the long-term effect of modeling the desired behavior.

As the children grow older, the family dynamic changes. And it must. As children grow, they need to be given and accept more responsibility, along with opportunity to learn how to make choices for themselves. As that happens, the interactions between the family members change. The parents need to accept that a child is maturing. The associated changes need to be *embraced*. As much as possible, Dad needs to resist the impulse to keep the child under unreasonably close supervision.

The oldest child is often the most difficult child to rear in that each stage of development is a new experience for the parents. Unless a child's father was raised by two parents himself who really knew what they were doing, then Dad might have a difficult time knowing what to do for each of these stages of development for his own kids. It would be a mistake for Dad to continue to treat a child who is eight years old in the same manner that he treated her when she was four years old. It would be just as big a mistake to treat a fifteen-year-old the same way Dad treated her when she was eleven years old. Usually, by the time a child is sixteen, she should know what is expected of her, know how to do what is expected of her, and be given the authority and responsibility to carry out the things that are expected of her. This does not mean that she is an adult. It simply means that she is responsible enough to do the things that are expected of a sixteen-year-old.

FUNCTIONAL FAMILY DYNAMICS

Under what circumstances is the family dynamic considered *functional*? It is when each member of a family knows what is expected of him/her, is held accountable for his/her own behavior, and behaves appropriately toward the other family members. In a functional family, each family member understands that they are a part of a family but at the same time they are able to *differentiate* themselves from the others. Members of functional families communicate openly and honestly, and they have respect and exhibit kindness for each other – even when they disagree.

In a functional family dynamic, both parents are in agreement as to how to raise their children. The parents agree on what philosophies (discussed in detail in Chapter 10) will be utilized to raise their children. They also agree on disciplinary and punishment strategies and when those strategies should become necessary. Parents from this type of family discuss issues openly, calmly, and consistently, and they provide a stable environment in which to raise their children. The parents provide a united front to the children, whereby the children understand that trying to play one parent against the other or sibling against sibling is not going to be successful.

A reminder: Parents in a functional family dynamic model the behaviors that they want the children to emulate. These parents are consistent with their parenting, and they would never even consider playing one family member against another family member. Individuals in this type of family are patient and kind toward each other, and the parents' every move, every motive, and every thought is focused on what is best for the family.

DYSFUNCTIONAL FAMILY DYNAMICS

Unfortunately, the dynamics just described are not found in too many households. All too often, many parents do not know how to manage and maintain multiple relationships within a complex family dynamic. This means that if there is more than one child in the family, the children may not all be treated the same. Too often, the "favorite" child shifts from one to the other depending upon the mood of the parent(s) and/or the behavior of the children. This is not acceptable for parenting multiple children in one household.

This type of interaction – not being able to manage more than one or two relationships at a time – is a part of normal development *of children* as they grow up and interact with peers. However, it is not acceptable *for parenting* children. For example, it is not unusual for a pre-adolescent – seven to eleven years old – to have difficulty managing more than one or two friendships. They also have difficulty understanding that other people do not necessarily see things as they do. For instance, if an eight-year-old boy is upset with one of his friends, he probably will not understand why another one of his friends is not upset with the boy as well.

Children of this age have difficulty with *differentiation*, which is being able to tell the difference between different members of the family and between different peers. They often believe that everyone else has the same likes, dislikes, and thoughts that they do. It is frequently not until adolescence when a child can recognize that individuals can differ in how they see things, feel things, and think about similar things and similar matters.

For an example of resistance to differentiation, when I was eighteen years old and in the Air Force, I was stationed at the Keflavik Naval Air Station in Iceland. I was taking a college class in biology, and the topic was the definition of life. In biology, in order for something to be alive, it must meet certain criteria. One of those criteria is the ability to reproduce. Another airman in the radar shop was a physics major, and he postulated the position that life was defined by molecular activity. I rebutted that if that were true then everything is alive in that every substance on earth has molecular movement. (Molecules by their nature have movement.) I could not convince him that the desk, for example, was not alive. He merely responded that if the desk had molecular movement, then it was alive. It frustrated me to no end that I could not convince him that the desk was not alive. Looking back, I wonder why it was so important to me for him to agree with my point of view, when the reality of it was that I could not see his point of view.

How many arguments have we engaged in merely because we cannot see the other person's point of view? When this occurs in a family, the family dynamic is altered sometimes to a point that is nearly impossible to correct. This doesn't have to happen. A dad has the influence to maintain a stable family dynamic.

THE DIFFERENTIATION FACTOR

One of the major problems in dysfunctional families (that is not to say that your family is dysfunctional or not) is that the individual members of the family have poor *differentiation*. Differentiation is the degree of *individuation* that each member of the family has in regard to the other family members. Individuation is how each family member is separate – or individual – from the other members of the family. I am aware that this may seem like a contradiction because I have been saying that family members are emotionally connected and feel similar things. Now I am saying that families not only need to act like a family but that individual family members also need to be able to differentiate themselves from each other. Well, one can be emotionally connected to their family while at the same time having the ability to differentiate themselves as an individual and be separate from the other family members.

Children may not be aware of this distinction, and they often have difficulty making a *separation* between themselves and their parents or siblings. This is generally the case and very normal with younger children. However, as the child reaches the middle to late teens, this distinction needs to be made. Separation and differentiation are other reasons that the developmental period of adolescence can be so difficult for the children and the parents. The child is trying, often unwittingly, to develop her own identity and individuality. Parents often resist this separation, while children often go out of their way to ensure that they are nothing like their parents.

In families that have poor differentiation, some members can become so enmeshed with each other that an unhealthy *codependence* can occur. Codependence is when one or more persons do not know who they are without the other person(s). This is typical of families where the children are not allowed, or not encouraged, to grow up but remain dependent upon one or both parents. It can also occur with other family members, such as grandparents, aunts, uncles, as well as other siblings. Keep in mind that the pendulum of dysfunction swings wide, and behaviors that might cause codependency in one family member may cause extreme differentiation in another family member.

One example is a family in which the parents did not allow their children to make any decisions for themselves. The children were taken to school and at the end of the school day were picked up and brought home by the parents. They were supervised twenty-four hours a day in an attempt to "protect" them from the ills of the world and to ensure that each child did as he/she was supposed to do as dictated by the parents. If the children did not do well in school, or had a problem of any kind, the parents took it very personally, as if the child's behavior was a direct insult to the parents. A parent would then often say to the child, "Why are you doing this to me?" The parents could not *differentiate* themselves from their children and the children's behavior.

In the above case, the teenage female was as helpless as could be. She got perfect grades in high school and presented with perfect behaviors, all the while suffering from major depression. The seventeen-year-old son, on the other hand, wanted nothing to do with the parents, even though he too had excellent grades and was not otherwise a behavioral problem. He had an eighteen-year-old girlfriend, and the parents were trying to have her arrested for having sex with their son, even though they knew they had not yet had sex. These parents were willing to file false charges to end the relationship. The son was rebelling, and the parents made it clear that if he wished to remain in their home after he turned eighteen he was to continue to do as they dictated. The son made it clear that on his eighteenth birthday he was moving in with his girlfriend.

This problem took a lifetime to create but could have been repaired in a relatively short period of time. However, the parents were positive that they knew what was best. They had even installed a chain link fence in the front yard so that the children, even as teenagers, could not leave the property. They were under the mistaken impression that they were protecting their children from the dangers of the world. Instead, they had been raising children who were unprepared for living in the world that the parents feared so much.

To summarize, poor differentiation can cause a child to become dependent upon her parents, or other family members, while on the other extreme the child may reject anything that remotely reminds her of her parents. This can be true for both parents or an individual parent. For example, it is not unusual for the children of an abusive father to either become just like him, or want nothing to do with him.

DYSFUNCTION KNOWS NO BOUNDARIES

There is something important to realize when we talk about dysfunction in the family dynamic or even just simple problems that can be resolved quite easily. This is that these types of issues are not reserved for any specific gender, race, religion, socioeconomic group, education level, or culture. Wealthy families have just as much, and often more, dysfunction as middle income or poorer families do.

I find it interesting, when treating patients of varying degrees of wealth or poverty, that the wealthier patients seem to have problems just as big as the poorer patients, with one very big distinction. That distinction being that people without a lot of money seem to believe that "everything will be okay" if they just had more money. Wealthy people know that money, in and of itself, will not make them happy and therefore their degree of hopelessness may seem much worse.

This is not to say that money will not make a family happier. But again, money in and of itself will not create a happy family. By the same token, the lack of money can cause significant interpersonal issues within families, and a major source of divorce is money problems or issues with the management of money. On a related note, dads need to understand that their wants and desires are last on the list. A man's family has priority, and a dad needs to make sure that his family is provided for before he worries about buying his own toys.

TYPES OF DYSFUNCTIONAL FAMILY DYNAMICS

Imagine living in a home where a child's entire life has been stable, consistent, loving, and caring. This child would not consider trying to play one parent against the other because she would never have been in an environment where that strategy would be effective. If one of the

45

parents tells the child that a behavior is not acceptable, the other parent agrees. If the parents do not agree on a topic, it is then discussed; this is often done in private if it is a parenting issue, but openly if it is not a parenting issue. A parent in this household would not try to use the children to sabotage the other parent's relationship with his or her children, or to try to gain favor with one of the children by being permissive when the other parent is being too restrictive. When these types of structural imbalances do occur, the family dynamic is described as *dysfunctional*. Some would describe family dysfunction as a "family that functions in pain."

Dysfunction within a family can be the result of structural imbalances, such as *malfunctioning hierarchical arrangements* and *boundaries* that are either too rigid or too diffuse. A malfunctioning hierarchical arrangement occurs when the parents do not see eye-to-eye on the way to parent, on how to discipline, and on the philosophies that govern their own lives. Therefore they have difficulty instilling such behaviors and philosophies into the lives of their children. This is when one member of the family tries, and may be successful, to be the one "in charge" and does not listen to the other parent or show respect for the other parent.

A malfunctioning hierarchical arrangement also occurs when the children are given authority or autonomy by their parents for an age other than their current age. This can be where the child is treated like a much younger child, or when a child is given too much autonomy over her life. Her status may even be placed at the same level as one of the parents. As a result, she may not listen to her parents, could expect her parents to obey *her* wishes, and could be the one who sets the boundaries – that is, what is and what is not expected of the child.

Boundaries that are clear, consistent, reasonable, and fair are paramount in the raising of well-adjusted children, for healthy parental relationships, and a healthy family dynamic. If the parents can exhibit good, clear, consistent, reasonable, and fair behaviors toward each other, the children, learning from their parents' example, accept such boundaries and most often operate within those boundaries. When parents have difficulty operating within the boundaries that they expect others to operate within, the children become confused and often have difficulty following even simple rules. Dad needs to lead by example and obey the rules that he sets for his children. It would be hypocritical for Dad to expect his children to function at a level that he can not handle himself.

Families, even those that are intact (that is, the parents are still married and living together as a family), can become *polarized*. Polarization occurs when one or more members of a family "choose sides" against one or more other members of the family. (This is generally not about a single issue or isolated case but more of a pattern of behavior.) It is often the case when the parents take sides against the children.

Another example of a polarized family would be when one parent sides with certain other family members (this could be their own children or other family members, whether living in the home or outside the home, such as in-laws) and against the other parent and one or more other family members.

A family that is polarized can develop several dysfunctional dynamics, such as triangulation, detouring, or a stable coalition. *Triangulation* is a dynamic where a child is caught in the middle of parental conflict with each parent wanting the child to side with them. In this dynamic, the child is often paralyzed, confused, or anxious. The child has difficulty concentrating and their grades at school can suffer. The parents operating within this dynamic might be looking for validation of the way they feel by trying to get the child to side with them. This is often the case when a marriage is having problems, or has already ended. For our current purposes, we will be more concerned with an intact family dynamic, rather than a broken family. Even so, Chapter 13 specifically addresses broken families.

Detouring is when the parents express distress through one child, who becomes the parents' focus in an attempt to deflect their own problems. In this scenario, the parents identify the child as "the patient" that needs to be protected or fixed. This type of family dynamic creates a false sense of harmony between the parents, who either blame the child as the source of their problems or unite together to protect the sick, weak

47

child. This too can be very confusing to a child, and when operating within this type of family dynamic, the child may very well take on the role as the source of the problem or as being weak or sick and act accordingly.

A *stable coalition* is a family dynamic where one parent unites with the child against the other parent. This often occurs when there is strife between the parents, and it can become more prevalent when the children become adolescents. A stable coalition might present itself as one parent and one of the children taking sides or being at odds with other members of the family or even picking on the other parent or a sibling.

A stable coalition often develops when a marriage is having problems, a divorce is imminent, or a split between the parents has already occurred. Some families seem to function in this mode for years or even decades, and the dynamic continues even after the children leave a parental home. This type of family dynamic creates a constant state of chaos and conflict. The children may willfully take sides in order to reduce the chaos and conflict, and they might grow to believe what is being modeled by the parent(s) – for example, that the other parents' behavior is wrong.

Another dysfunctional dynamic is when one or more of the family members are used as a *scapegoat*. Scapegoating within a family dynamic is when one or more children are singled out for unmerited aggressions. I have witnessed families that assigned one or two members of the family as scapegoats, and regardless of what happened, one of these family members was somehow made responsible for it.

DADS CAN MAKE A DIFFERENCE

In all of these dysfunctional dynamics, the father has significant influence to have a positive impact on his children, his wife, and the entire family. When a father can remain calm, consistent, loving, and nurturing, the rest of the family will usually follow suit. The strategies defined in this book will give the father the necessary information and know-how to make these differences.

In order for a father/husband to facilitate change, he must first see that changes need to be made. He also needs to be able to see that he has the influence to make that change and then act accordingly. Just the fact that a dad is a dad means that he has influence. However, in order for that influence to be effective, he has to utilize that influence and act in a manner such that the influence is used appropriately and without abuse.

WHAT'S NEXT?

In the next chapter, we will be discussing the importance of communication within the family dynamic. Men have a tendency to want to fix problems when often all that a dad needs to do is to listen to his loved ones. In Chapter 5, a discussion about being a good listener begins.

KEY CHAPTER POINTS

1. A family dynamic is the way in which each member of a family interacts with each of the other members of the family.
2. The larger the family, the greater effect that each member has on the dynamic as a whole and subsequently on each of the other members individually.
3. In a household where the father understands and effectively uses his influence, the entire family dynamic can be more functional and positive.
4. Influence is something that should be respected, used appropriately, and cherished by those who hold it.
5. Any member of a family can affect any other member of the family, either by *direct* or *indirect* interaction.
6. An infant has significant influence over her caregivers merely by her own dependence on the caregivers.
7. As children grow older, the family dynamic changes. As the children grow, they need to be given and accept more responsibility, along with opportunity to learn how to make choices for themselves.
8. In a functional family, each family member understands that they are a part of a family but at the same time they are able to differentiate themselves from the others.
9. *Separation* and *differentiation* are two reasons that the developmental period of adolescence can be so difficult for the child and the parents.
10. A family from any demographic, culture, ethnicity, socioeconomic group, religion, or education level has the potential of being dysfunctional.

5

Being a Good Listener

If there is one word that a man hates to hear, it is the word *communication* (almost as dreaded as the word *relationship*). When it is used in a sentence like "We need to improve our communication," men have a tendency to break out in a sweat. However, in order for a man to be a good dad, he must first be a good husband, and a good husband knows how to communicate. Communication is the key to *any* successful relationship, and the key to good communication is that ability to listen.

In being a good dad, it becomes very important that we practice *our communication and listening abilities in particular* with our wives, and apply what we learn to our children. Keep in mind that the success of a marriage is not measured merely by the length of time two people have spent together. There are many couples who have been married for years, even decades, who are both miserable with each other. In a successful marital relationship, both partners are happy, content, satisfied, and in love with the other. Being a good communicator supports all of this.

The topic of *communication* needs a great deal of clarification, especially for men who often would just as soon not communicate. It is not at all unusual that if a man can avoid a discussion about something he very often will do his best to do so. This avoidance, by the way, is a form of communication. Everything we do when we interact with someone, even when we do not interact with them, is communicating. In fact, most communication is non-verbal. Gestures, body language, sighs, eyeball rolls, and a host of other non-verbal cues can communicate nearly all of our thoughts, beliefs, needs, desires, and reactions.

I have spent thousands of hours counseling individuals and couples. The most often voiced complaint by a wife (and/or a child) is that she is not heard. What a wife means by this is that she is not being validated and she is not being listened to by her husband.

Everyone who is spoken to hears, although they may not listen. Even if someone listens, they still may not understand. A child who asks "why?" when the answer has clearly been stated is not really asking "why?" Instead, the child is asking to engage in a discussion on the topic. The answer may remain the same, but communication is the difference between a calm and happy home, and a loud and chaotic one.

WOMEN EXCHANGE INTIMACY BY TALKING

Women need to talk. Let me stress the word *need*. In some cases, if a woman does not talk she may physically explode. Many men do not have the *capacity* (or ability) to listen to their wives talk for very long; the reason is that they have a tendency to then feel that they need to own a wife's problems. But listening becomes much easier when men learn that talking is the way that women exchange intimacy, and that we do not need to own the problems being talked about, or fix them. Intimacy is exchanged when a husband can learn to listen to his wife in a way that is validating, caring, and patient.

There is a major difference in the way in which men and women exchange intimacy. Women exchange intimacy verbally; that is, by talking. When a wife verbalizes a problem to her husband, for example, she is not necessarily expecting input from him. In fact, most of the time, a woman is fully aware of what she needs to do to fix the problem. In all likelihood, as she discloses the problem, she merely expects her husband to listen to her. The husband's job at this point is to merely sit quietly, with genuine interest, and listen to what she is saying. A husband might engage in the conversation by asking questions to help clarify her meaning. However, we should try not to interrupt her train of thought or give her the perception that the discussion is about anything or anyone other than her.

During this part of the conversation, should the wife talk about a behavior of hers, a husband should not question this behavior as if the issue currently being discussed were her fault, even if it were. A husband should also not question his wife's feelings on the matter, as if to minimize her feelings, but be supportive and validating. For instance, your wife is talking about something that happened at work today; a husband might say something like "Well, that doesn't sound right" or "I'd be upset too." By doing this, we validate what our wife is saying and validate how she feels about what she is talking about. It is not the topic that is the issue here but that she is being listened to *by you*. This would not be a good time to point out anything that she may have done to contribute to the problem, if it is a problem that is being discussed, or suggest something that she might have done differently unless she specifically asks for that type of input.

Through the act of merely listening, a husband lets his wife know that he truly cares about her, and that she is worth his time, attention, and love. Listening makes the emotional connection between two people stronger, more fulfilling, and it keeps the spark of a relationship alive.

Now, for many men, this is hard pill to swallow. Again, one of the biggest problems that men have is not being able to listen to something without making a comment or trying to "fix it" so we can get back to whatever it is that we would rather be doing (remember that men are naturally selfish). An emotionally mature man understands that it is more fulfilling to give than to receive. This starts by being able to listen to your wife as she verbalizes her feelings.

MEN EXCHANGE INTIMACY PHYSICALLY

On the other hand, men exchange intimacy physically; that is, sexually – and that's about all there is to say about that. We're pretty basic, with not a lot of complicated underlying motives, dynamics, or frills. It's just sex – that is how we exchange intimacy. But then again, it is not quite that simple, is it? If it were that simple, then all a man would have to do is listen to his wife, validate her feelings, ask her if there is anything he can do to help, and give her a hug. A wife would then respond to her husband with sex. Now, with that said, we need to know how two people with ideas and needs of intimacy that are so different can fulfill each other's intimacy needs.

53

What is important for a husband to know about his wife is that, generally, women are 90% emotional and 10% sexual. Men, on the other hand, are 10% emotional and 90% sexual. A wife emotionally connects to her husband by talking to him. A husband actively listens to his wife as she talks to him, which validates her. This exchange gives the husband's 10% emotionality to his wife, which fills her up emotionally. Being filled emotionally makes the wife feel loved, validated, cared for, and heard.

Again, when a husband listens to his wife, validates her, and makes her feel important to him, *she fills up emotionally*. That is, the husband's 10% emotionality is given to his wife, which is added to her 90% for a total of 100%. When this happens, the wife is at 100% of her emotional capacity, and she will respond to her husband in a sexual manner (that is willfully and wantonly). When a wife responds to her husband sexually, that sexual response fills up her husband sexually and now he is fully satisfied. When this happens, both people are now filled emotionally and sexually and both people are happy, in terms of intimacy.

Now I am not saying that men are all a bunch of horn dogs with nothing else on their minds but sex, or that a relationship is nothing more than the exchange of intimacy. There is a great deal more than the exchange of intimacy that makes a relationship work. I will go over all of the factors that make a relationship succeed throughout this book. Right now, we are just looking at how intimacy is exchanged.

When one or both persons in an intimate relationship feel that their needs are not being fulfilled, the relationship starts to deteriorate. Over time, it can get to a point where one or both persons concede that this is the way it is supposed to be and that a relationship that is unfulfilling is normal.

Many couples do not realize that there is a real possibility of having an ongoing intimate relationship that is exciting, sensual, and everlasting. Certainly, this requires some effort, especially on the part of the husband. Women are generally very open to intimacy and doing whatever they can to increase the value of a relationship. There are always exceptions, but for the most part this is the case. Additionally, the husband has as much to gain in a good marriage, as does his wife. The difference is that the husband possesses so much influence in a marriage, and he needs to know what to do and what is expected of him to use it effectively.

In addition to fostering emotional intimacy with your wife by listening, it is also very important to have continued physical contact with her after making love. That is, it is a time to hug each other rather than rolling over and going to sleep. This is very important in the exchange of intimacy. Woman need to feel loved *after* sex, and much of the time, the caressing before and after sex is more important than the sex itself.

When a man does not fulfill his wife's emotional needs, she may feel that the act of lovemaking is a mechanical release and feel as if she is being taken for granted. Sex without intimacy can seem similar to masturbation or even sexual abuse.

One more thing… a man should only have physical intimacy with his own wife. Overall, intimacy with one's wife is something that should be very special and long lasting, something that is to be nurtured and treasured for the rest of a man's life. Without intimacy, the act of lovemaking is merely sex, and sex by its nature has a tendency to decrease its level of excitement over time.

Remember, one of the best ways to keep a marriage fun, exciting, and fulfilling is to exchange intimacy with your spouse. To do this requires the ability to communicate – that is, to listen – to put the needs of your spouse above your own, and to truly give yourself to your spouse.

OTHER DIFFERENCES IN INTIMACY

As I pointed out before, men like to do the right thing. Most of the time a man will do what is expected of him, given that he knows what is expected of him. Unfortunately, men have a tendency to believe that women like to be treated in the same manner as we would like to be treated given similar circumstances. This is a gargantuous mistake for a husband to make. For example, men have a tendency to want to be left alone when they do not feel well. Women, on the other hand, generally prefer to have their loved ones around them when they don't feel good. When men are in a bad mood, they have a tendency *not* to want to talk about it. Many women do not understand this, which often leads to arguments starting with comments like "You never talk to me" or "You always keep things bottled up inside." It is important for a man to let his wife know how he is feeling; he should also help her to understand that, as a man, he may not want to talk about things but just needs some space. That does not mean that he is shutting her out; he just needs his alone time.

Women, when in a similarly bad mood, generally have a *need* to talk about it. As you have learned, women talk to exchange intimacy, and the topic will hopefully not always be problems but also just normal daily activities. Men, on the other hand, are very content *not* talking about the daily activities at all. This is a major difference between the way men and women exchange intimacy.

It is also important to know that both men and women have emotional cycles. These cycles are usually twenty-eight days with half of the cycle being in a good mood and the other half being in a less-than-good mood. Men and women both cycle, with women cycling higher and lower than men. When a man is at a low point, he likes to be left alone. It is important for a man to be able to tell his wife, very compassionately, that he is just in a grumpy mood at the moment, that there is nothing wrong, and he will be out of it in a little while. When a woman is at the low point, she likes to have more contact and attention from her husband and those she loves.

It is important for a dad to understand his own mood cycles. When a dad is in the trough of the cycle, he may not be as understanding and caring toward his family. Dad needs to understand that he can compensate for it, knowing that he is just at a low point and that this too shall pass, and make it a point not to take his mood out on his family.

Intimacy is what makes a relationship grow, and it gives a relationship *emotional depth*. Without emotional depth, relationships become mundane, boring, and even laborious. So it now becomes obvious that in order for a man to be a good dad, he needs to know how to exchange intimacy, and there is no better person to practice intimacy with than his wife.

HOW THIS RELATES TO BEING A GOOD DAD

The exact same behavior of listening, validating, being calm, being strong, and being consistent with your spouse will work wonders with your children, both boys and girls. The ratio (90/10) of intimacy is different between a dad and his children. This exchange of intimacy is primarily emotional between a man and his kids, but with physical contact such as hugging, plus nurturing. The outcome of these exchanges is the children feeling validated, being given the feeling that she or he is important enough to be listened to and heard. At this point, it is easy to see that if a dad cannot be intimate with his wife, by being connected emotionally and responding to her emotional needs, then he cannot be connected emotionally to his children.

Dads who are appropriately connected to their children emotionally have kids who are more considerate, appropriate, confident, assertive, caring, loving, and nurturing. Children of fathers who take the time to listen and communicate with them have fewer incidents of negative behaviors, such as teenage pregnancy, drug or alcohol use, smoking, delinquent activities, and problems at school. These children also have a tendency to achieve higher grades and turn out to have better relationships with friends, teachers, employers, and other family members. Overall, these children do better in life. All because a dad knows how to communicate with his loved ones.

If we were to extend this same line of reasoning to outside the home, a man who can communicate, feel other people's needs, show empathy, genuinely care, and express himself calmly, appropriately, assertively, and consistently is going to be a very successful man. How that success is measured is the topic for a different time, however it is certainly not measured by how much money is made or what one possesses. Note that no amount of success outside of the home will make up for failure inside the home.

Children observe and learn by the way their dad acts, reacts, and responds to those inside the home and to those outside the home. Again, this behavior should be consistent. Children of any age can interpret hypocrisy when Dad is nice to them in public but acts differently at home. This type of hypocrisy is quite damaging to children of any age, as they realize that Dad is capable of being the dad they need when in front of others. The damaging part is that they are treated differently at home when no one is watching, giving the child a feeling of worthlessness. All kinds of issues can arise from this type of problem.

AN EXAMPLE CONVERSATION

The key to a happy marriage and subsequent happy home life is the husband *listening* to his wife and to his children. An example of this is when I came home from work one day and found my wife Carla sitting in the living room. It seemed clear to me that something was bothering her. So after I gave Carla a hug and kissed her, I asked, "Is there something wrong?" My wife replied, "Yes."

Now, my wife Carla is a very good communicator. And once she stated that something was bothering her, my next question was not what you might think it would be. Most people would naturally think that I would merely ask what was bothering her. But no, I asked, "Are you upset with me?" This was very important, because if the answer was "yes," I would need to be ready to exercise a great deal of self-control and refrain from trying to "pry" the information out of her. Usually this just makes Carla more resistant to discussing it.

However, at this particular time, my wife said that she was *not* upset with me. So my response was "Would you like to talk about it?" Actually, this would have been my response even if Carla had been upset with me. I just like to know exactly where it is I stand when we start these conversations and I know that she is upset about something. Anyway, she responded, "Yes." Once again, Carla did not expect me to drag the information out of her and she made an honest response.

What if Carla had responded that she did *not* want to talk about it? I would say, "Let me know when you would like to discuss it." I would not try to pull the information out of her, and I would definitely not try to guess what it might be if she had been upset with me. That has backfired for me on numerous occasions, mostly when I was younger and had less self-control. Generally, this leads to me bringing up things that Carla had forgotten about or previously did not know about. For instance, on one occasion, my wife was out of town for the weekend, and I discovered that a guitar amplifier that I really wanted had been marked down from $1,800 to a mere $600. I thought that was a really great price, and it was, and that she would understand if I just went ahead and bought it without discussing the purchase with her. When I eventually informed Carla about the great deal that I got, she did not share my enthusiasm with the purchase, and seemed only to focus on the fact that I had not included her in the decision to buy it. The price had exceeded my limit of spending that we had agreed to without a mutual discussion and consent by both of us.

Now, at this point on the day I found my wife in the living room, I had ascertained that she was upset, but not with me, and that she *did* want to talk about it. I sat down on the end of the sofa, not too close but not too far away either, looked at Carla and said, "Tell me about it." My wife started by saying that she was told at work, just before leaving for the day, that she was going to have to move her office from the second floor to the first floor, to a space next to the Vice-President's office. The VP had already left for the day, so Carla was not able to discuss it with him. She proceeded to tell me that she loves her office; it is a corner office with windows on two walls with a great view. Now, for me, the answer was simple; just tell your boss that you do not want to move your office. However, if I had suggested that, I would have made Carla feel unheard, invalidated, uncared for, and unloved. All of the things that I *never* wish to convey to my wife. So I merely sat there and listened. Meanwhile, the answer continued to be clear to me, but Carla was not searching for an answer. She just needed to talk about it. She went on for some time about how that office played a role in her decision to take this job and how it relaxes her.

After Carla had finished venting about her office, she went on to numerous other subjects. All the while I just nodded, listened, and sympathized with her. It was irrelevant whether or not I agreed with my wife's emotional attachment to her office, or if I felt that this was a workable problem. In fact, my thoughts about this situation and any potential solutions that I could come up with were completely irrelevant. The only issue that I had to deal with was to be supportive of my wife and listen to her as she talked.

After about forty minutes, I knew that Carla was done talking because when she is done, she sighs and has a relaxed posture. Often she will also say something like "I'm better now." At this point, and only at this point, I will ask, "Is there anything that you would like for me to do?" I say this because there have been times when I say nothing and then Carla will say, "Well, are you going to help me with this?" So I have learned to ask, "Is there anything you would like for me to do?" In this case, she responded, "No, I know what to do. Tomorrow morning I'm just going to tell my boss that I don't want to move my office." So I gave Carla a big hug and she said, "Thanks for listening." Then we continued on with our evening.

Now, what would have happened if I had dismissed Carla's problem as being trivial or senseless, or offered a solution to her problem rather than being a good listener? Well, she would have felt invalidated and unheard, that I did not care about her, and that I felt that she was incapable of fixing her own problems. This way, by me simply using empathetic listening, Carla felt as if I was genuinely concerned (which I was), and she saw that I listened to her problem, sympathized with her problem, and allowed her to be intimate with me verbally.

If I had not been a good listener, the woman that I love more than anything on this earth would have been in a much worse mood. This mood would have permeated throughout the entire house and every occupant in it, making life more difficult. Being her husband makes it my responsibility to act in a manner that will make my wife feel validated, heard, loved, and cared for. If I am not doing that as a husband, how can I expect to do the same as a father?

MEN CANNOT READ MINDS

There's one last thing about being a good listener, and this is that both spouses need to be honest when asked a question. This is very important. For example, if there is something bothering a wife and that wife's spouse asks, "Is there something bothering you?" and the response is "no," her husband may very well accept that response, even though he knows it is not true. Very likely, he will go about his business. It is important to tell the truth if communication is going to work. Husbands are not good mind readers, and if we get an answer that we are happy with, we are not likely to press the issue.

A good example of this came up when I was treating a husband and wife in therapy. The wife was livid with her husband because he did not know what to do to make her happy. The husband was at wits' end trying to please his wife, and he stated that he would do whatever she wanted him to do but that she would not say what it was. His wife replied, "He should know what I need without me having to tell him!" I suggested that she go ahead and tell him during that very session. She refused, again insisting that he should already know how to make her happy.

I then asked the husband to leave the office for a minute. The wife and I were now alone to discuss the problem without her husband. I asked her to tell me what it was her husband could do to make her happy. The wife then confessed that she did not know what she wanted him to do, but that *he* should know. I then asked the wife how her husband could possibly know what would make her happy when she did not know herself.

She had difficulty seeing that her unhappiness was within herself. That is not to say that her husband did not need to do things differently – like communicate better. However, she needed to understand her own needs and be able to communicate them to her husband. Like I have previously said, once a man knows what he is supposed to do, he will usually do it. In this case, it worked out well, once both persons were able to identify their feelings and needs, and communicate them to each other.

If a husband is not honest with his wife (and vice versa), there is generally a deeper problem in the relationship. Both husband and wife need to feel safe and secure enough to be honest with the other. Even so, honesty does not mean to say whatever is on your mind; the truth may be very damaging to a relationship, depending upon how it is said. To determine if something needs to be said, it should first and foremost be the truth, necessary, relevant, and kind. If a comment or statement does not meet with these criteria, it might be best to keep it to oneself.

Remember, our objective is to improve the relationship, not damage it. We always want honesty to help improve the relationship, like a tool that fixes; we do not ever want to use honesty like a club to bludgeon someone, especially someone we love, even if the statement is the truth. This same philosophy applies to our children. We do not need to point out all of the things that they have done wrong. Most people know when they have done something wrong, and they do not need to be reminded of it. Dad's objective is to improve the relationships with his family, and this is done by being a good communicator including being a good listener. When that occurs, the entire family flourishes.

WHAT'S NEXT?

In the next chapter, I will discuss the four different levels of communication and how the different levels increase intimacy and improve relationships.

Key Chapter Points

1. Communication is the key to any successful relationship, and listening is the key to communication.
2. Most communication is non-verbal.
3. Women exchange intimacy verbally; that is, by talking
4. Men exchange intimacy physically; that is, through sex.
5. Husbands need to be able to listen to their wives without making a comment or trying to fix the problem.
6. Remember the *90/10 Rule*: Women are 90% emotional and 10% physical; men are 10% emotional and 90% physical.
7. Intimacy is what makes a relationship grow; it gives a relationship emotional depth.
8. The feeling that one or both persons have when their emotional needs are not being met permeates throughout the entire home.
9. When a man does not feel well, or is in a bad mood, he prefers to be left alone. When a woman does not feel well, or is in a bad mood, she prefers to have her loved ones around her.
10. Honesty does not mean verbalizing every thought; some things are best left unsaid, especially if it will damage the relationship.
11. Children of father who take the time to listen and communicate with them have fewer incidents of negative behaviors. Overall, these children do better in life.
12. No amount of success outside the home will make up for failure inside the home.

6

Intimacy & the Four Levels of Communication

When we get to know someone, our intimacy (closeness, familiarity, and affection) has a chance to grow. We cannot get to know someone if we do not talk to them. Without communication, there is no intimacy; without intimacy, there is no emotional depth; and without emotional depth, relationships become monotonous, unloving, boring, and sometimes even painful. At that point, we could begin to take each other for granted, possibly even turn hostile and resentful. We can then develop behaviors that seem to say that our individual life is more important than our collective lives.

However, once we learn to be emotionally intimate with others, the depth of our relationships improves, and these relationships can remain in a state of continued excitement and newness. In order for this to happen, we have to be able to communicate with each other, and therefore we need to understand that communication is exchanged on four levels.

LEVEL ONE COMMUNICATION

Everyone who interacts with another human being uses the first level of communication. Simply stated, Level One Communication is the simplest form of communication. Most people engage in this very basic level of communication without exchanging intimacy. Level One Communication involves greetings such as "Hello," "Good-bye," and "How are you?" Even though it seems that "How are you?" is a question, one would really not expect an answer beyond, "Okay." Usually when one asks a question, their intention, whether conscious or not, is to initiate a conversation. Level One Communication often includes one-word answers to questions and does not necessarily require or solicit a response.

There is generally not much intimacy exchanged in this level of communication. However, that does not mean that Level One Communication is not important. Keep in mind that most communication is non-verbal, and the way in which a greeting is stated speaks a great deal beyond the greeting itself. How a dad responds to simple greetings expresses the way he is feeling, how much the dad cares about those he loves, and if he is really interested in what his wife or his child has to say.

It is safe to say that if Level One Communication is not going well, the next levels will be a disaster. For example, there are times when some couples, or members within the family, do not so much as communicate on Level One. When this happens, the relationship(s) is (are) in dire straits. There are households where people walk into the house, do not say a word to anyone, and go to their room or about their business. Unfortunately, this affects everyone in the household and not just the person(s) that is (are) the target of the silence. It is very important to understand that silence, or the "silent treatment," is a form of aggression and control, and it can be every bit as damaging as other forms of abuse.

Again, Level One Communication is the basic level. It is good for everyone to understand what Level One is, and this level would be especially necessary to grasp if your relationship(s) is (are) strained. As previously stated, if Level One Communication is not going well, it is likely that the other levels, the more intimate levels of communication, are either not doing any better or are not present at all.

The first thing we want to keep in mind when we attempt to initiate or improve communication is to speak Level One Communications in a positive, open, and honest manner. Good communication is honest, even though that does not mean "brutally honest." (The majority of people, at some point, say things that may not necessarily be completely true. The majority of "untruths" [over 80%] being told are intended to spare someone's feelings. Keep in mind that I am not supporting the concept of lying, but one can always be honest in a kind way.)

When communicating, it is not helpful to have standard, meaningless answers that are sarcastic or condescending. For instance, let's say that you are asked, "How was your day?" An answer such as "Greaaaat" said sarcastically would not be sincere. Sarcasm is generally negative, and it can be mean and insensitive even when intended to be in the form of humor. Even in the simplest form of communication, the slightest bit of sarcasm can be damaging to a relationship.

The tone of one's voice is also very important. A person who responds "Great" without sarcasm and means it is much more sincere and than a person who flippantly says "Greaaaat." On the other hand, a sarcastic response may be an invitation to initiate a conversation. (However, that is an advanced type of communication, and we are still on the basics.)

The use of sarcasm should be limited to rare cases, with the understanding that sarcasm is almost always negative. Additionally, there is most often a victim with sarcasm, and therefore it should not be used with one's children or spouse. Let your "yes" be "yes" and your "no" be "no." Talk honestly and openly without sarcasm to those you love. Sarcasm, although funny at times, is a mean form of humor and can be quite painful to the person at whom the sarcasm is directed. What might sound funny to others might be very hurtful to one's family, especially to one's wife and children.

In addition, approximately 70% of communication is non-verbal; that is body language, facial expressions, tone of voice, and any one of a series of sighs, grunts, or groans,. Many parents are painfully aware of the teenage eye-roll, or inappropriate sighs. During these moments of relative silence, even though no words were spoken, volumes were just exchanged. If a dad responds poorly to these childish behaviors, getting to higher levels of communication becomes much more difficult. It is important to remember that a dad does not need to respond to every non-verbal cue. Dad does not have to respond to every verbal cue either. Never forget that you are Dad, no power struggle needs to occur in that you already possess the influence. How one uses that influence is what's important when it comes to being a dad.

LEVEL TWO COMMUNICATION

The next level of communication would naturally be Level Two, and it involves an exchange of information. Most people have little problem in the exchange of information, as long as it does not become an argument. The exchange of information might be something along the lines of news reports, sports highlights, or political discussions. In terms of intimacy, Level Two Communication would be on a more personal level, and it may be an exchange started with a question like "How was your day?" This seems like a fairly benign question, but to the active and astute dad the answer becomes much more important. For example, if the answer is "Okay" or "Not bad" (both Level One Communicative answers, instead of Level Two answers), the communication process may not be going that well. That is not to say that a one-word answer means that the relationship is in severe trouble; however, when we are communicating on a higher level and the recipient responds on a lower level, there might be a communication problem.

Intimacy can begin at Level Two Communication, and it is a good place to start working on your listening skills. It is not enough to tell others about what is going on in your life, but more about listening and appropriately responding to what is going on in the lives of those in your family. You are the dad; you are the one who is strong, secure, consistent, caring, and loving. When we listen to our children, we, as dads, relay those attributes to our children. They, in turn, start to be strong, secure, consistent, caring, and loving. Again, it is best not to have standard answers, like "Same stuff, different day" when someone is genuinely asking you a question.

Men have a habit of using as few words as possible, often in an attempt to avoid an actual conversation. Children learn how to communicate from their parents. If the parent cannot communicate, the child will, in all likelihood, have difficulty with communication as well. This is where Dad should practice with his wife and actually engage in a discussion – for instance, about how your day went. Although the discussion might be short to begin with, it will hopefully be getting longer and more detailed as your communication skills improve. Again, practice with your wife and apply your new skills to your children.

Research shows that fathers have a significant effect on the way that their young children, and subsequently their adult children, interact with others. This not only includes the way our children interact with other family members, but also those outside the home. A dad's influence gives a child confidence to explore new ideas, new ways of thinking, and to be more social with peers and other adults. On the other hand, a dad's influence can also keep these skills from developing.

Keep in mind that good communication skills can improve nearly every area of a person's life, including home, work, school, and in the community. So learning to communicate effectively with your family is not only good practice for *other areas of your life,* it is also good practice for *your children and their lives* as well. However, know that it is not so much the topic of discussion that is important, but the verbal exchange. When Dad engages in effective, caring, and genuine communication with his child, it conveys to her that she is loved and that she *matters* to her dad.

This may seem very simplistic, and one might wonder, "How could something this simple have such a significant impact on a child?" Well, it does. When we communicate effectively, we are modeling behavior that we want to encourage in our children.

LEVEL THREE COMMUNICATION

Now that we understand the two basic levels of communication, we are ready for the advanced levels. In Level Three Communication, one person tells another how he/she feels, honestly and sincerely. At the third level, intimacy cannot help but be exchanged. In the Level Two Communication, intimacy can begin to take place when a person takes the time to engage in a discussion. Taking the time to be with someone and listening to what he or she has to say is intimate in and of itself. It shows that person that you care. Being able to listen to someone express to you how they feel is even more intimate.

In Level Three Communication, people often use *"I" statements.* These statements are worded like this: "I feel as if…" or "I feel that I…" I statements are meant for the person who has the feeling to own the feeling, to understand how he/she feels. That is not to say that others do not affect our emotions and that others cannot influence how we feel. People we love can have significant effects on how we feel, and how we feel about ourselves. That said, keep in mind that "I" statements let the individual own their feelings by letting others know how she feels.

In Level Three Communication, one person – in the case of the following example, let's say the husband – tells his wife how he is feeling, or how an event made him feel. In regard to the question "How was your day?" Level Three Communication would go further than merely exchanging information about the events of your day. It would also include an expression of how those events, and the persons with whom you interacted, made you feel.

In Level Two Communication, a husband might answer the question "How was your day?" by merely saying "Okay." However, in Level Three Communication, a husband could answer his wife's question with a more complete, sincere, and honest response. He might say, "Well, for the most part, it was a pretty normal day except that one of my co-workers was upset about something, and it made me feel uneasy. I didn't know if I should have said something to him or not..." This could then initiate an actual conversation, whereby his wife would then explain how things are going with her and how she feels about them.

An Inherent Risk of Level Three Communication

In Level Three Communication, intimacy increases, and when intimacy increases, there is an inherent level of risk attached. When we tell someone how we feel about something, it exposes our inner thoughts and our inner self to whomever we are talking with in that conversation. This does give the person we are talking to a certain degree of power, and vice versa. Therefore, when someone opens up to us, we have a responsibility to listen intently, with empathy, and not to minimize the other person's feelings or use that information in a manner that would make the person *feel worse*.

When a wife comes to her husband with a problem, it is important not to minimize the problem or her feelings. Men have a tendency not to want to admit that there is a problem. "If there is a problem, it must be a small problem and it certainly could not be my fault," the husband thinks. In Level Three Communication, we must resist the impulse to *fix* the problem that has been communicated or to minimize the feelings of the person who has entrusted us with this information.

One thing that we must *never* do is tell someone how they should or should not feel. This is a big one. If we expect someone, in this case our spouse and children, to tell us how they feel about things that are going on in their lives, we need to be empathetic. This means that we put ourselves in "their" place and understand "their" feelings and do not minimize their feelings by telling them, "You shouldn't feel that way."

Granted, there will be times when we will have no idea how the other person is feeling. Still, we can understand that whoever is talking to us about their problem is feeling bad and needs someone to share it with through conversation. (I am assuming that we are talking about a problem, in that rarely does anyone ever try to tell someone how to feel when the person is feeling good.) Again, the solution may be very simple and obvious to the listener (and it is probably just as obvious to the one we're talking with), but Dad's job in this situation is to merely listen to what the person is saying.

If a man can merely do this, he has come a long way in improving his relationship with his spouse. After practicing this type of communication with his spouse, he can then apply it to his children. And then, if you could muster up – at least every once in a while – a reciprocal response on how you feel about something, it would make the relationship much more intimate. In this way, the relationship grows and develops emotional depth.

Intimacy will increase if you merely listen to the thoughts and feelings of your loved ones. Additionally, when both persons share their thoughts and feelings, it allows both people the opportunity to be vulnerable and share a deeper sense of intimacy. Remember, this is how relationships stay alive, new, and fresh.

For example, sometimes my wife and I take a trip in the car that lasts four to five hours or more. She will start talking as soon as we get on the freeway and not stop for at least three hours. She will go through a progression of events that start with today and wind through a road of verbal soliloquies that includes the kids, family, friends, work, places she'd like to go, things she's already done, and the list goes on and on. Ultimately, she will say, "I'm really loving you right now," but the reality is that I have not done anything but drive the car and listen. I do not have to fix anything, comment on anything (unless, of course, I'm asked to), or share anything (even though that will happen). I just let her talk and let the intimacy grow. If I do not allow her this opportunity, or try to control the conversation, or cut the conversation short, our trip will not be as wonderful as they usually are.

This is not to say that I don't have things to communicate as well; I do, and my wife is very interested in the things I have to say. Yet I find it best to let her "go first" in what she has to communicate and then we talk about other things that might pertain to me. I am also not suggesting that a man does not have input or that his opinion should not be heard; it should. The issue is the way that a husband and wife communicate with each other.

When decisions need to be made, they should be made together after the issues and solutions have been communicated. Then a *summary of what was decided* should be stated. This will decrease miscommunication significantly. For example, my wife showed me a brochure for a cruise through the Panama Canal and asked if I had any interest in going. I told her that I would love to take a cruise through the Panama Canal. Next thing I know is we have a cruise booked from Florida to Los Angeles via the Panama Canal. I mentioned that I would like to go, meaning *someday.* My wife took my desire to go as a green light *to book it.* We did go and it was phenomenal. Two weeks alone on a cruise ship with my wife. What could be better? But you get my point.

Another example involves a colleague who was upset with her husband because he was taking a class so that he could purchase a firearm. They had previously discussed having guns in the house and she told her husband, "I don't want to hear about it." The husband took that to mean that he could buy the gun but not to tell her about it. Actually her intention was that she did not want any firearms in the house. Once she found out his intentions regarding the class, she was livid. After discussing it, they decided that the husband would also purchase a gun safe and put the safe and the gun in the garage. Hence, no guns in the house.

I feel the need to emphasize and point out, once again, that there is a big difference in the dynamics between Level Two and Level Three Communications. In Level Two Communication, information is exchanged, and you might very well disagree with the other person's position. It is not uncommon for arguments to start over Level Two Communication on such topics as politics, current events, or something like whether or not you believe that in the movie *Star Trek* the Starship Enterprise really could go faster than the speed of light. In Level Three Communication, it would be a monumental mistake to debate with someone about how they feel, and once again, *never* tell someone how they should or should not feel. In Level Three Communication, we accept how the person feels and empathize with them. That does not mean that we have to own *their* feelings, or even agree with *their* feelings in a given situation, just that we can understand what is being said.

LEVEL FOUR COMMUNICATION

Level Four Communication is the most intimate form of communicating, and it entails telling someone, usually a significant other, how *YOU* make *ME* feel. This is the highest level of intimacy, and it should be the most sincere form of communication. At this level of communication, a person is letting you know that you do have power (or control) over the way in which he or she feels.

Husbands and wives should have the comfort and security to be able to communicate to each other at this level. This level and Level Three Communication are not reserved only for problems. This is the level at which a husband can tell his wife how good she makes him feel about himself; that "If the world ended today, it would be okay because you were in my life." This is the level of communication where a husband can tell his child that she makes him feel proud, or that she makes him feel like she really does care about him.

Others Do Have an Effect on Our Feelings

Now, there is a great deal of literature that states that each one of us needs to own our feelings (using "I" statements), and that no one can *make* someone feel a certain way. That is simply not true. However, it is often very convenient for those who trivialize his or her own behavior to deny that his or her actions are capable of making someone feel something. For instance, a father yells at his child and the child cries. The father, in this case, may deny that his yelling caused the child to cry. This is exactly the type of trivializing that causes damage to a relationship, and it causes our significant others to communicate at Level One and Level Two, rather than on Level Three and Level Four.

People do have an influence over the way other people feel. One person can make another person feel a certain way, good or bad. Have any of us ever been afraid or in love? I have never had the feeling of being in love without the interaction of another person, nor have I ever frightened myself! It may be true that when we allow someone to affect our feelings, and the way we feel about our own self, we have allowed that person to have a great deal of power over us. However, it is through that intimacy of communicating openly and honestly, without the fear that what is being said will be used against us, that deep, long-lasting emotional connections are made. This is Level Four Communicating.

When a dad cares about how *he* makes his children feel, his children will, in all likelihood, respond to their dad with genuine respect, love, and honesty. These children will usually bend over backwards to make their dad happy with them. When a husband uses Level Four Communication, the relationship will develop emotional depth. Intimacy will grow, and the relationship will be better than one could ever imagine. That is what makes all of this worth the time and effort; the fact that as we mature emotionally, our relationships mature as well. We move into a more stable, meaningful, and fulfilling way of life. And since men have a tendency to place a great deal of emphasis on sex, just know that as one matures emotionally, the sex gets a lot better. It is amazing what emotions bring to lovemaking. This is something that women know, but men need to learn.

WHAT'S NEXT?

In Chapter 7, we will be discussing one of the most important facets of relationships – *expectations.*

Key Chapter Points

1. When we get to know someone, our intimacy (closeness, familiarity, and affection) has a chance to grow.

2. Without communication, there is no intimacy. Without intimacy, there is no emotional depth. And without emotional depth, relationships become monotonous, unloving, and boring.

3. Level One Communication includes greetings such as "Hello" or "Good-bye."

4. If Level One Communication is not going well, the relationship is in need of some help.

5. The "silent treatment" is a form of aggression and control, and it can be every bit as damaging as other forms of abuse.

6. Sarcasm is usually negative; there is almost always a victim.

7. Level Two Communication involves the exchange of information. Learn to *listen* to Level Two Communications.

8. Level Three Communication is where one person tells another how he/she is feeling. In Level Three Communication, never tell someone how they should or should not feel.

9. Level Four Communication is the most intimate form, and it is used when telling a person how that person makes you feel.

10. When a dad cares about how he makes his children feel, his children will, in all likelihood, respond to their dad with genuine respect, love, and honesty. These children will usually bend over backwards to make their dad happy with them.

7

Relationship Expectations & Communicating Problems

Next to poor communication, the biggest cause of relationship failure is disappointment related to expectations of the relationship. One person is expecting a certain set of behaviors, goals, and fulfillment, while the other person is expecting a separate, often incompatible set. Someone once told me that one of the problems with relationships is that a man expects the woman he met and fell in love with will never change. On the other hand, women look at a man and think, "I can change him; I can make him into something." That *something* is the man that particular woman *needs*. This reasoning on both sides is not rational. Numerous clients who I have worked with were disgusted with their spouse over things that both persons thought were cute and funny at the start of the relationship. Now these things have become a significant annoyance in the marriage.

A CLOSER LOOK AT OUR EXPECTATIONS

When we enter into a relationship, we have fairly specific expectations of the way we believe and hope the relationship will develop. We all have ideas of the way we believe we should be treated and how we should treat others. We also enter into a relationship with the expectations that the future will be brighter than the past. When these expectations either fail to materialize or are altered, there is stress placed on the relationship. This is one of the reasons that we want to keep our expectations of our partner realistic.

Most of us expect to be treated with respect, dignity, and love by our significant other and by those in our immediate family – and definitely by those in our home. However, it is difficult to fulfill the expectations of a particular relationship when we have not communicated what those expectations are. Often we go on about our lives believing that our wives are fully aware of our wants, our desires, our life goals, and our needs. We also, very often, go about our lives with the belief that we are aware of our wife's wants, desires, and needs, without ever really sitting down and communicating these expectations and needs with each other. This might very well be the case with the other members of our family as well.

This is clearly not something that can be done over a short period of time. That is why couples get involved in the process of dating, becoming engaged, and then being married – all of which takes time. We need to get to know each other, hopefully before we fall in love with the person. There are few things more disheartening than to fall in love with someone and find out that you really do not like that person.

It is important to like the person that we fall in love with. The best way to get to know someone is to talk to them. In this way, we get to understand what they want from life, what makes them happy, what makes them upset or angry, what lights up their life. Just the presence of my wife Carla lights me up. All she has to do is walk into the room and my day is made. This is the kind of love that I cherish. This is the kind of love that makes life worth living.

IMPORTANCE OF COMMUNICATING EXPECTATIONS EARLY

It is best for both parties to start communicating their expectations of the relationship as soon as possible. Miscommunication of what we expect from each other can result in disaster for the relationship.

An acquaintance of mine was a planner for a company that made radar systems. Before he got married, he worked on a pit crew for Indy cars. (Most of us guys can already tell this story is not going well.) When he met his wife-to-be, she came to every race, bragged to her friends about his job, and conveyed, at least in *his* own mind, that this would be the way things would stay. After they got married, the job became a sore spot; it was too dangerous, he was gone too much, and "What will we do if we have children and you're not around?" So he quit the job he loved with a passion and became a planner. Now, there's nothing wrong with being a planner, but it does not compare to the excitement of being on an Indy pit crew.

They remained married for thirty years until the wife died of cancer. They adopted five kids and were great parents, but the husband never forgot what he gave up and he always regretted it. Now I am not suggesting that we do not make concessions for our significant other, but this was clearly a case of miscommunication and faulty expectations.

EXPECTATIONS & OUR CHILDREN

In terms of expectations for our children, we need to keep what we expect to be *reasonable and realistic*. There are some dads who try to maintain expectations for their children that are unreasonable and unlikely. This might include something like expecting his twelve-year-old son to become a major league ball player, and meanwhile that child is currently not the star player in his current league. Dad just might be in for a disappointment and the relationship Dad has with his child might not develop in a positive manner.

I knew a father whose ten-year-old son raced motocross. This dad believed that this little boy was going to be his "meal ticket to the big time" and make him rich. He kept this young boy out of school to practice and the lad was really good. This son won most of his races and he loved to race, but the child's entire life revolved around his father's expectations. Unfortunately, the child got hurt and was unable to race anymore. The father blamed the child for being injured. When the boy returned to school, he was terribly behind his peers and sank into a deep depression. After all, what good was he if he could not race?

When we place too much emphasis on our expectations of our children, it stifles the child's true potential. More importantly, it damages the relationship that we have with them. There are situations where Dad's hopes are realized in their children. Still, in such cases, it should be the hope and dream of the child as well, and not the cornerstone of the father/child relationship.

Again, like with our spouse, we should have realistic expectations of our children. In addition, we need to communicate what those expectations are at whatever age is appropriate. In this way, the children will know what is expected of them. It is very frustrating to be held accountable for something that we were unaware of. In fact, to believe that our children "should" have known better is usually an unrealistic expectation. Expectations can be freely discussed when the lines of communication are open and a child feels comfortable talking with his dad.

We also need to be open to the expectations that *our children* have for *us*. Children have very basic, and sometimes unrealistic, expectations of their dad, and we need to be able to discuss such things openly and honestly. Sometimes we expect too much from our children and sometimes we do not expect enough. The same is true for a child's expectations of his dad.

COMMUNICATING PROBLEMS: A BASIC GROUND RULE

And what about discussing problems in your household? First, *adults should not discuss their problems with their children.* There is a significant difference in discussing adult issues with another adult and discussing them with a child. Children are not able to emotionally handle adult problems. They have a tendency to believe that they need to find a solution when they are aware of an issue. Since they are, in fact, children, they are usually incapable of adult reasoning, and therefore become stressed over problems they cannot solve. Therefore, it would be unkind, as well as irresponsible, to allow one's children to know about adult problems.

One of the most commonly discussed adult problems within a home is that of money. It is best that the children not become aware that there is a problem with money, or with work, or even health issues. That is, unless they are old enough to deal with the problem effectively. For instance, young children are too young to understand that there are financial problems and that the house is being foreclosed. All that a young child needs to know is that he is moving. To unduly burden children with details on such issues will cause problems. On the other hand, an adolescent should be able to understand the reason why the family is moving and an explanation should be given without going into too much detail about the adult problems.

DISCUSSING KIDS' PROBLEMS

It is usually the child's problems, issues, and their normal daily topics and events that are discussed with Dad. A dad would never tell a child that his day at work went anything other than "Just fine; it was a good day." There may be some events of Dad's day that would be appropriate for a child to be told, depending on the child's age. It might even be a growth experience for the child to understand the way things work in an adult's world. But generally, when dads and their kids discuss problems, it is usually a child's problems that are being discussed.

Progress in the relationship is being made regarding communication when one's children are confiding in Dad about things that are troubling them. This is when children talk freely about *their* day at school and about *their* friends and how *their* friends made them feel. It is important to ask your child how the events of the day made him feel, especially if it is obvious that the child is bothered by the event. Dad could empathize with his child's negative feeling by saying something like "That would make me feel bad too" or "Well, you didn't deserve to be treated like that." If it is a positive feeling, one might say, "That would make me feel good too; you must be proud." Remember what might seem insignificant to an adult might seem catastrophic to a child and to minimize one's feelings, anyone's feelings, would be insensitive and not help to improve the relationship.

It is also very important to be genuinely concerned and empathetic with kids and say what is true. It is not necessary to point out that the child might have contributed, in some way, to the problem that he is disclosing. If that's the case, Dad might ask, "Is there another way that you could handle such a situation should it happen again?" It is also important to let the child come to as many realizations on their own as possible, within limits, of course. Let's say that a child goes to Dad to vent his anger or to tell him about the day and then the problems that he discusses are blamed on the child. When that's the case, the child will very quickly stop talking to Dad. The bad news is that he will go and talk to someone else, and it could be someone Dad would rather the child not discuss the matter with. This becomes especially important in adolescence.

An important thing to remember is that you are working on improving the relationship with your children. Regardless of how good a relationship one has with someone, in this case our children, it can always be improved. Practice improving your communication skills with your wife, and then apply what you learn to your children. Again, always keep in mind that the content of the communication needs to be at an appropriate level for the child.

A DAD NEVER VENTS HIS ANGER AT HIS CHILDREN

The things that Dad says to his children and the way he communicates to them are extremely important for their development and emotional well-being. Remember that over half of communication is non-verbal. Therefore, the tone of voice and the content, as well as the words that are being used, are very important when communicating with a child.

A dad never vents his anger at his child, and he never makes derogatory comments to him about the child himself, his siblings, or other relatives. This is especially true about making derogatory comments about a child's mother. It is never appropriate and will only damage the relationship between the child and the father. A dad also does not make such comments about anyone where the children can overhear it. Relationships with family members can sometimes be trying; however, it is *never* helpful to denigrate a family member to a child – especially a child's mother or a sibling. If any of these types of behaviors do occur, it is best to apologize, explain that the behavior was inappropriate, and move on.

DEVELOPING MORE PATIENCE AS CHILDREN GROW UP

You will need to practice more and more patience as your children grow older. When kids are young or even into pre-adolescence (seven to eleven years old), they talk about things like school, friends, what they like, or what they don't like. They also talk about cartoons, video games, movies, and such. When a child talks about being scared, for example, a father sympathizes with him, probably hugs the child, and lets him know that everything will be okay. He says something like "I will always be here for you" (if that is true).

What occurs when we tell our children things that are not true or things that we cannot follow through with? The children will have a tendency to stop trusting us and stop believing *everything* we tell them. As children grow older, they might then listen more to their friends or someone other than their dad. It would be a great shame for a father not to be trusted by his children. Remember that one of a dad's greatest assets is that he provides "security" for his family. If a child cannot trust his dad, who can he trust?

ADOLESCENT TOPICS

In adolescence, the topics of discussion become much more relevant and very often concerning. Meanwhile, we want what is best for our children. When we have a good relationship with them, our kids will tell us what is going on in their lives, what's going on at school, in relationships, what their friends are doing, and when they need our advice. It is always a good idea to let our children make the decisions they are capable of for their lives. At the same time, we do not want to give our children more responsibility than they are prepared for, or more that they can manage. However, we do want to give them autonomy over their lives to whatever extent they can handle.

Being a good Level Three communicator (see Chapter 6) will make being the dad of an adolescent much easier. You can tell when your adolescent child is comfortable with discussing things in his life with you when some of the things he might say will drive you crazy. At times, you might even wish you could lock him in his room until he's about thirty years old. Resist the temptation to offer unsolicited advice. When your child tells you that he tried marijuana last week, the proper response would be "What prompted you to try it?" or "So, what did you think of it?" and not "You're grounded for the rest of your life, young man." (Note: About 50% of all adolescents at least try marijuana, so it would not be unusual for your adolescent child to try it as well. The same is true for cigarettes with about 50% of children trying it, and over 70% of kids at least sample alcohol before graduating high school.)

The point is that you want your communication to be open, honest, and valued by your children. Again, a dad knows that his relationship is improving when his children tell him things that might normally get them into trouble or things that, when they are disclosed, Dad's first instinct is to strangle them. This does not necessarily mean that when a child tells Dad about something like that, he gets a pass for the behavior. Often, the child will know he is in trouble, but will feel as if he must tell his dad about it anyway. (You'll find more on discipline in Chapter 15.)

With Level Four Communication, the emotional depth of the relationship grows even more, and the child will feel more assertive, competent, and social. He will also have a sense of belonging. Belonging is a key element of a person's life, and it contributes a great deal to how a child feels about himself.

As discussed earlier in this chapter, communicating one's expectations (and needs) is central to a successful relationship. Children need to learn that they are allowed to express themselves in an appropriate and respectful way. Children learn how to communicate effectively by watching the way their parents interact. When the parents communicate with each other in a manner that is honest, respectful, and congruent with their behaviors, children and adolescents have a tendency to mimic those behaviors inside and out of the home. Conversely, if a husband yells at his wife and calls her derogatory names, for example, there is a very good chance that the children will behave in a similar manner.

Still, children need to be taught that they have the right to be assertive and stand up for themselves. Children and adults have the right to express their needs and desires. Kids need to know that they have the right to say "no" to something that they feel is wrong and to say "yes" to what they believe in.

NO ONE SHOULD ARGUE FOR INAPPROPRIATE BEHAVIORS

There's one last thing to discuss before ending the chapter. This is the expectation that our children will be accountable for their behaviors and not try to justify an inappropriate behavior as if it were appropriate. Dads need to communicate to their children that there is a monumental difference between engaging in an inappropriate behavior and trying to convince others, or himself, that the behavior is appropriate.

It is very important that children, as well as adults, understand that an inappropriate behavior is, for the most part, always inappropriate. The fact that a behavior is inappropriate does not mean that a person will not engage in the behavior. For example, it is not appropriate for someone under that age of twenty-one to drink alcohol in this country under most circumstances. However, the majority of people will at least sample alcohol prior to being twenty-one. It is necessary to understand that the drinking of alcohol prior to a person's twenty-first birthday is an inappropriate behavior. Any illegal behavior is by default inappropriate.

The same would apply to driving a car faster than the posted speed limit. This is not to say that no one drives faster than the posted speed limit, but understand that the behavior is not appropriate. As an adult, we make decisions for ourselves and we pay the consequences of those decisions. If we speed, we could get a traffic ticket, and in this case, we may literally "pay the consequences" for our actions.

When a behavior is inappropriate, trying to make excuses for the behavior or trying to legitimatize the behavior only makes matters worse. A high percentage of the population does not like to admit that they have done something wrong. It is a mature person who can acknowledge that a behavior was/is inappropriate. That is not to say that the behavior will not continue; it is just that it is important to understand that the behavior is inappropriate.

Trying to argue that something is okay to do is different than acknowledging that a behavior is inappropriate but doing it anyway. For example, a seventeen-year-old boy was admitted to the hospital for having suicidal thoughts. He had been arguing with his father. The initial argument occurred when his dad told him he could not go to a party where alcohol would be served with no parental supervision on a school night. The teen then snuck out of the house and went to the party anyway. However, when he got home, the house was locked up, and the boy tried to stumble his way through the garage to get in. He tripped over a few things, which awakened his father. That's when the next argument started.

I asked the young man what the second argument had been about. The boy explained that it was about him going to the party, getting drunk, and coming home late. Again, I asked, "So, what was the argument about?" He repeated himself and again I asked the same question. Finally, the boy realized that there should not have been an argument in that the boy's position and behavior were indefensible.

This is an example where the boy's behavior was completely inappropriate but he did it anyway. Additionally, he was not sorry for his behavior anymore than I am sorry for sometimes driving faster than the posted speed limit. This is an important point in that this lesson is not only for children, but for adults as well. Fathers want to model appropriate behaviors, and when Dad's behavior is not appropriate, he should not try to make excuses for it. Children learn from their dad; if it is okay for a dad to do this, then expect your children to do the same thing. Remember that children generalize behaviors.

In the above example, the son went without permission to the party serving alcohol, and there was absolutely no rationale for an argument. The adolescent was clearly wrong. He should have apologized for disobeying his father and gone to bed. His punishment could have been discussed in the morning because it does not make much sense to try to discuss something with someone who is drunk.

WHAT'S NEXT?

Arguing is a big problem in families, and it has a detrimental effect on all members of a household, regardless of who is involved. Arguments will occur from time to time but should be kept to a minimum. While this is not the case in all households, one national survey reported that 25% of married couples in this country argue with each other *every single day*. The next chapter discusses arguments.

KEY CHAPTER POINTS

1. Next to poor communication, the biggest cause of relationship failure is disappointment related to expectations of the relationship.
2. It is best to discuss expectations as soon into the relationship as possible and as issues arise.
3. In terms of expectations for our children, we need to keep what we expect to be *reasonable and realistic*, and any expectations should be age-appropriate.
4. When there's too much emphasis on our expectations of a child, it stifles his true potential and damages the father/child relationship.
5. Dads need to be open to discussing the expectations that their children have for them, and what might be realistic or inappropriate.
6. When Dad discusses problems with one of his children, it should be about the child's problems and not adult problems.
7. Progress is being made in the dad/child relationship when the child feels comfortable enough to talk about things that are troubling him.
8. Issues that might seem insignificant to an adult might seem catastrophic to a child.
9. A dad never vents his anger toward his children, and he never makes derogatory comments to a child, about the child, the child's siblings, or other relatives (including the child's mother).
10. The older a child becomes, the more patience a dad needs to practice.
11. There is a monumental difference between engaging in an inappropriate behavior and trying to convince others that the behavior is appropriate.

8

A Discussion of Arguing

One of the most damaging interactions to a relationship, and one that can affect the development of a child, is arguing between those within the home. In this chapter, it is assumed that when there is arguing, the argument is accompanied by yelling and, very likely, name-calling and derogatory comments. (There will be more about yelling – without arguing – in the next chapter.) Much of this chapter is about arguing with our children; however, the same applies to the parents. When parents argue with each other, the emotional damage that is being done to the children is significant. In homes where parents do not argue with each other, there is a much lower chance that the children will argue with the parents.

Arguing within the home creates a hostile, unsafe, insecure, and unloving environment for all occupants. The younger the child, the more damaging parental arguing is to her. Even if the child is too young to understand what is being said, the act of arguing is, by its nature, hostile, regardless who is arguing with whom. A child interprets arguing as an act of aggression and reacts, at least internally, as if *she* is being attacked. Anyone with an infant or young child in the home can attest that when her parents argue, the child will often cry or hold her hands over her ears.

THE "LITTLE ALBERT" EXPERIMENT

The following is an example of how quickly a child involuntarily responds to external stimuli that is perceived as dangerous, such as the case with arguing and yelling. An experiment in the 1920s involved a one-year-old child named "Little Albert." (This type of study would not be permitted today because it has such devastating effects on a child.) The study was conducted to verify the researcher's belief that a child's reaction to loud noises was prompted by fear. Little Albert was allowed to sit on a mattress and play with a white rat. Albert showed no signs of being fearful of the rat.

The next phase of the experiment involved striking a metal bar with a hammer when the baby touched the rat. It took only a few times of striking the steel bar with the hammer when Little Albert touched the rat for Albert to fear the rat *without* someone striking the metal bar. Albert also became very distressed just by the sight of the rat as well as generalizing his fear to other furry objects, such as a non-white rabbit, a seal-skin coat, and a Santa Claus beard made of white cotton balls worn by the researcher.

Little Albert was discharged from the university hospital shortly after the experiment was concluded without any additional desensitization or follow-up to determine any long-term effects. However, the stimulus (hitting the steel bar with a hammer) was discontinued after seventeen days. For long after the stimulus was discontinued, Little Albert continued to shows signs of distress when in the presence of small furry objects.

ARGUING

Arguing seems to be a very natural part of communicating and to an extent it is. Recall from the previous chapter that one national study found 25% of all married couples in the United States argue *every single day!* It is easy to see why arguing is bad now that we know arguing creates a hostile environment to raise a child in and does significant damage to a relationship. This does not mean that you will never argue; however, it is important to understand why we argue, what happens when we argue, and what the alternatives to arguing are.

WHAT HAPPENS IN THE BRAIN WHEN WE ARGUE

So what happens when we argue? Why does it seem that we lose control of our common sense? The answer is simple. We do in fact lose control of our common sense or, more specifically, our *ability* to reason.

We, as human beings (along with most other mammals), have a structure in our brain called the amygdala. This is the fight-or-flight area of the brain, and although it might not be as developed in humans as in other mammals, the amygdala still drives our behavior, if we allow it to do so.

Let me briefly explain. If one is walking down a hallway and someone jumps out of a doorway, the person walking down the hallway is generally startled (being startled is an innate reflex behavior and does not have to be learned). The person being startled, internally and automatically, either prepares to run or prepares to fight. In other mammals, they may react without hesitation, or control. A deer pausing to drink from a calm brook may bolt into a fast run at the sound of rustling leaves. No danger may be apparent; the deer's amygdala just took over and the deer ran. On the other hand, a mountain lion, in the same situation, may prepare to fight or may attack the perceived threat without warning.

Since humans have a more developed brain, they can learn to control the instincts of the amygdala to some degree. However, the instincts are still there. (It is important to recognize that it may not be possible to repress innate reflexes.) When a person senses danger, the amygdala activates, and the cognitive ability of *reasoning* becomes impaired – this is not optional. The reason is because all sensory perception goes directly to the amygdala. The sense of sight, hearing, smell, touch, and taste all go directly to the amygdala (this is simplified, of course, but for our purposes it will suffice). Once the stimulus is processed in the amygdala, the data is sent through two very narrow neuronal pathways to the front (pre-frontal cortex) of the brain for processing a reasonable response. So if someone becomes angry, their amygdala becomes activated, and the person may very well react without the benefit of the higher brain function of reasoning.

When we are yelled at, our amygdala senses danger and activates. When *we* yell at someone else, our own amygdala senses danger and activates. As long as it remains activated, our reasoning is impaired and we may not, most likely will not, be very reasonable, or rational. This is why it is important to stay calm and not yell. It takes a very short period of time, maybe one-third of a second, for the sensory data inputted to the amygdala to reach the pre-frontal cortex, the area of the brain in the forehead.

When agitated, it is best not to let one's inner-instincts take over. Remember, your own state of agitation – being upset and yelling at someone else – will activate *your* own amygdala, and *your* own ability to reason *will* be impaired and your actual reasoning will not be sound.

As a consequence, while in this state of mind, we have a tendency to act in a manner we often later regret. Additionally, when we argue, one's memory may also be impaired. A person may not remember exactly what was said, by one's self or the other person, which can easily lead to even more arguing. Next, defending one's self by denying something that was said generally leads to more arguing.

Even if we win the argument and get our way, we may not feel good about the manner in which we got it. That is not to say that everything said was not true and that everything said was not relevant; however, it becomes a question of how we treat those who we love. And above all else, and in everything we do, we want to act and behave in a manner that expresses our love for each other.

The easiest way to avoid conflict – and the subsequent foolishness that accompanies it – is to listen to what is being said and wait a couple of seconds to think about what was actually said. Do not be thinking about what you are going to say in response to what was said. Rather, listen, pay attention, stay focused on what is being said, and then reply calmly. If something that is said arouses feelings of anger, it would be best to take a break and recompose yourself so that you can respond appropriately. People will say things that are upsetting; your objective is not to respond in a manner that will damage the relationship. It is also a good idea to keep in the forefront of your mind that the person you are speaking to is someone you love, so try to behave like it. Try to convey a feeling of love to those who love you, even when *their* behavior may not be reflecting those same feelings.

WHAT STARTS AN ARGUMENT

What starts arguments? A difference of opinion, conflicting points of view? Not getting one's point across? Being controlling? Not having one's needs met? One of the biggest things that causes people to argue is the individual's *need to be right.* It's an issue of *self-esteem,* the way people see themselves and the way that people perceive the way others see them.

For many people, the logic is "I can't be wrong in that it would make me feel (and look to those around me) less important." In other words, it would damage their self-esteem. I have listened to many people argue about one thing or another, and even when faced with the facts, they still will not admit to being wrong. Their self-esteem just will not allow them this, even though an admission of being wrong is not what we were looking for at the time. They just had to be right. (The importance of self-esteem will be discussed in greater detail in the next chapter.)

DIFFERENCES IN ARGUING, DISAGREEING & DISCUSSING

There is a significant difference between *arguing, disagreeing, and discussing.* When we discuss something, we do not usually get angry, we do not accuse, we do not bring up past wrongs, and the objective is not to "win." When the entire objective of someone – child or adult – is to win, reason is no longer a factor; winning, or being right, becomes its own reward. When this happens, the discussion is over and the argument has begun. (I'll get to disagreeing in a moment.)

Another dynamic that relates to arguing is that of *being heard.* Children, especially adolescents, will argue endlessly when in reality they just want to be heard. They would probably also like to be right and to win, but more than that they need us to *listen.* When we stop arguing and start listening, children feel as if we are beginning to hear them. The outcome of the discussion may not change, but the child will feel that Dad at least cares enough to listen.

I want to clarify something about my suggestion to "never argue." I do not mean to imply that you will actually never argue, but to encourage you to understand that arguing usually does not help *any* situation. Not arguing does not necessarily mean that the outcome is going to be any different; you will just have gotten to the same outcome in a more pleasant and less damaging way. Then again, the outcome may be different once you *discuss* whatever it is that needs to be considered. This concept can be applied to every relationship that people have, whether it be with your spouse, your children, your own parents and siblings, your employer, your instructors, your friends, and even those you encounter during the course of a normal day.

A *disagreement* merely means that the participants in the discussion do not agree on the topic, the facts, or their opinions. We, as adults, can disagree with someone and not have it turn into an argument. This is a sign of a person who is emotionally an adult. Adults do not feel that they have to be right *all* the time or that everyone has to agree with them. We just need to be open to the possibility that there might be another point of view that makes more sense than our own point of view or of our own knowledge in a particular area.

One of the problems with having to be right all the time is that someone then has to be wrong all the time. No one wants to be wrong all the time and, in fact, no one *is* wrong all the time. Often men can bully their point across merely because of their size and the loudness of their voice. This influence has to be exercised with extreme caution in that no dad wants his child (or spouse) to feel bullied, especially by their father (or husband). By definition, dads do not bully people. Dad provides security, which is the opposite of bullying, and therefore, when a man bullies his family, he is not acting like an adult man, much less a dad.

WHAT PEOPLE ARGUE ABOUT

People argue about a multitude of things. If we summarized the reasons, we could group them into three categories:

1. Arguing over facts (*John F. Kennedy was the thirty-fifth President.*);
2. Behaviors (*Why have you not cleaned the kitchen?*); or

3. A combination of the two (*If you have cleaned the kitchen, why are there dirty dishes in the sink?*).

In the above list, I omitted another possible topic of arguing and that is *arguing about the way a person feels*. One cannot effectively argue over the way a person feels, therefore it is a complete waste of time to do so. When someone expresses how she feels, a mature person acknowledges it and the *discussion* goes on from there. For example, a wife tells her husband that she "feels" he does not love her. Any debate at this point would only make her feel less loved. The proper response would be to say, "I do love you. What can I do to show you that I love you?" And let the discussion go from there.

Again, discussing is different from "arguing." When we argue, one or more persons involved in the argument wants/needs to be "right," i.e., wants to "win." When our objective is to be right or to win, reason ceases to apply. When we argue, tempers flare, we get upset, and we might say or do something that we will later wish we had not. This does not mean that what was said was not true, but it may not need to have been said to get to the same conclusion. Remember, when we communicate with our children, our objective should be *to help them*. The relationship will be well served if you understand the objective of the discussion before engaging in the discussion. This could be applied to every other person we communicate with as well.

THE WORD "WHY"

One way to turn a potential argument into a discussion is not to start a sentence with the word "why." When a sentence starts with the word "why," an argument is about to begin. It creates a question, and men especially do not like to be questioned, neither do children. The truth is that no one likes to be questioned but when a man or child is questioned, they have a tendency to be more defensive than a wife might be.

Very often, there is not a good reason for the question of "why." In the above example – "Why have you not cleaned the kitchen?" – there is usually not a good reason for why it was not done. The child becomes defensive and generally says something that is unacceptable. The parent then responds to that as well and the argument is on.

I am reminded of a time when my wife Carla called our eighteen-year-old daughter Nicole on the phone to ask her to do the dishes before Carla got home from work. When my wife got home, the kitchen sink was still full of dirty dishes. Nicole was standing next to the sink when Carla walked into the room. Carla asked Nicole, "Why have you not done the dishes?" Nicole's "knee jerk response" was "I did do them." I was standing next to Nicole and merely looked at the sink full of dirty dishes. Nicole responded, "Oh, those dishes." Her first instinct was to defend herself rather than say something like "Oops, I forgot, I'll do them right now."

Rarely does a child have a good reason for why something is not done. Another example might be the question, "Why is your homework not done?" What answer to this question is acceptable? The truth would probably get the child in as much trouble as a lie. "Because I'm lazy and I don't care" might be the truth but an argument is then about to start. It would be better to ask "Is your homework done?" and if it's not done, merely to state, "Go do it," or something along those lines. The same would apply to chores. There is generally not a good reason as to why they are not done and a reminder to do them is better than an explanation as to why they are not done.

In reality, it does not matter why the chores are not done, or why the homework is not done; it just needs to be done. The way Dad conveys this to his children can have a significant impact on his relationship with his kids. A similar approach works very well with adults as well, even at work. Being in charge of people, one might ask, "Is there a reason that ____ is not done yet?" This is far better than "Why has ____ not been done?"

When a sentence is started with the word "why," it brings with it a certain amount of hostility and negativity – whether intended or not. People have a tendency to defend themselves when they *perceive* that they are being attacked, even if that is not what was intended. This simple change in communication can have quite an effect on the interactions one has with others. This is another time to practice with your wife and apply what you learn to your children. You could also practice this same technique in other milieus, such as at work or in the community.

DOES SOMETHING NEED TO BE SAID? THE TEST OF THREES

Another reason people argue rather than discuss is that things are said that do not need to be said. To decide if something needs to be said, consider whether it passes the *Test of Threes*. First, *is it true;* are the facts correct? And true does not mean only to one's self or some convoluted interpretation of the truth. For example, "The dishes were not washed" is significantly different than "the dishes were not washed well enough." Additionally, in terms of "facts," we want to avoid making global or universal statements such as "you *always...*" or "you *never...*" Those types of statements are judgmental; they minimize a person's positive behaviors, and are usually not true. They do, however, have very long-lasting negative effects on relationships, even when said in moments of anger. Once something is said, it cannot be unsaid – even when you apologize for it. However, apologize for it just the same.

Other statements to be avoided are those that attack someone's character, such as "You are such a liar," "You are so inconsiderate," or "You don't care about anyone but yourself." These types of statement are usually not true either, even though the person making the statement may feel as if the statement is true at the time. Dads must be careful about making such statements to their children as kids have a tendency to meet our expectations. If Dad communicates to his daughter that he believes *she* is a liar, she may very well become one.

The second part of the *Test of Threes* is the question *"Is it helpful?"* If it is not helpful, there is no need to bring it up – at least at this point in time and while discussing the current topic. When we are trying to discuss something with our child, it is best to remember what our main objective is, and that would be to raise a self-governing adult with all the necessary tools to be so.

If something said is not helpful, it should probably not be said. Every thought does not have to be verbalized. We *can* keep things to ourselves. For instance, "I told you so" is a very good example of something that virtually *never* needs to be said. Most of the time when someone has made a mistake or failed to do what they were supposed to do, that person is painfully aware of the mistake and does not need to be reminded of it. And what if you are on the receiving end of an "I told you so" comment. Well, it is best to apologize and acknowledge that "You were right; I wish I had listened to you." This quite often will send the discussion/argument into a more positive and helpful direction.

And the last part of the *Test of Threes* is *"Is it necessary?"* If it is not necessary, there is no reason to bring it up unless it can be discussed appropriately. Again, when we are discussing something with our child, we are trying to help her. We do not want to make her feel as if there is something wrong with her personally, but that instead there is a behavior needing to be corrected. There is no reason to bring up something that has nothing to do with the current discussion. This is not a good time to bring up all the other things that the child has done wrong in the past.

Unfortunately, many arguments are prolonged due to non-adherence to any or all of the above. An argument can become so convoluted that the participants no longer remember what the original argument was about.

It is not uncommon during an argument that things are said that really are hurtful. What could have been resolved with merely acknowledging that a mistake was made has now turned into a major problem. This dynamic of keeping it simple and to the point works the same with adults as it does with kids. The truth is that people do not always do as we wish that they would.

WOULDN'T IT BE NICE

Wouldn't it be nice if kids always did what you told them to do – *every time*? And wouldn't it be nice if when you have given them the same chore to do every day – like taking out the trash – that they would do it every day *without being told*? With everyday chores, this might be the case in a perfect world, but it would probably be best *not* to expect that kind of dedication to something like taking out the trash. Children usually need at least occasional reminders. (This could apply to any of their behaviors or your other expectations, such as doing homework, coming home on time, taking a bath every day, etc.)

Another issue is that I try not to expect my kids to perform at a higher level than I do or even at the same level as me. With some families, it seems that minor behaviors, like taking out the trash, can become a major issue. In our home, for example, I did not take out the trash for about thirty years; it was always the job of one of the kids. I found that it would be foolish to expect the kids to do such a routine chore, daily, without at least an occasional reminder.

Now that all of our kids are grown and out of the house, I am the one whose job it is to take out the trash. My wife has to ask me at least once a week if I could somehow work emptying the trash into my busy schedule. Now I know the trash needs to be taken out, but I just do not want to do it. So why then, when the kids were the ones taking out the trash, would I expect them to take it out every day without being reminded every so often? It's easy to see that it is just *not* realistic to expect our kids to perform at a higher level, or even the same level, as an adult. Now, one would certainly expect that a child *could* successfully take out the trash every day without being told, and I applaud those who do. I just do not like to make a big deal out of something that can be remedied by a quick reminder.

I find it extremely bothersome when dads resort to yelling, name-calling, or making derogatory comments like "How do you expect to be successful in life if you can't do a simple thing like take out the trash every day without being told?" These kinds of behaviors are damaging to the relationship. Additionally, there is no correlation in the research literature that indicates that a person will perform better or worse in a career with how well that same person does their chores at home.

Another important thing to remember is that people have differing ideas on how things should be done, and whether or not something is done correctly. For instance, my wife's idea of a clean bathroom and my idea of a clean bathroom are two completely different ideas. My wife Carla was cleaning the house one Saturday when I came home. I asked her, "Is there anything I can do to help?" She suggested that I could clean the hall bathroom. Naturally I said, "It would be my pleasure." I walked into the bathroom, took a look around and decided it looked fine without any further effort needed by me. Carla came to me later on and told me that this bathroom was filthy. Instead of arguing with me, she sent me to my room, which is where I really wanted to be anyway.

In that same light, when our daughter lived at home, my wife would tell her, for instance, to clean her room. Our daughter Nicole's idea of a clean room was significantly different than my wife's idea of a clean room. On numerous occasions, it had been explained to our daughter what was expected when we asked her to clean her room; however, there continued to be some confusion. It would have been a mistake to make a big deal about how our daughter cleans her own room, and this would only lead to arguing and ill feeling within the house. There came a point when Carla and I decided that our daughter's room belonged to her and that she could keep it the way she wanted. This was not the case with our children while they were younger. The reasoning was that they got an allowance, and part of that was for keeping their rooms clean. When our kids were about sixteen, we stopped giving them an allowance for cleaning their rooms and left the cleanliness of their rooms up to them. There was one caveat, and this was that the doors to their rooms needed to be kept shut and that no odors could be detected outside of the rooms.

Now, in terms of taking out the trash, I was not certain that there might be an incorrect way to do it, or at least until a certain situation happened at our house. Let me start this story about trash with a little background. From time to time, my wife would buy things from the Home Shopping Network. Things that one might never imagine needing, like a punch bowl specifically engraved for February 29 (which means it can only be used once every four years).

A pile of unopened boxes accumulated in the garage, and I still have no idea what is inside of them. I often wonder if she even knows. But they are there if she should ever need them. One of these boxes was of good size, about twenty inches long, twelve inches wide, and six inches deep. When my wife took the item that she had purchased out of this box, the package was still full of white-popcorn-type packing material. There did not seem to be any space left over for a product. Anyway, after opening it, Carla asked our youngest son Sammy to take the box out to the trashcan. Sammy said, "No problem," and he took the box outside.

We live on a hill in Simi Valley. For those of you who do not know, Simi Valley is an Indian expression for *Valley of the Wind*, and the wind blows at our house. Instead of putting the box and its contents *inside* the trashcan, Sammy put it *on top* of the trashcan. The wind whipped up that night and blew that white popcorn stuff all around the backyard. It looked like we'd had a blizzard the night before and it snowed white packing popcorn.

The next day was Saturday, and Sammy wanted to go to his friend's house. He was about fourteen years old at this time, and before he could go play with his friends, I asked him to "Pick up all of the white stuff in the backyard and come and let me know when you're done." If something was important enough for me to tell him to do, it was important enough for me to ensure that he did do it. Kids learn really quickly. If you do not monitor their work, they may not do a very good job. And don't forget, what we as parents are trying to do is produce a self-governing adult, and fourteen years old is an age where kids really are not invested in doing a job correctly, but more along the lines of just getting it done. I knew that, and I also knew that if I were the one who had to pick up all that popcorn, I too would just want to get the job done.

A few minutes after Sammy started the task, he came in and told me that he was done. I went out to the backyard and, although it was a lot better, there was still quite a bit left to pick up. I said to Sammy, "I don't think that I have explained the objective completely (notice I did not ask a "why" question). I want you to pick up *all* of this white stuff. So, as you stand here, you should not see any white stuff. Also, as you walk around the yard, you should not see any white stuff. If you do, pick it up and then come let me know that you're done."

At this point, Sammy was upset. Now I ask the question, does he have a right to be upset? The answer is "Of course he does." I know that he has a right to be upset because if I were the one having to pick up all the white packing popcorn, I'd be upset too. I know that I would not want to pick up all that stuff in the backyard, so why would I expect him not to be upset about it? So I very patiently said to Sammy, "Son, you have the right to be upset; I would be upset myself. However, what you do when you're upset matters. Don't make matters worse and just finish the job."

The reason I said this was that in the past Sammy had a habit of slamming things around when he got upset, and I did not want him to make matters worse. Keep in mind that if one member of our family has a problem, or is feeling bad about something, it ripples through the entire family whether we want it to or not.

So Sammy cleaned up the backyard again and came to my office to tell me that he was done. And again, when I checked the backyard, the job was not done yet. At least this time he seemed to understand that all of the white stuff had to be picked up. I walked back into the house again and started down the hallway. In the hallway, Carla came towards me saying, "Don't you just want to strangle him?"

I asked, "Why!"

"Because he's not doing it right!"

I responded, "It makes little difference to me how many times it takes him to finish the job; it's up to him." It seemed that this letting our son be responsible for his actions without getting upset was easier for me than it was for Carla. However, I was able to console her and convince my wife that everything would be all right. Now, if I had allowed her being bothered by the situation to get me upset, then all three of us would have been upset. One could easily see how the arguing or the denigrating comments would then begin.

Notice a couple things that I did not do or say to Sammy during this interaction. One of them was that I did not get upset when our son was upset. When both, or all, parties in an interaction are upset, not a whole lot of good emerges. The other thing I did not do was rub his nose in it by saying something like "If you had done it right the first time, you would not be out here picking it up now," or "How do you expect to be successful in life if you can't do a simple thing like pick up trash?" Additionally, there was no doubt in my mind that Sammy had already come to know a couple things. One was where the box should have gone, and second was that if he had done it right the first time he would not still be out there picking up packing material. There was no reason for me to state this to him.

None of the above interactions would have helped the situation. More importantly, any of those actions would have damaged our relationship. My objective was to help Sammy become a self-governing adult. If I had berated him, or his performance, it would only have taught him to be angry and unreasonable in situations that are uncomfortable for him. The way that it was handled ensured the job got done to my satisfaction. It also allowed Sammy to go on about his day without getting into an argument, which would only have made matters worse, and might have resulted in his being grounded.

OLDER CHILDREN HAVE A TENDENCY TO ARGUE MORE

The older the child, the more inclined they are to argue. This is perfectly normal, and I would hope that we could all agree that we do not want to raise our children to be passive rather than assertive. We do want our children to be able to verbally stand up for themselves. Then again, standing up for oneself is not necessarily arguing. Remember once more that all behavior is learned. If a child has been raised in an environment where there is arguing and not so much discussing, the child will probably develop a propensity to argue. And who is the child more inclined to argue with? That would be the parents, the very persons who are telling the child what to do and the ones who modeled the behavior of arguing in the first place.

We want to teach our children to discuss things calmly and reasonably. This is more easily done by not arguing ourselves, especially with our spouse, and to a lesser degree with our own parents and our own siblings. Again, this is a behavior that Dad needs to practice with his wife and then apply it to the kids.

EASIER TO DISAGREE OVER FACTS

When we disagree with someone, it seems to be easier to disagree without arguing over facts rather than behaviors. A fact would be something that is irrefutable, for instance, today's date, or that the world is round. There are those who would argue these types of facts, and in such cases, it would be best to allow them their beliefs. Arguing opinions is more difficult, and discussing would be a much better way to persuade someone's opinion. However, once one sees that a person is being unreasonable, it would be best to disengage from the discussion before the argument starts. Arguing with people who are unreasonable is generally a waste of time and leads to more problems.

Arguing related to behaviors can be about facts or perceptions. Let's say that a child is supposed to be in the house by a certain time and the child is not; well, he is late. This is a fact, and there is absolutely no need to argue over it. Unfortunately, children, and especially adolescents, often feel the need to be heard and offer an explanation – even when they are clearly wrong. It would be wise to listen to the explanation and allow the discussion to start. The outcome of the discussion will probably not change but the interaction is what is important. When a child feels heard, she is much more likely to be compliant, even though the outcome may be the same.

Dads are often confronted with deciding which behaviors are acceptable and which ones are not. This can certainly lead to disagreements. Disagreements are not necessarily bad. Everyone disagrees with someone at some time in his or her life, and it is likely that we will have disagreements, or discussions, with those we interact with on a daily basis. That is not to say this happens every day, though I would hope that we do have discussions every day with family members.

However, disagreeing does not equate to arguing. Disagreeing can be a good way of discussing things that need to be discussed and having one's point of view and feelings heard. Arguing usually equates to one's need to be right, the need to control others or the situation, and the need to be angry. Once anger rears its ugly head, reason ceases to function.

In moments of anger, I have made some of the most meaningful statements I have ever lived to regret. Just because something is true does not mean we have to say it, and once something is said, it cannot be "unsaid." No matter how many times we apologize, the words were already spoken. The listener believes that what was said is true, even if it is not. They are likely to conclude "You were thinking it," so therefore "You must really think it is true."

103

YOU DON'T HAVE TO BE RIGHT ALL THE TIME

When Dad is secure in who he is, he does not have to be right all the time. He does not need to have his point of view constantly validated, nor does he feel that being right makes him any better than anyone else. With some people, it is easier to be wrong than it is with others, and being proven wrong by such people can be frustrating, embarrassing, and even annoying. But let's not worry about things we cannot change. The objective here is that we are able to have discussions with those we love, without damaging the relationship we have with them – and without damaging *their* self-esteem. This is especially crucial in terms of conversing with our wife and our children.

WHAT'S NEXT?

In the next chapter, we will look at such issues as self-esteem and perception, as well as more ways to be a good dad. Our children need to feel our love and support in order to develop healthy self-esteem, and what we model will help them build good social skills.

KEY CHAPTER POINTS

1. Being exposed to arguing within the home is very damaging to a child's emotional growth, and such arguing creates a hostile, unsafe, insecure, and unloving environment for everyone in the household.

2. In homes where parents do not argue with each other, there is a much lower chance that the children will argue with the parents and each other.

3. There is a significant difference between arguing, disagreeing, and discussing.

4. One of the problems with being right all the time is that someone has to be wrong all the time.

5. There are generally three categories of arguing: (1) over facts, (2) over behaviors, and (3) over a combination of facts and behaviors.

6. One cannot effectively argue about the way someone feels.

7. Try not to start a sentence with the word "why."

8. To decide if something needs to be said, it should pass the *Test of Threes*: (1) Is it true? (2) Is it helpful? (3) Is it necessary?

9. Try not to expect children to function at or above the level of an adult.

10. Older children have a tendency to argue more than younger ones.

11. It is easier to disagree over facts without arguing than over behaviors.

12. When a person is yelled at, his or her brain senses danger, and the same is true if a person yells at someone else. In both cases, the listener's amygdala activates, and reason is impaired.

13. Memory may also be impaired during arguments, and a person may have said something that they do not remember saying. This can lead to more arguing.
14. Protecting self-esteem is easily the most salient reason why people argue and stay engaged in an argument.

9

The Influence of Self-Esteem, Perceptions & Emotions

Simply stated, self-esteem is the way in which a person feels about himself or herself. Self-esteem is what gives the person a sense of personal worth and competence, and it includes the degree to which one possesses self-respect and self-acceptance. Extremely important in the development of self-esteem is the love, warmth, and acceptance demonstrated by one's parents during all stages of development. The attributes contributing to one's self-esteem – love, warmth, and acceptance – will ultimately develop into a sense of trust, especially in infants and toddlers. Such attributes provide the infant with a feeling of basic security, which is necessary for the infant to meet the challenges in his environment. These attributes remain effectual well into adolescence and adulthood, and they safeguard the person against anxiety in coping with the stressors of life.

Briefly summarized, there are multiple types of self-esteem: *realistic*, *poor*, *unstable*, and *unrealistic*. People with realistic self-esteem are those who see themselves appropriately, have a fairly reasonable sense of their abilities, and are not easily hurt or angered by what other people say or think. People with poor self-esteem usually look upon themselves as inferior, even when it is not the case. Those with unstable self-esteem have a tendency to overreact and become easily angered. People with unrealistic self-esteem are those who overestimate their self-worth and abilities.

Self-esteem is extremely important for the psychological well-being of an individual, not only in children but also adults. Still, it is not as fragile as many theorists would have us believe. Even so, as discussed in the last chapter, continued arguing between parents and an environment of inconsistency and chaos can have long-lasting detrimental outcomes for children and their self-esteem. Damaging factors include the derogatory comments, yelling, and insecurities that go along with arguing.

PROTECTING ONE'S SELF-ESTEEM

Self-esteem issues cause more problems than any other personality trait. Many arguments are started because of the way that other people perceive us, or more specifically, the way *we* perceive how *other* people perceive us. To protect one's self-esteem, people will exaggerate and even lie about who they are, what they do for a living, where they live, how much money they have or make, their level of education, their accomplishments, trouble they have been in or not been in, how much they drink, what drugs they use or have used, how many sexual partners they have had or not had, how old they are, and much, much more. People will assault others, risking going to jail for years for being "disrespected" – just to protect their self-esteem. (As if going to jail because you were disrespected is going to improve your self-esteem.) But you get the point that people will go to great lengths to protect the way in which they believe *others* perceive them.

Very often, the way other people perceive us is not representational of the way we may perceive ourselves. We often believe that other people are aware of our thoughts, our mistakes, and our flaws, when in reality this is seldom true. However, this type of belief causes us to act to protect our self-esteem so as to not let others see us for who we believe we are. The truth be known, people with poor, unrealistic, or unstable self-esteem are usually wrong about the way that others perceive them. For our purposes, what is important is the way our children perceive Dad and the influence that a father has on his children's self-esteem.

It is very important for Dad to just be a dad and not try to protect his self-esteem around his family. His family loves him for who he is, not who he would like them to believe he is. Dads need to be genuine with their family. That is not to say that Dad should be open with everything that is going on in his life. However, he should allow his children to see a dad who is compassionate, not cold; sensitive, but not dramatic; protective, but not angry; understanding and not closed-minded.

What difference could it possibly make what other people, who are not close to us, feel about us, or what they believe about us? A wise man once said, "It is a small thing for me to be judged by you." On the other hand, those who are close to us are very aware of the truth – good or bad. What benefit is it to a dad if the world sees him as a really great guy, or a tough guy, or a wealthy guy, or a handsome guy? We want our children to see us as Dad. Our children do not care about the way in which we perceive ourselves, or the way others perceive us. That is, unless we ingrain it into them and they become as shallow and empty as the person modeling that type of behavior.

As dads, we want to be able to treat our family in a calm and nurturing manner that always shows love, caring, consistency, kindness, and understanding. That may sound like a lot; however, it is really quite simple. When we listen to our children, when we let them state their case, when we let them be heard and then respond in a way that keeps an ever-watchful eye on the relationship, we are doing all of those things.

Again, this is something that a husband should practice with his wife and then apply to his children. It could work the other way as well, but it is usually best to treat your wife as the most important person on the planet. And that is regardless of how she treats you. We have already discussed how to communicate and be a good listener, and that's half the battle to improving relationships with those you love.

THERE IS NO NEED TO DEFEND YOURSELF

When a father (or anyone else) feels he needs to verbally defend himself, he has already lost. This may not be the case 100% of the time, but it usually is. When two people start to argue, there is most often one person who is right and one person who is wrong. When you know which one you are, then there is no need to defend yourself. If you are the one who is wrong, a better plan would be to apologize for whatever it is, make amends, and get on with life. As discussed earlier in the book, trying to defend a position that is inappropriate is a waste of time, and this demonstrates to those we love all the things we do not want to convey – that is, that they are not being heard or loved.

If you are the one who is right, it would be best not to argue about it but to discuss it calmly. If the person you are trying to communicate with is not reasonable, it does no good to argue about it. When we are discussing things with our children, there is virtually never a need to argue. Children need to be heard. Often just discussing something with them will be enough to help the child understand why he can or cannot do something.

THE ISSUE OF PERCEPTION

The issue of one's *perception* is often encountered when communicating and this can lead to an argument. Perception is the way a person looks at something or is something that someone believes. Two people, observing or experiencing the same thing, may have differing perceptions. One example that was used previously in the book was the difference in perception of a bathroom being clean or a bathroom being dirty. What constitutes "clean" is a matter of perception.

People's perceptions are their realities. Often people will rationalize and protect their perceptions in similar ways as they might protect their self-esteem. If a child has the perception that his dad loves him, then he is loved by his dad regardless of how the father actually feels about the child. The same is true when a wife holds the perception that she is taken for granted or not loved. In her mind, she *is* taken for granted and/or *not* loved, regardless of what the intentions of the husband are. It is important to try to accept the other person's perceptions and not argue over them. If you have done something wrong, apologize for the behavior, find out if there is anything you could co differently, and move on. But do not argue about the way someone feels. And if they bring it up again, apologize again and ask if there is something that you can do differently.

On the other hand, people do have the ability to change the way they feel and change the way they view things. For example, when our daughter Nicole was nineteen years old, going to college, and living at home, she was supposed to be in the house no later than eleven o'clock. Well, she was always on time except for one night. That night, as my wife Carla and I were getting ready for bed, Carla noticed that it was 11:15 and our daughter was not at home. Very concerned, Carla called Nicole's cell phone, and when Nicole answered, Carla asked, "Are you okay?" Nicole answered that she was fine and at a friend's house. Carla, now upset (remember that anger is rooted in fear), said, "You need to get home right now," and then she hung up the phone.

A few minutes later, Nicole walked through the front door of our home and very defensively stated, "You don't trust me!" Now, before the argument could start, I chimed in that everyone should just go to bed, and if it was necessary to discuss anything, we would talk about it in the morning. So everyone went to bed.

The next morning, my wife went to work before I got up. When I arose, Nicole was in the kitchen slamming cupboard doors and banging pots in the sink as she was cleaning the kitchen. Being a highly trained mental health professional, I surmised immediately that there was a problem. So I asked, "Pumpkin, is something wrong?" Nicole said, "Mom doesn't trust me!" My response was that she could believe anything she wanted to believe but, for me, I'd prefer to believe the truth. So I asked Nicole, "What was the first thing your mother said to you when you answered the phone last night?" Nicole responded, "Are you okay?"

"Right, does that sound like she doesn't trust you?"

"Oh, she was worried about me."

"That's right, she was worried about you. However, you believe whatever you want to believe, but me... I prefer to believe the truth."

Nicole got a big smile on her face and said, "My mommy loves me." And from then on, Nicole was able to see that her mother's concern for her was an act of love.

The point of this example is that we can change the way we perceive issues when given more information or change the way that we interpret a behavior or emotion. It also incorporates the fact that some emotions come up and we initially have little influence over them. We do, on the other hand, have a great deal of control over the accompanying behaviors. These emotions are love, anger, and jealousy. When these emotions arise, there is usually little we can do about them except to take care with how we behave in reaction to them.

Here is another example about perception and emotions. A man walks into his home one night after work and sees his wife in the arms of another man. She sees her husband and looks surprised. The husband immediately feels jealousy and anger but has the ability to control his reaction. His wife says to her husband, "Honey, I'd like you to meet my brother who just got back from Norway." The husband was aware that his wife had a brother who had been away since he was twenty years old. The wife then says, "I'd like you to meet his family also." As the husband looks around the corner, he sees his brother-in-law's wife and three children sitting on the family-room sofa. The husband feels very relieved and greets his new family members.

This example demonstrates that the husband's initial emotions of anger and jealousy changed when he received more information. As I told my daughter, people have the ability to believe whatever they want to believe; however, it would be best to believe the truth.

WHEN YOUR WIFE BRINGS UP AN ISSUE

Another truth is that in a lot of households, it is often the wife who is very much in tune with the way things are going. This includes issues with the children, the parental relationship, and even the physical condition of the home. When problems arise within the household, such as one of the children not doing well in school or the clothes dryer not working properly, it is usually the wife that brings them to her husband's attention. As we discussed earlier, men have a tendency to minimize problems, often discounting them altogether. Once a man finally admits that there is a problem, it is without a doubt, at least in his mind, a small problem and "it is not my fault." In other words, bringing a problem to a man automatically puts him on the defensive.

When a wife comes to her husband with an issue, the husband usually perceives a low level of hostility that comes along with the issue. The wife does not intend to come across as being hostile; it is just the way a husband *perceives* it. A wife can bring an issue to her husband with all the love and patience in the world; it is the way the husband *perceives* the issue that triggers him. The issue is secondary to the way the husband feels about himself and the thought that *he* is responsible for the problem that is being presented to him. If the husband defends his actions or minimizes the issue, an argument often starts, or worse, the wife stops talking altogether. In contrast, when a husband calmly listens to the issue, without preconceived notions, and without taking it personally, a discussion begins instead.

For example, a wife comes to her husband with the issue that their little boy is not doing well in school and "we need to do something." The husband might interpret this as meaning that he has not been a good father, or that he did not do something he should have already done. If the father is emotionally connected to his child's behavior, and derives self-esteem from his child, the father will, in all likelihood, become defensive.

His wife may merely be presenting this problem so a discussion can get started. Rather than defending oneself, blaming the child, the teachers, or minimizing the problem, it might be better to say something along the lines of "Tell me more" or "What do you think we should do?" This lets your wife know that you are at least interested in listening to her and discussing the problem. Keep in mind that a wife may merely want to talk about the problem without a solution being needed. Additionally, she may already know what the solution might be and just needs to be validated by her husband through him listening to her.

LEARNING NOT TO YELL

People with poor, unrealistic, or unstable self-esteem have a tendency to become angry very quickly. They then have a tendency to yell at those who love them. People very often yell when they argue with someone. It is also not unusual at all for Dad to yell to get his way or to get the kids to do what they are supposed to do. By the same token as

113

arguing, when we yell at someone, whether we are arguing or not, this stimulates our own amygdala as well as the *other* person's amygdala. This holds true as well for everyone within earshot of the yelling.

When people are yelled *at,* they do not reason well, they do not listen well, and they do not respond well. The main reason for this is that the amygdala part of the brain has taken over and reason is not functioning very well. Also, keep in mind that the pre-frontal cortex of the brain, the area of executive functioning and reasoning, does not fully develop until the late teens and early twenties. Expecting a person younger than that to be able to communicate, respond, and reason as an adult would be unrealistic.

In addition, when we yell at someone consistently, whether it is our wife or our children, they have a tendency to tune us out. So the yelling loses its effectiveness as it is often ignored. When a person who has a tendency to yell is ignored, it generally increases the yelling. Then the person is further ignored, or is yelled back at in return, which increases the yelling even further.

Another common response when there is consistent yelling is that the person it is directed toward internalizes the anger and becomes depressed and/or withdrawn. (This reaction will be discussed in more detail in Chapter 16, which addresses the depressed child.) This is where the influence of Dad becomes extremely important. A dad who can stay calm when those around him are not being calm is exercising his influence. A dad does not have to be loud, does not have to be tough, and does not have to always be right. But in order to be effective as a dad, he has to be calm, consistent, caring, and concerned (*the 4 Cs*).

If a behavior – such as yelling – is not working, stop doing it. If something is abusive, especially by its nature, stop doing it. (Yelling, just by its nature, is abusive.) Why on earth would someone yell at someone they love (because they were trained to)? Why would someone verbally abuse someone they love (because they were taught to)? This would be a good time to end that cycle and treat each other like you love one another. I am certain that most children know their father loves them. What I am suggesting is to merely act like it in that *actions* speak so much louder than words, especially when yelling.

One of the quickest and easiest ways to improve the relationships we have with those we love is *not* to yell at them. Again, practice with your wife and apply what you learn to your children. However, I must make a disclaimer in that most people at some time will yell. This is something that is very common, but it is something that needs to decrease and even stop altogether.

If you're a dad and you find yourself yelling at your child, remove yourself from the situation. Calm down, think things through, and apologize to your child for yelling, as well to the other members of the family. This does not mean that you were wrong; it means that you are sorry for the way you communicated. Note that the end result may stay the same. For example, let's say the child did not take out the trash, and he got yelled at for it. He still needs to take out the trash. The apology is for the way he was treated and the way you communicated that the trash needed to be taken out.

WAS IT REALLY YELLING?

There are times when people being accused of yelling were not really yelling, but it was perceived as such. For instance, someone may feel they were being yelled at when in fact the tone of voice of the other person had not gone up at all. A child may interpret something that they do not want to hear as yelling. This is a different case than yelling or arguing but it still needs to be understood.

For example, it was the first day of school when my youngest son Sammy was starting eleventh grade. I got a phone call from the high school stating that he had not attended sixth period English. Now the train of thought in our home was that when a child begins high school (in our community that is ninth grade), he knows what he is supposed to do. So for the most part, being a dad at that point is monitoring how well he can function on his own and advising him as necessary. As long as I did not get a phone call from the school, I assumed that a child was doing everything he was supposed to do, and I pretty much left that up to him. This philosophy is difficult for a lot of parents to agree to and follow. In this scenario, the child needs to be brought up knowing what is expected of him, being held accountable for his actions, and being taught the things that he needs to know to be successful. With this, there is a very real possibility that the child will do as he is supposed to do. (Note: This hands-off approach only works if the dad/child relationship is such that when the child is having a problem he feels safe and secure enough to come and discuss it with his father. If that type of relationship does not exist, the child will generally go out of his way to hide the problem and even lie about the problem should one come up. The good news is that relationships can be improved at any age, and old behaviors can be replaced with new behaviors.)

So when I got that phone call on the first day of school, I was a little puzzled. Naturally, I did not jump to conclusions or jump down Sammy's throat by yelling, "Why didn't you go to sixth period English?" But I did ask him if it was the case and, if so, what happened? Sammy replied rather defensively (remember that when men are presented with a question/problem, they often take the presentation of the issue as hostility). He explained that the football coach had talked to him during first period PE and asked him to come to football practice during sixth period, which is what he did. The problem was that his schedule of classes showed he had English for sixth period and now he had been absent from English.

My comment at this point was merely "So you didn't go to sixth period English?" Sammy's response was that the coach told him to go to sixth period football practice and that he could not see why I was upset and yelling at him. Now it was clear to see that I was not happy with his choice to skip English in lieu of football practice, even though his coach told him to do this. That obviously was being conveyed to him by non-verbal cues. My tone of voice and volume were normal, however kids can interpret the content of what is being said as yelling. At this point, Sammy continued to be defensive and was not seeing that he should have gone to sixth period English or had his class schedule changed. Since Sammy was getting upset, I suggested we take a break. I mentioned that I had planned to take a shower, so when I got out we would continue the discussion.

When I got out of the shower, Sammy was watching TV. I simply asked him what his intentions were. He muted the sound of the TV and explained that tomorrow morning before school started he would go to the counselor's office and have his first period PE class changed with his six period English. This way, he could have football practice during sixth period and English class during first period. And Sammy further stated that he would bring me a copy of his new schedule after school tomorrow so that I could see it. I concurred with his plan and praised him for thinking it through. I also asked him, "Can you see where my frustration came from?" He responded, "Yes, I can. I should have had my schedule changed before I missed the English class. I will make sure this does not happen again."

At this point, the fact that Sammy had missed English class becomes irrelevant. There is absolutely no reason to discuss it further or whether there are to be any repercussions or consequences. This was a mistake, but Sammy honestly felt that he was doing what his football coach said to do. However, the football coach certainly did not give him permission to miss English class. The coach just wanted him on the football team. This was a learning experience for my son; he learned that just because a person is in a position of authority does not necessarily make him right and that *he* himself needs to decide how to handle a situation as it comes up. He might rather have told the coach that he had English class during sixth period and that he would have it swapped by the next day and be in football practice tomorrow rather than today.

Children and especially adolescents need to know that they can question authority. They are allowed to stop, think, and reason for themselves, as well as feel that they have the authority to make decisions for themselves and to follow through on those decisions. Also notice that I was not the one who resolved this problem. I also did not contact the school, the English teacher, or the football coach. This was my son's problem and he handled it well. There was no reason for me to get involved any further. If there was a need to become involved, I would have; however this is one of those instances where my son would learn a lot more by fixing the problem himself.

Problem resolved – no yelling.

SELF-ESTEEM AND NAME-CALLING

Self-esteem is affected when one decides to argue rather than communicate or discuss. A related issue is name-calling. As with yelling, name-calling is inherently abusive. If we call our child "stupid," he may very well fulfill our expectation and act stupid.

There was a sitcom that I used to watch every week, *That '70s Show*, whereby Red, the father of one of the teenagers, would refer to his son Eric as "Dumbass" at least one time per episode. This is a very good example of something that people find humorous when in reality it is abusive. I thought the show was funny, and when the series came out on DVD, I bought all of the seasons. When I was in my home office and working on numerous things, I would usually have something playing on the TV and therefore I was playing episodes of *That '70s Show* back-to-back. Listening to Red call his son Eric "Dumbass" time after time became annoying to me. Eventually I could not listen to more than one or two episodes at a time. The show was hilarious but listening to a father repeatedly call his son names was bothersome to me.

A dad should never call his child, his spouse, his own parents, or his in-laws a derogatory name. There is never an excuse to call someone we love a derogatory name. It is degrading, it is judgmental, and it goes against everything that makes a man a dad. Additionally, there is little distinction made between calling someone a name and stating that they act that way. For instance, in the example of *That '70s Show*, there would be little comfort to Red's son if Red said, "Stop acting like a dumbass" rather than calling him "Dumbass." Note also that, to the listener, there is virtually no difference in saying something like "I love you, I just don't like you very much right now" and "I don't love you." What a child hears is "I do not love you and I do not like you."

Again, keep in mind that all behavior is learned. If your child is saying things or engaging in behaviors that he should not, let him know that the behavior is not appropriate. If he learned an inappropriate behavior such as name-calling from you, apologize to him. Let the child know that you were wrong to say what you did or that the behavior you used was inappropriate and that you will not do it again.

MORE REAL-LIFE EXAMPLES

I was treating a couple in therapy because their eleven-year-old son refused to go to school and was a behavioral problem at home. The child was also being very rude to his mother, who was a stay-at-home mom. The father was a doctor. The parents came to see me for parenting advice. After a couple of sessions, I asked the father what he did when the boy was rude to his mother. The mother chimed in and said, "He does nothing. He cares more about his own mother than he does about me." It got real quiet in the office at that point, and then the father said, "Well, she makes fun of my accent." The wife started to laugh and said, "It's funny."

This started several weeks of couple's therapy where I worked to help the parents understand that the child was mimicking their own behaviors. He was also generalizing their behaviors to both parents. If the mother made fun of the father, the child felt it was okay to make fun of either of them. The mother would throw things at her husband, so the child felt it was acceptable to throw things toward either of them. The parents discovered that, at this child's age, the father possessed a significant amount of influence over the son. If the father responded differently to the actions of his wife, the son would understand the proper way to treat his mother and subsequently others.

The parents were acting like a couple of kids themselves and then wondered why the child was not listening to them. The parent/child relationships were more like peer/peer relationships and therefore the child was not listening to his parents. After all, peers do not tell peers what to do, and you can say whatever you want to a peer, being aware that, of course, they might retaliate. The mother was home all day with this child who was making her life miserable. When the father came home, he did not want to deal with it so he would take the child out for dinner or some fun activity. This merely reinforced to the child that his behavior all day long with his mother was acceptable. The problem for the father was that if he did not continuously do something for the child, the child made his life miserable as well.

The parents tried to set boundaries, but rarely followed through with any consequences. Therefore the child's poor behaviors were intermittently reinforced, which, as you might recall, is the most difficult type of reinforcement to extinguish. The child's behaviors got worse for a couple of weeks. Yet, eventually, this child figured out that things had changed. For instance, the parents learned how to present themselves to the child as a united front. When the child made a derogatory comment to his mother, the father explained very firmly, "That is my wife. No one talks to my wife that way. Is that clear?" It seemed to make it very clear. The key to this of course was to model the desired behavior and make sure that the dad did not talk poorly to his wife. Also, the father had already explained to the child that the behavior was inappropriate.

I had another couple who came to treatment because their nine-year-old son was wetting the bed. I talked with the parents for an hour and then I scheduled another appointment with them for the next week. At the end of that second appointment, we scheduled another appointment for a week later. At the end of the third appointment, I asked the couple to come back. The couple asked, "When are you going to talk to our son? He's the reason we came here." I asked if their son had continued to wet the bed. They replied that the bed-wetting had stopped over a week earlier. I responded by saying that the reason the child had been wetting the bed was because of the frequency and intensity of the parents' arguing. Now that the parents were getting along better, the child's level of stress had decreased, and he stopped wetting the bed.

It's easy to see through these two examples that children are affected by arguing between parents, as well as by the other ways parents interact together. When we talk about relationships, it is always about how we communicate with one another. Every word, gesture, and behavior communicates to those around us.

COMMUNICATING FEELINGS

Most relationships revolve around what is being said to each other. Granted, much of what is said revolves around behaviors. However, when we communicate our expectations of behaviors and express our needs appropriately, then behaviors have a tendency to change. Changes come to both the one improving the way he or she communicates, and also the ones he or she is communicating with.

In addition to communicating about behaviors, we want to ensure that we can also communicate about our feelings. Just as important, or even more important, than being able to communicate about our own feelings is being able to listen, validate, and empathize with the feelings of those we love. Arguing, yelling, and name-calling, regardless of the content, damages relationships. Continued exposure to these types of interactions will do more than cause kids to have poor relationships with their parents. It also teaches them these same means of communicating with teachers, peers, and other people they come into contact with in the community. As the children become adults, the way they communicate will affect the relationships with their own spouse and their own children as well as others in their world.

In fact, more than half of a person's success in life revolves around social skills, which involves communicating. Along with the ability to communicate, the assertiveness to communicate needs to be implanted as well, and there is no person with more influence in this area than Dad.

Fostering your child's ability to communicate and be successful in social situations is every bit as important as his intelligence and level of education. This will also help build his self-esteem.

WHAT'S NEXT?

In the next chapter, we will be discussing philosophies that govern the way we want to live our lives. Philosophies also help to solidify the way we treat each other, and they help us to develop the consistency that is so important in creating a calm and caring environment for our families.

KEY CHAPTER POINTS

1. Self-esteem is the way in which a person feels about himself or herself.
2. Self-esteem is extremely important for the psychological well-being of an individual, not only in children but also adults.
3. Self-esteem issues and attempts to protect self-esteem cause many relationship problems.
4. It is very important for Dad not to try to protect his self-esteem around his family. He should allow his children to see a dad who is calm, compassionate, protective, and understanding.
5. A person's perception is their reality. One thing that is very important is the way a child perceives his dad.
6. People have the ability to change their perception of things when given additional information.
7. In many households, it is often the wife who is very much in tune with the way that things are going. It is usually the wife who brings issues about the household to the husband.
8. Husbands often perceive a low level of hostility in someone bringing them a problem, even when there is no hostility intended.
9. People with poor, unrealistic, or unstable self-esteem tend to become angry very quickly, and they also have a tendency to yell at their loved ones. Arguing, yelling, and name-calling, regardless of the content, damages relationships.
10. When people are yelled at, they do not reason, listen, and/or respond well.
11. One of the quickest and easiest ways to improve the relationship we have with those we love is not to yell at them.
12. As with yelling, name-calling is inherently abusive.

13. A dad should never call his children, his spouse, or even his own parents or in-laws a derogatory name in that it is inherently abusive.
14. I am certain that most children know their father loves them. What I am suggesting is to merely act like it in that *actions* speak so much louder than words.

10

Philosophies to Live By

Some of the things discussed in this chapter might seem obvious but we need to understand what makes relationships successful. As you read in Chapter 7, one of the major reasons that relationships fail is due to unmet expectations. We have expectations in nearly everything we do, starting with what we expect from our wife and children, from our friends, from our parents, from our employer, and from our government.

In a marriage or romantic relationship, it is important to discuss how we are going to treat each other and how we will live our lives together, which will aid in the fulfillment of one's expectations. This can be done in terms of philosophies, which state how we want to live our life, treat others, and expect to be treated by others. For example, before my wife Carla and I got married, we sat down and discussed, over a period of time, the philosophies we would use and how we were going to treat each other and raise our children. At that point, my six boys were grown and either in college or out on their own. My wife still had two children at home, a ten-year-old son and a seventeen-year-old daughter.

At the time, neither of my wife's children had had a father in their life for the past eight years. Throughout our entire dating process, Carla and I decided that we would not involve the children until we were sure that the relationship was going to go the distance. We certainly had some interaction with the children, in that we would occasionally go to places like Magic Mountain, out to dinner, and things like that with the children. But for the most part, they were not a part of our courtship.

My wife was and remains one of the most delightful people I have ever known. She is all the things I could have ever asked for in a wife, a companion, and a friend. Carla is all the things that I would pray to God for in a wife. She is my best friend; she is my confidant; and she is my soulmate. I knew that I wanted to spend the rest of my life with this girl.

PHILOSOPHY TO ALWAYS TREAT EACH OTHER AS IF WE LOVE EACH OTHER

As I explained, before we got married, my wife Carla and I sat down and developed some philosophies. The first philosophy, and clearly the most important, was that we would always treat each other as if we loved one another. This philosophy extended not only to each other, but to our children as well. We knew that the children would mimic the behaviors that we modeled in our own relationship, and if we treated each other well, this would show the children how to treat others, including us.

Years earlier, I had worked for over six years with adolescent patients and their families at a psychiatric hospital. The overriding issue the adolescents conveyed was that each one did not feel as if he or she was loved. (This feeling was often accompanied with a much deeper feeling that he or she was not worth loving.)

After talking to the parent(s), it was obvious that the child was loved very much; however, that love was not being conveyed to the child. In short, the child's perception was that she was not loved. When I would then suggest that the family go home and treat each other as if they loved each other, the parents would usually get very tearful. They were aware that the love they had for their child was not being conveyed. They realized that they had gotten into the habit of having unrealistic expectations. This was also coupled with communication that was conveying the wrong message, as well as parenting behaviors that were making matters worse. In most cases, the parents were doing the best that they could. However, they had not learned the necessary strategies to solve the current problems or to keep the problems from happening in the first place.

Very often the parents would see that the younger children were developing problems similar to the older children's. Parents sometimes blamed the older children for teaching maladaptive behaviors to the younger children and to some degree this was true. When we consider that all behavior is learned, siblings will learn from each other. It would, however, be naïve to believe that the younger children's behavioral issues were entirely a result of being around the older children.

Most parents are very eager to learn strategies that will not only address the problems that are currently happening but also head off upcoming issues. The way that a dad deals with issues within his family has long-lasting and far-reaching influence on everyone in the house, especially the younger children. If a father is treating one of his children in an unrealistic or uncaring manner, the other children within the home may very well develop those same or similar attitudes toward their *father* or toward other family members. It would be best to stop using parenting techniques that are not effective, including yelling and name-calling (as discussed in the last chapter).

If an approach to parenting is not working, stop using it. A parent, in all likelihood, is not going to say or do something that will "shock" the child into compliance. However, the same comment or behavior could do severe damage to the relationship and adversely affect the child's self-esteem and subsequent behavior. A wise man once said, "If you find yourself in a hole, stop digging." Get back to such basics as "Love is patient, love is kind." If we all treated each other that way, imagine how well we would all get along.

When dads make changes in how they interact with loved ones, this does not mean that the rest of the family will make the same changes right away. Behaviors take time to change, and even after these changes are firmly in place, there may be (probably will be) times when an old, unacceptable behavior pops up (this happens with dads too). Stay calm, consistent, loving, and caring; use the skills that are being discussed within these pages and move on. If, as Dad, you mess up and revert back to yelling or worse, apologize for the behavior (even though what was conveyed might have been correct – the way it was conveyed was not) and move on. If the child brings it up again, apologize again because this shows that the child is clearly not over it yet.

When dads get angry, it can be very frightening to one's wife and children. Men are generally larger than women and children, and even if they are not that large, there is a certain amount of power that accompanies a dad merely because he is Dad. That needs to be taken very seriously and that power needs to be controlled. When a dad backslides and yells or throws a temper tantrum, maybe after not having acted like that in months, the fears that the children and the wife previously felt come back from within themselves. It might take some time and reassurance from the dad to help them settle back into their new expectations of Dad's behaviors.

Most feelings (about 90%) that a person experiences in any given situation are from previous experiences of a similar nature. Let's say that a child was terrified when her father used to yell at her mother, but now that same dad is being calm and loving. Then suddenly there is an outburst from Dad, and all those old feelings of terror come up in the child during this isolated incident. Ninety percent of what the child is feeling in this situation is from past experiences, and only 10% is from the current experience. However, what the child is currently feeling is 100% of the emotions from the combined experiences. Also, it is important to remember that a child's, as well as an adolescent's, brain is not yet fully developed – which would affect her ability to reason. Adults may have difficulty rationalizing away their feelings in these scenarios as well, and additional compassion and empathy will most likely be necessary.

People make mistakes, people get frustrated and revert back to old behaviors, and others within the home might not be making the same progress that Dad is making. This is an opportunity to exercise one's influence and remain calm, consistent, caring, and concerned (*the 4 Cs*), regardless of what the other family members are doing. *Always act as if you love each other.* Even if others are not acting that way, dads must use their influence to be a good example. "Love is patient, love is kind" *always*, regardless of how *you* are being treated. When Dad acts in a manner that shows his children that he loves them, children generally mimic those behaviors. This gets us to our next philosophy, which goes

hand-in-hand with treating each other like you love each other –
modeling the desired behaviors.

PHILOSOPHY TO MODEL THE DESIRED BEHAVIOR

This topic has been discussed previously but needs a little more
clarification. As you read through this book, you should start to
understand the importance of modeling the behavior that Dad wants his
children to use. This would apply not only to behaviors that Dad wants
his children to mimic, but also behaviors that he does *not* want his
children to establish. If Dad does not want his children to yell, for
example, then Dad should not yell. This holds true for virtually every
other behavior that Dad does not want his children to develop.

It is very difficult to tell a child not to do something when a parent is
engaging in that very behavior. These behaviors might include smoking,
drinking, sex outside of marriage, infidelity, and the entire gamut of
possibilities, including the way we communicate with each other.

When modeling the desired behavior, it is also important to realize
once again that children are not capable of performing at an adult level.
Therefore it would be unrealistic to expect a child to be as responsible as
an adult. This is age-dependent but in general younger children need
much more supervision than older children, and they need more help
from Dad with activities like homework and chores.

When a child does not perform at an adult level, it's important that
Dad maintain his love for his family members, and that he understand
that children do the best they can. If a child needs help, it is best to give
her that help.

PHILOSOPHY OF CONSISTENT PARENTING STYLES

The *Philosophy of Consistent Parenting Styles* has to do with the
parents cooperatively deciding how they are going to raise their children.
This is very important because inconsistency in parenting styles creates a
chaotic and insecure environment in which to raise children. Also, as you
are learning, kids learn many of the skills necessary to become a
successful adult by the way their parents interact.

Parents need to be calm, consistent, caring, and concerned when deciding what is and what is not appropriate for a child. As you read through this chapter and the rest of the book, my hope is that it will become clear that *behaviors matter*. Parents do not always see eye-to-eye with each other as to rules and what appropriate behavior is for their children. Often this is due to an issue of control, which is never a good thing if the objective is control. The objective should be *what is best for the family and for the individual child.* What is best for the individual parent should be considered, but not at the cost of the parental relationship.

One of the philosophies that has worked well in our home is that one "no" is no and it takes two "yeses" to be yes. In other words, if one parent told one of our children that she could not do something, then it was no. If one of the kids wanted to do something, it would take an affirmative response from both my wife and me for the answer to be yes.

This should not be taken too far because many of the day-to-day decisions are made by whichever parent is home. An example might be if one of the kids, when she was ten years old, wanted to go next door and play with a friend. My wife and I would not have to discuss that. However, if the answer were "no," regardless of what the child wanted to do, the other parent would not give a different answer without a *private* discussion with the first parent.

An example. My wife Carla loves to have parties at our house. One time, only our fourteen-year-old son Sammy was still at home, and on this night, the guests were starting to arrive. I was in my office working when Sammy came to me and said that there was nothing for him to do during the party. Still, his mother told him that he could not go to his friend's house.

I asked Sammy if there was a reason his mother would not allow him to go, and he said there was not. He also said that there were only going to be adults at the party and that there would be nothing in his room to do for the evening. He was correct, in that he did not have a television, computer, or video games in his room. Sammy asked me if I would talk to his mother for him. I asked him to wait in his room as I talked to her.

My wife was very busy and anxious about the party. I asked if Sammy was in trouble, and she said "no." I asked if there was a reason that Sammy could not go to his friend's house for the night. She responded that Sammy had two weeks to figure out what he was going to do for the night, and that she did not have time to take him across town to his friend's house. I asked if it was okay for Sammy to go if he could find a ride. Carla said that she had no problem with him going, but that he should have thought about this before now and she would not take him. My wife also reminded me that I could not take him either (this had never crossed my mind, but my wife knows how I like to get out of these parties). Instead, I was supposed to be helping her greet the guests, who were now arriving.

I went to Sammy's room and told him that his mother and I had agreed to allow him to spend the night at his friend's house if he could get a ride. Sammy called his friend's mother who volunteered to come pick him up. There are valuable lessons in this story, in that a child needs to be responsible for his behavior. Indeed, he should have planned ahead. Second, he was able to see that his parents were on the same page in terms of what he was or was not allowed to do. Third, and maybe most importantly, he learned that his parents were not unreasonable, and they were able to talk things over and come to a sensible conclusion. And fourth, he fixed the problem himself by finding a ride.

It is important, as the above example illustrates, that parents work cooperatively together to do what is best for each member of the family. If my wife had continued to hold her ground, I would not have permitted Sammy to go to his friend's house. (This would probably never happen because we try to always have a reason for our decisions and the reason for this one was that we could not take him. Once that problem was resolved, there was no reason that he could not go. Keeping him at home under these circumstances would have been unfair to our son.) I also would not have made my wife out to be the bad guy. I would have publicly supported her decision, even though I may not have been supportive in private with her. Parents always need to present *a united front* in the way they parent their children. The next philosophy relates to this, as it is about non-confrontation in front of the children.

PHILOSOPHY OF NON-CONFRONTATION

The *Philosophy of Non-Confrontation* has to do with not discussing parenting issues in front of the children or where the children can hear. When parents do not agree on what is best for their children, or whether a child is allowed to do something, this should be discussed in private away from the children if at all possible.

When a child learns she can get the answer she wants from one of the parents, that is the parent the child will, in all likelihood, go to when she wants something. Children also learn very quickly that if they can split the parents, they can often get what they want. This is very true when the parents are not getting along.

Remember that being a parent means to do what is in the best interest of the child. Even when the parents are not getting along, they still need to do what is in the best interest of the child. It is not necessarily bad that children witness their parents disagreeing – everybody at some time will have a disagreement. What's important is that children learn how to disagree without it becoming personal or abusive.

Still, a non-confrontational philosophy centers on not arguing, or even discussing what a child can or cannot do in the presence of the child. As mentioned, children will pick up very quickly which parent is on their side and try to exploit that. This can create a very dysfunctional family dynamic, and that is not a position a dad wants to be in. It would be better to give in to his wife's position, than to argue it in front of the children. Once the children are out of earshot, the parents can discuss it in more detail – all the time remembering that the job of a parent is to raise their children to be self-governing adults.

I cannot tell you the number of times I have heard parents say that all they want for their children is for them to be healthy and happy. I agree with the healthy part, but the happy part I will take exception to here. If not going to school, taking drugs, being disrespectful, or being a delinquent makes a child happy, I would certainly not be in favor of that. Happiness comes from doing what a person is supposed to do. Happiness is a byproduct of doing what is right and appropriate. I prefer my children, as for myself, to be healthy and do what is right.

131

PHILOSOPHY THAT KIDS DO THE BEST THEY CAN

As explained earlier in the book, we cannot expect our children to perform at an adult level. Also, it should be apparent by now that kids do the best that they can. If a child is not doing what she is supposed to do, there is a reason. That reason is very often that she has not been modeled the behavior necessary for success or has been modeled behaviors that are inconsistent.

Dad's influence is so great that most children will go to great lengths to make Dad proud. But this is only true if the relationship is something that the child cherishes. When the relationship a child enjoys with her father is coupled with appropriate parental modeling, a child will excel. However, it is important to understand that not all children excel at the same pace or in the same manner. For example, not all kids are good at sports; not all kids are good at math; not all kids are good at art or creativity. Some kids are not especially good at any one thing but have attributes that are unique only to her.

Once again, kids do the best they can. When a child is having problems, it is imperative that she be able to go to her father with confidence. She needs to know that her dad will help her, sympathize with her, and let her know that he still loves her – no matter what.

Yes, kids do the best they can. Sometimes the bar seems pretty low, but that just means it is going to take a little more time to help the child do better. There is nothing more fulfilling to a dad than when he sees his child making progress in an area where she has previously been struggling. Practice being patient and kind, and always remember that kids do the best they can.

So now let's say that a child is doing the best that she can, and Dad knows what the child is capable of. At this point, Dad needs to allow the child to be responsible for her actions at a level that is appropriate for the child. When Dad acts in a manner that shows that he is responsible for his own actions, it models the same philosophy to his children.

PHILOSOPHY NOT TO MAKE COMMENTS
ABOUT A CHILD'S PHYSICAL APPEARANCE

The title of this section pretty much sums it up. In today's society, it might be difficult not to make a sarcastic comment about the way some people choose to present themselves. The key term in this example is "choose." What is never acceptable is to make a comment in a derogatory manner about how one's own child looks.

This would include making a comment about a child's physical characteristics, such as a feature of her body or face. Most people have little control over many of their physical features, and it would be abusive to make fun of them. One related subject that is getting a lot of attention today is children's weight. It is *never* appropriate for Dad to *ever* make a derogatory comment about his children's physical characteristics, especially his daughter's weight. This is another one of those areas that applies to a man's wife as well. It is *never* acceptable to make derogatory comments about a spouse's weight or other physical characteristics.

PHILOSOPHY TO ALLOW EACH PERSON
TO BE RESPONSIBLE FOR HIS OR HER OWN ACTIONS

The next philosophical point that my wife and I agreed to is that each member of the family must be responsible for his or her own actions. This is very important for each member of the family, including children.

It is not unusual for parents to hold older siblings accountable for the actions of their younger brothers and sisters. While there might be occasions where the older sibling is tasked with watching the younger ones, the littler children should still be responsible for their own actions. This would also be true when a parent is watching over his or her own child. The non-compliant child should be responsible for his or her own actions.

In these cases, holding the younger sibling responsible for his or her own actions should be within reason. Let's say that an older sibling is watching a three-year-old and the three-year-old gets into something that she should not have had access to using. If the older sibling was not watching her carefully enough, then obviously the older child is responsible. However, as children get older and understand the difference between right and wrong, they should then be held accountable for their own behaviors. Even so, this needs to be within the design of sufficient and appropriate supervision.

The degree of responsibility needs to be dependent on the age of the child. Of course, a two-year-old is not as capable of controlling her behavior as an eight-year-old. An eight-year-old is not as capable of controlling her behavior as a sixteen-year-old. Dad needs to keep in mind that the overall objective is to raise a child into a self-governing adult. Often this requires that a dad let the child suffer the consequences of her actions, possibly without any disciplinary action from the dad. He lets the *natural consequences* of the child's actions be her own punishment or reward. This should be within the reasonable limits that continue to provide for the child's safety.

PHILOSOPHY OF NATURAL CONSEQUENCES

Natural consequences are another philosophical point that needs to be addressed. The parent does not always have to be the one to hand out punishment in that, very often, the natural consequences are sufficient. Natural consequences are a very powerful method to help a child learn to be responsible. It also teaches the child that there are consequences in life beyond the punishment or consequences imposed by a parent.

As a dad, we try to protect our children when in reality children need to make decisions for themselves as often as possible. Natural consequences are an excellent way of helping a child grow into a self-governing adult. For example, I was asked to help a fourteen-year-old girl who lived with her grandfather improve their communication skills and relationship. The young girl had lived with her grandparents for her entire life. Her grandmother had died five years earlier of cancer, and the grandfather had dedicated his life to raising this young lady on his own.

At our first meeting, the two argued like an old married couple. The relationship seemed to be more of a peer/peer relationship rather than a parent/child relationship. Even so, the grandfather still invoked his parental authority. Note that arguing at the child's level while also trying to exert parental authority creates conflict and confusion within the child and frustration for the parent. Dad is always dad and should act like it – *always* (even when a grandfather is acting as Dad).

One of the issues they argued about was whether the child could have a work permit. In Ventura County where this family lived, a person under the age of eighteen years old needed a work permit from the child's school in order to obtain a job. The grandfather did not feel that the girl was incapable of holding down a job but that no employer would hire this child because she was only fourteen.

In the absence of the child, I suggested that the grandfather go ahead and sign the work permit, which the girl would then present to the school. What this did was relinquish the grandfather from being blamed for the child not being able to work. He and I both knew there was a very good chance that no employer would hire the girl because of her age, even with a work permit. Still, all the reasoning in the world had not convinced this extremely intelligent young lady that most likely she would not be hired.

After the grandfather signed the permit, and the school subsequently issued it officially, the entire burden and responsibility of getting a job had been placed onto the girl. She was about to learn for herself what her grandfather already knew. When she could not get hired, at least that argument ceased. The young lady learned by a matter of natural consequences that it would be difficult for her to get a job at fourteen years old.

This situation would most assuredly have been different if the girl had been sixteen years old or older. Even then, a staggering number of parents refuse to sign a work permit in Ventura County because of their belief that the child's grades are not good enough, that she was too irresponsible, or that the child is not trained to do anything. None of these is a good reason not to allow a child who wants to work to try to find a job.

In our household, sixteen was the age when our kids would get part-time jobs for no more than twelve to sixteen hours a week. Additionally, they had to maintain their grades at school and the other activities that they had committed to previously. In the case where a child is struggling in school, there is usually a reason, and getting a job may actually help to improve the grades. A parent has absolutely nothing to lose – except for control – by allowing a child to try.

When a child reaches the age of sixteen, she should be allowed to start making more important decisions for herself. In our home, the children started playing sports at about five years old. They often took music lessons or karate lessons as well. By the time they were sixteen, they had the option of no longer playing those sports in lieu of other organized activities. Almost unanimously, the children decided that they would like to get a job and earn their own money.

It is important for parents to know that just because children do not do their chores without being told, are not doing well in school, or have difficulty following instructions does not mean that they will not be successful at work. Also understand that any of these problems might occur in your household. However, there are valuable lessons for our children to learn through these problems. In addition, there is no research that indicates that a child will do better at work if they do their chores well at home. Quite often a child's level of responsibility and compliance increases, as well as their grades and participation at school, when they get a job.

This is true for many reasons. One of them is that it gives the child a feeling of responsibility, a sense of achievement, and an experience of control over their own life when they earn their own money. It also gives a child an experience of working at the type of job that does not require an education. This alone is often motivation enough for a child to do better in school.

Getting back to the example, this same girl later asked her grandfather if she could sing in a musical band with other teenagers her own age. Once again, the grandfather pointed out all the pitfalls that would beseech her in trying to put together a band with other teens. And again, the young lady was accusing her grandfather of not allowing her to express herself and have responsibility over her life, when he was the one who continuously lectured her about being responsible.

After some discussion, the grandfather gave his consent for her to sing in the band. The granddaughter wrote a contract that stated that this activity would not negatively impact her schoolwork and the other obligations that she had committed to previously. Within three weeks, this young lady came to the realization (something her grandfather had previously realized) that adolescents have a very difficult time keeping to schedules, adhering to rules, even self-imposed ones, and finding times when five of them could get together for band practice.

The grandfather had been suggesting for months that the church choir would be a very good place for her to obtain experience singing on a regularly scheduled basis. After several weeks, the newly formed band had only practiced once. The child then made *her own decision* to join the church choir.

PHILOSOPHY TO LET KIDS MAKE
AS MANY OF THEIR OWN DECISIONS AS POSSIBLE

The next philosophy goes hand in hand with the philosophy that children should be accountable for their behaviors. Starting as soon as possible, it is a good idea to allow children to make as many decisions for themselves as they can. This would generally start with simple choices like "What kind of ice cream would you like?" When a child is very young, you would not offer them every flavor of ice cream, but you might ask, "Would you like vanilla or strawberry ice cream?" As a child gets older, the number of choices can get broader with the hope that practicing decision-making will help with the quality of those decisions. It would be unrealistic for someone to believe that if a person were not accustomed to making decisions, they would start off with making good ones. The more decisions children are *allowed* to make, the better decisions they ultimately *will* make.

Let's say all goes well in the rearing of a child. Then by the time she is sixteen or the beginning her junior year in high school, the child should be prepared to make most of her own decisions. Usually, by this time, children understand what is expected of them, that the rules are not optional, that they have certain capabilities, that there are consequences to their actions, and that often the consequences are natural consequences. For instance, my wife and I no longer checked our children's homework once the children started high school.

In general, the younger children saw what would be expected of them as they watched and learned from the actions of the older children. They were also aware of exactly what would be expected by the consistent parenting of the older siblings and the discussions we had with each of them.

When children are growing up, it would be naïve to believe that they would do their homework well without supervision or while in their room alone. From the time when a child begins school, the parent needs to check the homework. They should also have a place where the child does her homework, with the parent either sitting with her or near enough to watch and help the child as needed.

Without adult supervision, it is far too easy for a child to be distracted away from homework by all the other things in her room or elsewhere in the house. With your supervision, this can become a bonding experience for both the parent and the child. In addition, this can also be a time when the child develops a love of learning. When Dad uses *the 4 Cs* (calm, consistent, caring, and concerned), it gives the child the sense that learning is fun and something she would like to do rather than being laborious. It would be very frustrating for a child who is doing her homework if the parent is *not* calm, consistent, caring, concerned, and helpful. In such circumstances, learning becomes negatively reinforced, and when something is negatively reinforced, the child often avoids the behavior – in this case, homework. That is not a good idea if we expect our children to do well in school.

Taking the right approach with our children naturally applies to other areas of behaviors as well. I had the displeasure of overhearing a neighbor who was working with his eight-year-old son in their backyard on how to hit a baseball. The father was angry, distracted, and derogatory toward his son. When this father thought his son should not have done something during the lesson, the father would bark, "Who taught you how to do that?" or "Why did you do it that way?" or "Who taught you to do it that way?" Needless to say, the baseball practice lasted only for a few minutes with the young boy crying and the father yelling at him to go in the house. This was one of those times when I really wanted to explain to the father that he was failing miserably as a dad and offer some help. However, my expectation was that he was not in the mood for any constructive criticism.

I must also point out that there are times when a child needs to understand that the decision is not hers to make. This is much easier for the child to understand if she has a lot of experience in making decisions for herself. Examples of these types of decisions would be if a behavior were against the law, if it is unhealthy, or it goes against your moral fiber. This would include such things as smoking cigarettes or drinking alcohol prior to the proper age. It also includes behaviors that are dangerous, like being out alone after a certain hour.

These are things that are important for children to be taught. That way, when they grow older, they will not be surprised. For instance, smoking of anything is not allowed in our house. Children have the right to decide for themselves whether or not they want to smoke; however, they do not have the right to do it in my house. It is illegal for any person under the age of eighteen years old to smoke cigarettes in the United States. Therefore, I would expect my children not to smoke cigarettes until they are of legal age and even then *never* in *my* house.

With that said, I am not naïve enough to believe that if one of my children wanted to smoke cigarettes, I could forcibly keep her from doing so. Children have to make decisions for themselves; they need to decide what is best for them. There are limits to what a parent can force a child to do or not do. Yet, if a child cherishes the relationship she has with her dad, then in all likelihood she will engage in behaviors that would further that relationship and make her dad proud of her. In the example of smoking cigarettes, it would be unrealistic for a father who smokes them to expect his child not to do so. It would also be highly hypocritical for him to use the excuse "You're not old enough" or "They're not good for you."

Remember, a parent should model the desired behavior, and children generalize the behaviors of their parents. Without proper modeling, a child can make unwise decisions. For example, when I was an adolescent, my mother's boyfriend was living with us in my mother's house. At fifteen years old, I had my first serious girlfriend. My mother lectured me every chance she had – on the rare occasion when she would see my girlfriend and me holding hands or kissing – that we were not married and should "not be having sex." She was unaware that we were having sex, and my response to her was "But you're living with someone you're not married to!" Her rebuttal was that she was an adult and responsible for her own actions. I, on the other hand, was not responsible in that I was only a fifteen-year-old child. Subsequently, this author (a child at the time) and his girlfriend got pregnant and at sixteen years old had our first child. Eventually my mother and her boyfriend did get married, and then she would use the excuse "We have a license" to have sex. My response at that point became "Well, I have a learner's permit."

Needless to say, I never had a very good relationship with either of my parents. Both of them spent years in prison, on numerous occasions, while my brothers and I spent those same years and more in an orphanage, foster care and in group-homes.

I was angry with my mother for many years for some of the things that had happened as I was growing up. It was not until later in life, when I became a dad, that I came to realize that even though she was not the best parent, my mom did do the best she could. My father, on the other hand, never even tried. I give a person a lot of credit for trying.

My mother and I did not have the type of relationship where we could sit down and have a discussion. Generally, she would talk and I would pretend to listen. I did not trust her. Therefore, anything she said was of little consequence to me. It was not until I was twelve years old that my mother bought a house, and my sister and I lived with her full-time. I learned very quickly that if my mom were at home, it would be best for me to be somewhere else. Luckily for me, she was not home very often.

PHILOSOPHY NOT TO ALLOW EVENTS OUTSIDE HOME
TO AFFECT LIFE INSIDE HOME

Another one of the philosophies my wife and I devised was that we would not allow events outside of the home to make our home life miserable. This extended to how the kids did in school. This is not to say that school is not important or that kids do not need to perform well in school. It is just that very few activities outside the home are worth damaging relationships and causing problems inside the home.

For example, if things are not going well at *work* (and sometimes things can be going terribly at work), we want to keep that from having a negative effect on the relationships at home. This can be difficult because our work-life is extremely important. The money that work generates dictates the lifestyle that we will live, and it also contributes to one's self-esteem.

It would be a big mistake (and I know this because I made this mistake for years) to believe that the kids are as interested as the parents in living a better life. Living a better life, in my old way of thinking, was a bigger house, a nicer car, nicer and more expensive clothes, jewelry, and all the things that one might (like I did) imagine would make others envious of my life. What other people think about me personally or how much money or possessions I have are things I no longer care about.

This point was made clear to me by one of my younger sons, Aaron, when he was about seventeen years old. I used to work twelve or more hours a day and sometimes seven days a week for most of my children's life. Two years before this particular night, I had resigned my position at work to take time off to get to know my children. My son had been working part-time at a restaurant. At night, I would stroll over to the restaurant and walk home with him. As we walked home one evening, we were talking about various things and Aaron said something that brought tears to my eyes. He told me, "I know it isn't true now but when I was little I thought you worked all the time because you didn't like me very much." I immediately apologized for making him feel that way and he said that I had made up for it.

I apologized again for all the lost time. I saw that Aaron did not care about our house, cars, clothes, or anything else. He just wanted his dad, and when his dad was not at home, he assumed it was because I did not like him very much.

Kids generally just want to be kids and to have the things that kids have. More importantly, they want their dad. They want to spend time with their dad, go places with their dad, and be able to go to their dad when things are going well and when things are not going well. It is very deflating to go to your dad, tell him something that you are really happy about, and he does not share in that excitement, or worse, points out that it is not so great or all the possible problems it might cause. This is not to say that the child might very well be overly enthusiastic; yet to crush that enthusiasm would be a shame. On the other hand, it would be a shame for a child to come to his dad with a problem, and Dad dismisses it, or minimizes the problem, or tells the child that he does not have time to deal with it.

School was another area that we tried to segregate from the home. We understood that punishment at home for something that happened at school is often confusing for children and only leads to more problems at school. If a child has been appropriately punished at school for a behavior, there is often no reason to further punish the child at home. Young children have a very difficult time understanding that they are not allowed to do something at home because of something they did, or did not do, at school. There will be more on this topic in later chapters. For now, it is enough to try to not let things that happen outside the home negatively affect relationships in your household.

PHILOSOPHY TO RESPECT EACH OTHER'S FEARS

Adults and children alike have fears – real or perceived. It is always a good idea to respect those fears regardless of how irrational they might be. There comes a point where a fear may be a phobia, and this is something that still needs to be respected but might also need a professional intervention. A good place to start would be at one's primary-care physician.

What I am stressing here are fears that many people have, like someone driving too fast, or taking chances behind the wheel of a car that do not need to be taken. For example, if you are driving a car and your child asks you to slow down, it would be best to not go as fast. This should start a discussion on her fear, if there is a basis for it, and what Dad should do to help the child. Naturally if Dad is driving irresponsibly, this would be a good time to change that behavior.

Other examples of fears might be one's wife has a fear of being late to the airport and miss a flight, or of running out of gas even though the gas gauge shows enough gas to go a little farther. Then there is always the fear of bugs, which is something my wife and many other women I have known are afflicted with.

When a husband hears a blood-curdling scream coming from the bathroom, it is a good idea to respond as quickly as possible. When you arrive and it is only a spider, try not to laugh. Instead, discard the creature immediately, without putting it in your wife's face to show her that it is harmless. Even though this might be funny to some, it is rarely funny to someone who is frightened, especially children.

There are those who look at life with rose-colored glasses, and it would not be advisable to try to disenchant them. And when one member of the family has a fear, it is best not to try to minimize or rationalize it away. Instead, it helps to solve it. Perhaps this is something as simple as making hotel reservations to ensure that a room is secured. There is little that is more frustrating than minimizing a problem like "We're going to miss the plane," and then getting to the airport late and missing that very flight.

This is a good example of what happens when one member of the family does not respect the fears of another family member. In the above example of missing the plane, the entire family just learned something by the process of natural consequences.

PHILOSOPHIES ARE PRO-ACTIVE PARENTING

You have now read about some of my family's biggest philosophies, and I hope that they are helpful. Other philosophies might cover what a family does at holidays, whether or not they go to church, sitting down together for dinner (anywhere from one to seven times a week), at what age and under what circumstances a child can get a driver's license, etc. These are just a few examples of things that parents need to talk about and decide long before an issue arises. I call this *proactive parenting*; that is, know what you are going to do ahead of time before there's an issue. The first child is often the most difficult to raise in that every stage is new. By thinking things through in advance, children get the impression that the parents actually do know what they are doing. Thus kids are often much more compliant.

WHAT'S NEXT?

The following chapter helps Dad to understand what children are capable of as they grow up. This includes information about the way children develop as well as the way that parenting skills need to develop as well.

KEY CHAPTER POINTS

1. Philosophies help parents govern their lives, and they provide guidance for the way that they are going to raise their children.
2. Probably the most important philosophy is to *always treat each other as if you love each other.*
3. If a parenting technique that you're utilizing is not working, stop using it.
4. People make mistakes, people get frustrated and revert back to old behaviors, and others within the home might not be making the same progress that Dad is making. This is an opportunity for Dad to practice the *4 Cs: calm, consistent, caring, and concerned.*
5. Dad's and Mom's parenting styles need to be consistent with each other. This helps you follow the rule to not argue about the children in front of the children.
6. Kids do the best they can.
7. Never make derogatory comments about your children's physical appearance.
8. Another philosophy is to *allow each person to be responsible for his or her own actions.*
9. Another philosophy is that of allowing children to experience *natural consequences.*
10. Another philosophy is to *let the kids make as many of their own decisions as possible.*
11. The more decisions a child makes for herself the better decisions that will be made. It would be unrealistic for someone to believe that if a person were not accustomed to making decisions they would start off making good ones.
12. There are times when a child needs to understand that the decision is not hers to make.

13. When children are growing up, it would be naïve to believe that they would do their homework well without supervision or while in their room alone.
14. Adults and children alike have fears – real or perceived. It is always a good idea to respect those fears regardless of how irrational they might be.
15. Another philosophy is that *events outside the home should not have a negative effect on life inside the home.*
16. Very few activities outside the home are worth damaging relationships and causing problems inside the home.

11

Child Development & Parenting

A person's emotional development plays a significant role in their overall functioning for all of a person's life. If a person's emotional development is stifled anywhere along the way, it will, in all likelihood, remain in that emotional stage – unless an intervention is achieved.

It is important to know and understand the different stages of development. *Child development* starts at conception and seems to go on endlessly, or at least until the child is self-sufficient. Development of the child's personality begins some time after conception but still within the mother's womb. As discussed earlier in the book, whatever feelings the mother is experiencing are conveyed to the unborn child. Even before a child is born, the environment in which the mother lives already plays a role in how the child will develop emotionally, and it will affect the personality development of the child.

DIFFERENT TYPES OF CHILD DEVELOPMENT

Children develop in three different ways: *physically, intellectually, and emotionally.* Most children develop physically and intellectually, regardless of the environment. This is not always the case, but it is under most circumstances, barring extraordinary circumstances like genetic defects, malnourishment, or acute trauma.

147

It is easy to know and understand what to expect for a child's *physical* development, as measured by standard, normalized milestones of child development. A child's physical development will usually achieve those normalized milestones, regardless of the environment in which a child resides.

In terms of *intellectual* development, a child's intellectual *ability* will most likely develop along normal milestones regardless of the environment. Whether a child exercises his intellectual abilities or not, those intellectual *abilities* will still develop. In other words, if a child never went to school and had not learned to read, write, or do math, the child is still *capable* of performing intellectually at the proper age once given the instruction. For example, eight-year-olds are generally not taught how to do algebra. This is due to the fact that the brain of most eight-year-olds is *not capable* of performing abstract thought, which is required to perform algebra. Once a child reaches the developmental stage of adolescence, the child is capable of abstract thought and can be taught algebra.

School-age children are generally taught at the intellectual developmental pace of the majority of children, and most children's abilities develop at a steady pace. If a child who never went to school enrolled in a community college at eighteen years old, after approximately one or two semesters of remedial classes in basic reading, writing, and math, the young adult would in all likelihood be *capable* of performing at the college-level.

This is merely an example of a child's intellectual development and not an endorsement of a child not going to school. The chances of a child doing well in college without having attended school earlier are very low. The reason for this is that going to school teaches a child much more than how to read and write. There is a great deal of evidence that indicates that a child who engages in school activities from an early age will clearly perform better in college, in their career, and in life in general. Additionally, there is more to going to school than merely learning facts. At any rate, the point that I am stressing here is that regardless of whether or not a person intentionally exercises their intellectual abilities that ability is available to the individual just the same.

EMOTIONAL DEVELOPMENT

The development of emotions is unlike the development of physical or intellectual abilities. Very much like developing physically and intellectually, emotions develop *in stages*. However, unlike the other two, if a child does not master the current stage of emotional development, he will advance into the next stage without being fully prepared. This would be similar to trying to teach a child how to perform multiplication when the child has not mastered the function of addition.

Unlike physical and intellectual development, emotional development is not as straightforward. Once a person advances from one emotional stage to the next, it becomes difficult for the child (or adult) to gain the attributes that were supposed to be achieved in the previous developmental stage. If they did not achieve them, the child also acquires fewer skills in the current stage. It then becomes difficult to develop into the more advanced emotional stages, and one's psychological development will be incomplete.

Each stage of emotional development has certain attributes as well as conflicts that need to be resolved in order for the child to move to the next emotional stage. For example, a newborn baby's first developmental stage is about acquiring the attribute of trust. This is done without any input, effort, or knowledge on the part of the infant. It is entirely the outcome of the infant's environment and how the infant's parents/caregivers interact with the infant.

In an environment where an infant does not develop the attribute of trust, as the infant grows older, he will have a difficult time with this attribute. Since each of the emotional stages of development depends on the previous one, it is easy to see that the first developmental stages of emotions are critical. These emotional stages and how well each of the attributes is learned in each stage forms a person's personality and subsequent behaviors.

ONLY 25% OF ADULTS ARE EMOTIONALLY ADULTS

If a child does not master each of the stages of emotional development, eventually emotional growth will become so difficult that the person will stop developing emotionally and remain in that specific stage. Some estimates are that the emotional development of approximately 50% of Americans has stopped in the pre-adolescent stage (seven to twelve years of age). Of those that continue to develop into the emotional stage of adolescence (twelve to eighteen years of age), only 50% of those develop into the emotional stage of a young adult. That means that 50% of all adults in the United States have the emotional abilities of someone who is under the age of twelve years old. Twenty-five percent of all adults in the United States have the emotional abilities of someone who is between twelve and eighteen years old. Only 25% of American adults act as if they are emotionally adults (emotional abilities of someone eighteen years or older).

It is now easy to see why grown adults can act so immaturely, especially when participating in an intimate relationship. I know men who are very affluent, who own their own company, have advanced college degrees, and can solve the mysteries of the universe. But put those same men in an intimate relationship, and they act like a four-year-old. Four-year olds are impulsive, selfish, egocentric, insensitive, and uncaring. They believe that the world revolves around them and that the entire world has the same thoughts as they do. A four-year-old cannot see another person's point of view, and they cannot see how their actions affect others.

Now, for a four-year-old, that type of behavior is expected. No one would expect a four-year-old to have the slightest idea of what it feels like to be someone else or to realize that there is anyone in the world more important than he is. It is also important to note that the four-year-old does not consciously know any of this, very similar to the adult whose emotional development was arrested at four years old. The difference is that a four-year-old is not *capable* of acting differently whereby an adult at least has the capacity to *act* like an adult.

With these thoughts in mind, it becomes easy to see why so many marriages end in divorce… why there is so much crime… why there are so many teenage pregnancies… why there is so much substance abuse… why there is such a big problem in this country with education, debt, and personal responsibility. When 75% of the nation acts like they are emotionally under the age of nineteen, it is no wonder why we have the problems that we do in relationships and elsewhere in our lives.

Additionally, people are emotionally attracted to others who are at their own level of emotionality. For example, if a forty-year-old man is at an emotional age of ten, he will in all likelihood be attracted to a woman whose emotional age is ten as well.

People of all ages seek others who have their level of emotional functioning or level of emotional dysfunction. The results are often disastrous when two people with low levels of emotional maturity fall in love and try to form a lasting, mature relationship, and then add children to the equation. Regardless of the physical age of the parents, the emotional age is what drives people's behaviors. When Dad's emotional age is not in the adult range, there may be some fairly big problems in his relationships.

Men are *naturally* selfish up until their late twenties or early thirties – we are born that way. Only *if* a man develops emotionally to an adult level will he grow out of that and learn that giving love is more fulfilling than receiving love. Stated differently, a man will learn that it is more fulfilling to give than to receive. However, if a man's emotional growth is arrested at an early age, he will, in all likelihood, remain self-centered, egotistical, and selfish all the days of his life. It makes it hard to be a good dad when the most important person in your life is yourself.

Only when a man's emotional maturity reaches an adult level can he sustain a healthy, caring, nurturing relationship where the other person is the priority. The mature man gets a great deal of satisfaction from acting in this way and the emotional depth of the relationship grows.

When a relationship has emotional depth in both persons, intimacy grows. The relationship stays new and exciting, the partners treat each other well, and the relationship lasts.

THE DECISION TO START A FAMILY

This might not be a good time in the process to discuss whether or not to have children, especially if you already have kids! Still, it is an important topic to address. I will keep it brief. There are a few things to consider before the decision to propagate is made. First, it would be best to wait to have children until both parents are more mature. The reason for this is that it gives the would-be parents time to pursue educational and career goals, both of which can interfere with parenting children. Parents who are better educated and are established in their careers generally have more income and financial security.

Parents who are older when they have children also had more time to mature emotionally, and as you are seeing, this becomes extremely important. Parents who are emotionally mature have a tendency to be more effective and consistent in their relationship with each other. Consequently, they are also more effective and consistent in their parenting and in the disciplining of their children.

MARITAL SATISFACTION AND CHILDREN

Something important to know, whether you already have children or not, is that marital satisfaction *decreases* when a child is born. This happens even in the best of marriages. The focus of the relationship changes from each other to the child, and this will continue for the next several years. However, research does indicate that marital satisfaction declines less after the baby is born if the father participates more in the infant's caregiving.

The addition of a baby does not affect each individual or every couple in the same way. Briefly, marriage is comprised of three basic elements: romance, friendship, and partnership. *Romance* emphasizes physical intimacy. *Friendship* emphasizes mutual interests, supportiveness, and the thought that the married couple genuinely enjoys spending time together. *Partnership* emphasizes working together in an efficient and effective way, often toward similar goals. Adding a baby to the marriage may affect each of these areas differently. Men have a tendency to be selfish, so consider this. The less a husband/father does to support his wife with the new baby, the less time she will have to "play" with her husband. She will also be less inclined to want to "play" when time permits.

Like marital satisfaction, the frequency of sexual relations also generally decreases after the baby is born. It also has a tendency to decrease during pregnancy too. This is another reason for the husband to help with the care of the child, aside from all the positive effects it will have on the child as he develops. There is personal growth for the dad in this, and the wife will then be more inclined to want to have sex with her husband.

The single biggest reason the frequency of sex drops after a baby's birth is because the mother is too tired. If the husband/father is helpful in caring for the infant/children, which is often very appealing to wives, your wife will not be as exhausted and will be more receptive to sex. Note that a husband's chances of having sex decreases precipitously in the following scenario. He does not help with the care of the infants/children, and also sits around and complains about not "getting enough."

For the most part, having children is worth it. Children can be a wonderful addition to one's life. Know that this works a lot better if you, as Dad, are aware of what to expect and can remain calm, consistent, loving, and caring. If a man is not a good husband before the children are born, he will, in all likelihood, not be a very good father and a much worse husband after the baby is born.

Once the child is born, the focus of the relationship becomes "all baby." For men who have not developed emotionally, this can be very frustrating and often causes such severe problems within the relationship that a separation is imminent. What will help the transition from being a couple to being a family is for the father to be prepared for the new baby. To do this, take parenting classes, read books, talk things over with your wife, and take an active role in preparing for the baby's arrival. If you have children already, still do these things. That way, you can better understand what works well and what will help the whole family to act like a whole family.

If there are already problems within a household, it is not too late to make changes. Remember that a dad has significant influence, and it would be naïve to believe that the rest of the household will make changes if the dad does not. Always lead by example. Apply the principles contained in this book and just be a dad.

As you read earlier in the book, it would be a big mistake to expect something from a child that they are incapable of. This is also true of adults who have not emotionally matured into adulthood. The difference is that an adult is fully responsible for his actions regardless of his emotional level of maturity. He needs to act like an adult, emotionally, as well as physically and intellectually.

STAGE ONE OF EMOTIONAL DEVELOPMENT – TRUST

During the first stage of emotional development (*birth to one year*), the attribute that needs to be learned is *trust*. In the event that an infant does not develop trust, he does develop the attribute of *mistrust*. During this stage of life, the infant's parents are the main source of caregiving and the ones who can best provide a sense of trust in the infant. This is done merely by meeting the needs of the infant, by caring for the baby, by holding, loving, and nurturing the baby in a calm, consistent, caring, and concerned (the *four Cs*) environment.

When an infant cries, he is sending a signal to his caregivers that something is wrong. When a parent responds by meeting the infant's needs, the baby learns that the parent will respond and the baby begins to trust the parent(s). This is not done consciously but is an innate reflex. Newborns cannot cognitively, or intellectually, rationalize that they are, for example, hungry, and therefore cry until they get fed. Instead, a child is born with the instinct to cry when uncomfortable, or in pain. It would be a mistake to allow a child who is uncomfortable, or in pain, and communicating that by crying, to continue to be uncomfortable or in pain. This sends a message to the child that his needs are not important and that the caregiver cannot be trusted.

When I was a child, my mother was under a mistaken impression. She thought that if a child cries, it was best not to fulfill the need immediately but rather to let the child cry for a while. This behavior was commonplace in the 1950s, and it was also written in some of the parenting literature. The intention was not to allow the child to believe that crying would result in immediate gratification. My mother made it very clear to me that a crying baby should not have his needs met. Rather, she allowed the baby (me) to cry for ten to twenty minutes in order to "let him know who's in charge."

This type of child-rearing practice fails to allow the child to develop a good and sound sense of trust. Babies whose parents are consistently insensitive to their signals, such as crying, may come to feel that they have little effect on their environment. Babies need to learn that they can trust their caregivers to provide their basic needs.

Remember that behaviors are learned. Behaviors, such as crying, that are reinforced continue to be used, even at a reflex level. Parents can quickly learn to anticipate the infant's needs prior to the infant crying, and they can fulfill that need without him needing to cry. Babies give signals that they are hungry or uncomfortable from a wet diaper. A baby will most generally become "fussy" before starting to cry. When a dad learns these signals, caring for the baby becomes much easier for him and the child learns trust.

It is difficult at times not to be annoyed at a baby's cry. However, crying is supposed to illicit a response; if it were pleasant, one might not respond to a need. It is important to understand the difference between merely responding to a baby's cry and responding appropriately. Babies have to have their needs met *immediately*. When a baby is crying, just understand that he is learning a great many things. When a dad satisfies the child's need prior to the start of crying, he will convey to the baby that he truly does care about the baby and can be trusted.

It is also important for Dad to realize that an infant needs to be held, cuddled, talked to, and shown expressions of love. Infants need to have frequent, appropriate physical touch. On that note, consider this. In ancient times, a king conducted an experiment with babies. The study used one-hundred newborn infants divided into two groups. One group was treated normally but was not talked to. The other group had no human contact whatsoever except to care for their basic needs, and even then the infants were not held or nurtured. The group that was not held, nurtured, nor given human touch all died, showing that an infant has a *need* to be physically nurtured.

155

In more recent studies using rhesus monkeys, surrogate mothers made out of chicken wire provided food from a bottle to the babies. Another surrogate mother made of chicken wire but covered with soft burlap was also available to the babies but she provided no food. When frightened, the baby monkeys would inevitably seek comfort from the surrogate burlap mother rather than the wire-frame surrogate mother who provided the food. This indicates that a child is more attached to his caregiver who provides comfort and affection over a caregiver who merely provides sustenance.

Up to one month of age, the infant is not cognitively, that is intellectually, aware of the world around him. A baby will respond much more to a gentle reassuring touch coupled with a soft tone and gentle language and speech. Touch should always be done as to convey loving, nurturing, and caring, as should speech and language. This, of course, should continue to be the case as the child grows older.

Naturally, as the child becomes mobile and tests the parents' boundaries, the tone of voice a parent uses can have quite an effect on the child. A firm tone is only useful when the child is old enough to understand its meaning, and then it should be used only in moderation. Less is better in this case, because a young child will become startled by a harsh, loud, or cruel tone. Such a continual response from Dad will have long-term negative effects on the child, especially an infant or toddler, which may not be truly evident until adolescence.

It is important to focus on the baby when performing caregiving functions. Try to avoid allowing one's mind to wander or to daydream. As I have stated before, it is not the actual changing of a diaper that is important but how the baby interprets the experience. A dad has the option to initiate a relationship with the infant as soon as the child is born by making baby sounds, holding the baby in a loving, nurturing way, and being completely present when caring for the baby.

From birth to four months, the baby cannot differentiate between himself and his primary caregiver, which is generally the baby's mother. In other words, the infant cannot tell the difference between himself and his mother during this stage. That would be similar to someone looking at himself in the mirror and not being able to tell there is a difference between the real person and the reflection. This phenomenon is resolved by about ten months of age, whereby the child can distinguish between himself and other objects.

STAGE TWO OF EMOTIONAL DEVELOPMENT – AUTONOMY

Once a baby attains the age of one year old, he is a toddler. The child becomes mobile and has the ability to be inquisitive about his immediate surroundings and the world around him. This second stage of emotional development occurs between the ages of *one to three years*. During this stage, the toddler's developmental challenge that needs to be mastered is the attribute of *autonomy*. In the absence of developing autonomy, the child develops a sense of *shame and doubt*.

Children in this stage become more self-sufficient, attaining the ability to walk, to eat without help, to talk, and go to the bathroom independently. Their behaviors are more intentional and the things they say are very literal. This is a time when children learn, and use, every word they hear, and take the words and behaviors of their parents very literally.

This is also a time when Dad needs to be very careful in what he says and does. For example, toddlers are very inquisitive, everything is new to them. When a toddler gets into Dad's belongings, help him to see what it is all about – *without scolding*. A toddler mimics the behavior of Dad. Try not to get upset over the child's inquisitive nature and remember that imitation is a high form of flattery.

Here's an example. My twin boys were three years old, and my sister had brought her car to our house to prepare it for a new paint job. As we were sanding my sister's car, we left some used pieces of sandpaper on the driveway. One of the twins picked up one of those pieces and started to sand my completely rebuilt 1964 Chevy Malibu (which had a flawless paint job). After my heart started to beat again, I redirected his efforts to the car we were working on. I also made sure that we did not leave pieces of sandpaper on the ground. My son was merely doing what he saw his dad doing, just on the wrong car! It would have been damaging to him to discipline him for doing what he saw me doing. By letting him and his brothers help us with my sister's car, it allowed each of them to feel a sense of belonging by participating. Generally, when a dad allows his children to help him, it teaches his children how to be helpful and how to do things that they may not otherwise learn.

This is also a good time for parents to start allowing the toddler to feel successful in his newfound independence. This will help the child not to doubt his abilities and to not feel shame over failures. Failures will come; however, it is important to allow the toddler the ability to make decisions, at a very rudimental level. This should be in areas that are safe, like what toy he would like to play with or what flavor ice cream he would like. Doing so gives the child a sense of autonomy, and the belief that he is capable.

The Importance of Not Being Overprotective/Overreactive

It is very common and a natural reaction for Dad to be overprotective, trying to keep the child from getting into a situation that might be harmful. However, it would be counterproductive not to allow a toddler to be inquisitive and explore his world, out of fear that the child may be hurt, or the fear that the parent will lose control over the child's behavior. Still, during this phase, adult supervision is imperative so that the child does not become hurt.

At this point, the child's world may mainly be his bedroom or the family room. Of course, the child will also be in the other rooms of the house. To the best of Dad's ability, the house (and especially those particular rooms) should be safety-proofed in such a way to allow the child to feel a sense of autonomy at his early stages of development. If this autonomy is not encouraged, a rebellion may be coming when the child reaches adolescence.

Attachment

During this stage of development, at between twelve and twenty-four months of age, the child develops *attachment behaviors*. That is, behaviors that show that the child gains and seeks out comfort from the primary caregiver. For example, in unfamiliar environments, the toddler stays close to Mom, wandering away from her side as he becomes more secure with the environment. In unfamiliar environments, the child will, in all likelihood, return to his mother's side for comfort and security if a stranger enters the room.

A child can attach to more than one person; however, there is usually a primary attachment figure (mother) and then secondary attachment figures (including father). In normal development, a child will seek refuge, comfort, and safety through his mother. In the absence of the mother, a child of this age will generally seek out his father. It is not until about the age of eight or nine years old when a great deal of influence shifts to the father. The shift is gradual but is usually well established by fourth grade.

Object Permanence

There is another interesting addition to the toddler's abilities at this stage. Between the ages of sixteen and twenty-four months, the child develops the ability to maintain *object constancy*. This is the ability to understand that an object continues to exist even when the child cannot see it. Up until this time, if a child is playing with a toy, for example, and the toy is covered up or falls out of the child's sight, the child believes the object no longer exists and will not seek it out.

Somewhere between sixteen and twenty-four months of age, the child becomes aware that the object still exists and will look for it. This ability to understand that an object continues to exist extends to the child's parents. At this age, it is not uncommon for toddlers to cry when their parent(s) leave them with the babysitter. Early on, this is often due to the toddler's inability to realize that Mom or Dad will be back later. The toddler now knows the parent(s) still exists though he cannot see him or her. Children also have difficulty with cause and effect at this age; even when they come to realize that Mom or Dad will return, they may continue to cry upon their departure. This can simply be because the child does not want him or her to leave and not be an issue of object permanence.

The roles of the parents are often different in this stage of development. The mother tends to engage in more caregiving activities, such as feeding, diapering, and bathing, while the father tends to engage in more play activities. When mothers do play with their children at this age, it tends to be more conventional play such as Peek-a-Boo or Pat-a-Cake. Father's tend to play in more active, physical, and unpredictable ways. Both ways are important, and they teach the child to play, think, and behave in different manners.

Parental Development at Two to Five Years

As a child develops through these stages, so too must the parenting skills of the mother and father develop. As early as two years old and continuing until five years old, the *parents* enter into the *authority stage* of parenting. This is the time when the child's behavior dictates when a parent becomes more or less authoritative. During these years, it often seems that a power struggle is in play between a child and his parents. Always remember that you are Dad and use that power/influence wisely.

This is a critical time for the child's development. Being too forceful will create self-esteem and self-efficacy issues, while being too lenient will create very similar issues. Both parenting styles, being too harsh or too lenient, create significant behavioral problems for this stage of development and set the stage for the next ten to fifteen years. This is a time when the development of good parenting skills is a necessity to relieve significant problems later, as the child grows older.

During this stage of parenting, Dad faces the task of accepting the responsibility of his authority over the child; he must establish communication and enforce limits. He must also be able to cope with conflict with the child in a manner that is beneficial to the child and his relationship with the child. I cannot stress enough that failure at this stage of parenting can have long-lasting and far-reaching effects on the entire family. This is not the time to be stubborn, self-centered, or overly controlling with your child. Always do what is in the best interest of the child.

The same is true for developing a good working parenting relationship with the child's mother. Together you will determine your expectations of the child within the child's abilities. Cooperatively decide upon the means of communication you will use with the child by using appropriate words and statements. Also determine the means and methods of discipline before the need arises.

Keep in mind that a child between the ages of one and five years has the brain of a sponge; everything he comes in contact with is learned. If a parent does not want a child to learn something, this is a good time not to teach it to the child. At this age, a child does not know what is appropriate and what is not unless taught so. If a child comes in contact with something, he will assume that it is appropriate and allowed. Children learn by example, and this would be a good time to model the desired behavior for your child.

An example of using appropriate words and the literalness with which children interpret them would be in teaching a child to share. A child needs to *learn* to share, and one of the easiest ways is for Dad to share with the child. Let's say that a child is told "Do not play with my things" when he gets into something that he should not play with. There is a good chance that he will mimic that behavior when someone tries to play with *his* things. A more appropriate rationale would be not to play with something because "That is not a toy," as opposed to not being able to play with something merely because "It is mine," or because "It is not yours."

Again, a child needs to be able to investigate his world. He needs to be able to see and understand the things that his dad is doing. From this, he learns what to do, what not to do, and what he is capable of. When a child gets into something he should not, *gently* explain why he cannot play with it. This works well with children of all ages but young children will not be able to cognitively evaluate right from wrong, and *should* from *should not*, unless appropriately taught by example and modeling. When a child sees his dad playing with something, he will assume it is okay for him to play with it as well.

STAGE THREE OF EMOTIONAL DEVELOPMENT – INITIATIVE – THE PRESCHOOL YEARS

The third stage of emotional development (*three to six years of age*) contains the attributes of *initiative*. In the absence of acquiring this attribute, the child develops the attribute of *guilt*. This is a stage when children often try to act too much like an adult and overstep the limits set by the parents. Children at this age may defy their parents in an attempt to have more initiative, like crossing the street when they know that they are not supposed to do that. At this stage, Dad must therefore try to impart to the child a balance of self-reliance and responding appropriately to others and rules set before him.

This is a period where children become more able, and they create a sense of their personal abilities and independence. This is a time when the child starts to separate from the parents, as he grows in awareness of his own existence as an individual.

Children in this stage of development have a tendency to think illogically. They have difficulty considering the point-of-view or feelings of others; they are very egocentric. Children in this developmental stage have a good sense of themselves, but they are not able to take into consideration the perspectives or needs of others. They may not take responsibility for their actions, and instead blame their own behaviors on others. For example, a five-year-old boy accidentally shut the sliding glass door to the patio on his three-year-old brother's hand. When his brother cried in pain, the five-year-old replied, "He shouldn't have had his hand there."

It may be difficult not to become angry when a child makes a comment like that, especially when his little brother is crying with a mangled hand. However, this is the way a preschool child thinks. Be calm and explain that, even though it was an accident, it still hurt his brother.

Although many children of this stage appear to be egocentric and almost hedonistic, they are also capable of *prosocial* behaviors – such as altruism or selflessness out of concern for someone else. Children at this stage can exhibit such prosocial behaviors as sharing, helping, compassion, cooperation, protecting, nurturing, and kindness. This is often the case when the parent is sensitive to the needs of a child. Parents must model these behaviors because otherwise the child will not know that they (the behaviors) exist!

Children of this stage also have difficulty with cause and effect, and they will often account for their behavior or feelings as the result of *illogical consequences*. For example, a child may believe that his brother got sick because he was thinking bad thoughts about him, when in fact his brother just got sick.

This is a good period for Dad to break away from the typical father-gender roles. For example, a dad should respond to a child's hurt feelings and tears with sensitivity. Meanwhile, it is also a good stage for a dad to exercise the freedom to be different from his wife in the way a Dad interacts with his children. It is very common for Dad to play with his children in a manner considered to be more like *roughhousing* than the way a mother would interact with the child.

A final note on preschool-aged children. It is about teaching them to learn academic skills at an early age. It is best to allow a child to be a child. Rather than teaching them formal academic skills, motivate interest in the child to have excitement and enthusiasm for learning in general. This is not difficult to do in that preschoolers are eager to learn new and interesting things. Trying to have them mature too quickly can lead to severe problems later. For more information about the dangers and pitfalls of children growing up too quickly, read Dr. David Elkind's book, *The Hurried Child: Growing Up Too Fast Too Soon.*

STAGE FOUR OF EMOTIONAL DEVELOPMENT – INDUSTRY – SCHOOL-AGED CHILDREN

Stage Four of emotional development (*seven to twelve years of age*) is that of *industry* with the fear of *inferiority* needing to be overcome. School-aged, or pre-adolescent, children are learning to be more competent and productive in mastering important academic and social skills. If they fail to develop these skills, a sense of inferiority develops and the feeling that they are incapable or incompetent to do anything well.

During this stage, Dad must answer a lot of questions, provide information, and help children wade through the myriad of moral issues that will help the child develop their own moral values. A great many of these moral values should have been taught already by modeling. In this stage of development, a great many of these behaviors are now *discussed verbally.*

This is a time when children become more independent, focus on many social and academic activities, spend more time with peers, and explore friendships in more depth. This is an age where children can learn to take more responsibility for their activities at home and at school, including chores and homework. Throughout this stage, it is important that Dad assist the child with chores and homework, gradually shifting more and more of the responsibility to the child.

Learning (academic, moral values, and appropriate behaviors) at home will be enhanced by a cooperative environment where homework and learning activities are valued, where television and other forms of media are limited, and bedtime is stable. Setting up a routine with normal schedules for doing chores, homework, and recreational activities is paramount in establishing a stable, consistent environment for children of all ages. The earlier in the child's life this is initiated the better.

Most children, by the age of twelve, come to understand that household chores and homework are not optional, and they resolve themselves to the fact that it is easier to "just do it" and get them over with. (It is essential for parents to be persistent and consistent so that children eventually come to this realization.) If a child is not at this level of responsibility, it is not the fault of the child, but a parenting issue. If the child still needs some prodding at this age, resist the temptation to ask "why" something has not been done and merely remind the child to do it. It is important to mention again that when a sentence is predicated with the word "why," people (adults as well as children) get *defensive* and an argument is about to start. There is usually not a good reason as to "why" something is not yet done.

Doing chores helps a child to develop social and cooperative behaviors, but only to the extent that the parents interact in helpful and cooperative ways. If Dad is short-tempered or verbally abusive, the experience of doing chores or other tasks such as homework feels painful rather than cooperative. Power struggles between the child and Dad will likely develop.

Collaborative Parenting

Dads of pre-adolescent children are most effective when they engage in *collaborative parenting*. Collaborative parenting simply means that parents and children cooperate, share responsibility, and have mutual respect for one another. Dad starts to take more of a guiding role, within the framework of age-appropriate boundaries, and allows the child to be more of an active participant in the decision-making process.

Remember that the ultimate role of a dad is to raise a "self-governing adult." From the day a child is born, the parents' job is to prepare him for living independently. It is important that Dad always keep an eye on the relationship he enjoys with his child, while at the same time allowing him to develop, at the proper pace and time, to be independent.

There is a balance between allowing a child more responsibility over his life and in the decisions that he makes, and pushing him to do so too quickly. Even though some children need to be "guided" with more rigor than others, the process should take place naturally with gentle prodding from Dad.

The issues that all children encounter during this stage of development will seem less significant to the child and the parents when a stable and consistent routine is established for the child and the family. This should be coupled with consistent, calm, and nurturing parenting skills. When this is done, it makes the next stage of development, adolescence, much more enjoyable for all concerned.

WHAT'S NEXT?

The next chapter is dedicated entirely to adolescence. Adolescence is the most difficult stage of development for children and the most difficult stage of child development for most parents.

KEY CHAPTER POINTS

1. A person's emotional development plays a significant role in their overall functioning over the entire lifespan.

2. Child development starts at conception and seems to go on endlessly or at least until the child is self-sufficient.

3. Children develop in three different ways: *physically, intellectually,* and *emotionally.*

4. Emotional development is unlike physical and intellectual development in that if a child does not master the current emotional stage he moves into the next stage unprepared.

5. A person's emotional development can be arrested at any stage.

6. Fifty percent of people do not develop *emotionally* beyond the stage of pre-adolescent (seven to twelve years of age). Only 50% of those who continue to develop emotionally into the adolescent stage (thirteen to eighteen years of age) move on to enter the young adult stage (over eighteen years). Note: Age ranges are the typical ages for each stage but vary from child to child.

7. Seventy-five percent of adults in this country have the emotional abilities of someone who is eighteen years of age or younger.

8. Men are naturally selfish until they are in their late twenties or early thirties.

9. It makes it hard for a man to be a good dad when the most important person in his life is himself.

10. Marital satisfaction decreases when a baby is born, even in the best of marriages, due to the focus becoming *all baby*. Marital satisfaction increases when the father helps with child-rearing and household activities.

11. It would be a mistake to believe that children of any age will always do what they are supposed to do merely because they are supposed to do it.

12. If Dad is short-tempered or verbally abusive, the experience of doing chores or other tasks such as homework become quite a painful experience. This is in contrast with it possibly being a cooperative experience. When it's painful, power struggles between the child and Dad will likely develop.

13. Dads of pre-adolescent children are most effective when they engage in *collaborative parenting*, which simply means that parents and children cooperate, share responsibility, and have mutual respect for one another.

14. It is a good practice to allow a child more responsibility over his life as well as the decisions he can make. But remember that there is a difference between that and pushing him to do so before he is ready.

12

Adolescence

Every developmental stage has new challenges, and *adolescence* is no exception. Parenting an adolescent is *advanced parenting*; it's not for the skittish or the faint of heart. It requires patience, resolve, and the ability to let the adolescent make decisions for herself and suffer the consequences – within reason, of course.

FOND MEMORIES OF YOUNGER YEARS

Many dads of adolescents look back at earlier stages of their child's development with fond memories. They remember a time when the child actually obeyed Dad without questions, or asking for an explanation. I cannot recall how many parents of teenagers have said to me, "I'd just like to have my darling little eight-year-old son back," or "What happened to my cute little girl?" I can say with all the confidence in the world that they are gone. But in their place is a *developing adult*. This is the time when a dad can really prove what kind of a person *he* is and how much he loves his child. It is a time when a dad can show just how patient he can be, and how much love he has in his heart because "Love is patient, love is kind."

Adolescence is a time when parents are tested over and over again. It is a time that will question your decision to have ever had children in the first place. It is also a time that can make a dad proud to see the little boy or girl that he and his wife have loved and nurtured for the child's entire life developing into a successful adult. It may also be a time when a troubled youth turns around and starts to make better decisions as she develops into adulthood. In both instances, Dad is a significant influence in how difficult or how enjoyable adolescence will be. Like the other stages, adolescence has attributes that need to be learned.

THE ADOLESCENT STAGE OF EMOTIONAL DEVELOPMENT

In this stage of emotional development, the psychosocial crisis that needs to be resolved is that of *identity* versus *role confusion*. The age-old question of "Who am I?" is never more prevalent than in the stage of adolescence. Unfortunately, if the child has not developed a strong sense of self, role confusion may have a long-lasting impact.

For adolescents, figuring out "who I am" is much different than determining "what I want to be." The question of "who I am" involves what kind of a person a child wants to develop into. Many teenagers would answer the "who I am" question in very standard terms of being honest, caring, reliable, and loving. The "what I want to be" issue is an occupational choice, but it can also include personality attributes. There are a surprisingly high percentage of adolescents who do not have an answer to either of these two questions. The same is true for many adults.

Dads play a significant role in the solution of both of these questions, as kids often mimic the behaviors and personality attributes of someone they respect. Kids also go out of their way not to mimic behaviors and traits of those they do not respect. It is important for Dad to play a valuable role in the life of his children. That way, these types of questions are answered more readily. It feels good when a teen is asked the question, "What kind of a person do you want to be?" and the answer is "I want to be like my Dad."

This Should Be the Most Difficult Time of Life

Adolescence *should be* the most difficult time of a person's life. I use the phrase "should be" for a reason. Life gets a lot easier (for the teen and her parents) if an adolescent successfully navigates this very difficult stage of development and moves into young adulthood. In contrast, being an adult becomes extremely difficult if the child does not learn the things necessary to be an effective adult during this stage as well as the stage leading up to adolescence. Also, as mentioned, the adolescent stage is when being a dad can be very difficult too.

Many parents report feelings of being less competent and less effective during the adolescent years. Much of this is about the fear of the unknown, expecting problems (that do not have to happen) and not knowing how to let their children grow up and not be reliant upon their parents.

The stage of adolescence brings with it a wide array of difficulties. The difficulties that a teen has navigating through adolescence can very often translate into problems for the parents. Some of the problems that confront teens are obvious ones –hormones, body changes, peer pressure, parental expectations, more difficult school studies, and a host of environmental and social challenges.

Environmental and social challenges would include easy access to illicit and prescribed drugs, being bullied, the possibility of living in an unsafe neighborhood, not fitting in at school, not fitting into the neighborhood, or the feeling of not fitting in at home. The feeling of belonging and being able to associate, or fit in with, a specific group becomes more and more important to the teen.

In fact, a sense of belonging becomes paramount during this developmental stage. Teens will go far out of their way and do things that they know are inappropriate, including things which may even feel very uncomfortable, just to *belong*. When a child feels secure and comfortable within her own family, the pressures to belong to groups outside the family that might be inappropriate decline significantly.

THE BRAIN IS DEVELOPING INTO AN ADULT BRAIN

Certainly there are a lot of additional pressures during the teenage years. However, the biggest issue contributing to an adolescent's behavior is the fact that the adolescent's brain is developing into an adult brain. Adolescence is the period when the brain is changing and acquiring the intellectual power of an adult. This transition can be extremely difficult for the teen, as well as for the parents – especially if the parents do not understand the reasons the teenager thinks and behaves the way she does.

A crucial factor that makes being an adolescent so difficult is that the brain's function of "reason" has not yet fully developed. As a result, what might seem reasonable to a teen may not seem reasonable at all to an adult. Considering that, one can easily see the difficulties of developing through the adolescent stage. Add to this another issue that I have already discussed – that a person is able to develop physically and intellectually, but without developing emotionally at the same pace. Also, mix in the fact that teenagers generalize behaviors, especially those modeled by their parents.

The developmental stage of adolescence can seem like an eternity if Dad's parenting skills are not up to the challenge. This is a stage when being a parent will require all of the aforementioned fundamental skills, in terms of being consistent, calm, caring, concerned, and nurturing. It is easier for the dad to initially practice these attributes and parenting skills as the child is growing up. However, if you find yourself parenting adolescents and have not yet developed these attributes, this would be a good time to develop them. Once again, practice with your wife and apply your new skills to your children.

THE FIRST CHILD CAN BE THE MOST CHALLENGING

If a dad has not yet experienced the raising of an adolescent, the first child can easily be the most challenging. Again, this is because every stage of development is different and new. Being a dad becomes much more challenging when a parent does not know what to expect or what a child is capable of.

With my first child, I remember every stage of development being wonderfully new and exciting. I remember noticing when he was just five or six months old, that he was developing a personality. I loved him so much that first year, just the way he was, that I never wanted him to change. However, as he did change, every step along the way my son was just as new and exciting, and I had those same thoughts – that I did not want this new stage to end. Every step, every phase, every stage of development was a new experience for me, and I loved every part of being his dad.

Along with every new stage comes new challenges, and with challenges come problems. When the groundwork has been properly laid, the problems during adolescence will be less frequent and of less magnitude. If the groundwork has not been laid (for any number of reasons, with *not knowing any better* being the most common reason), problems become more prevalent. Adolescents will test you every day of the week, and if they see a weakness, they will exploit it.

It is imperative to use the skills you have learned in this book, especially in regard to remaining calm, consistent, caring, nurturing, and loving. If you are having difficulty with any of it at this point, read the book again, take notes, underline important passages with a highlighter until you know it by heart, and apply it *your* life. Don't just read the words of the book; *do what it says*. Love is patient, love is kind.

WHEN A CHILD TURNS SIXTEEN, DAD BECOMES MORE OF AN ADVISOR

Adolescence is a stage when children should be able to make more and more of the decisions in their lives. By age sixteen, if all has gone well, a dad is more of an advisor than a dictator. (If all had gone well up to this stage, Dad *never would have been* a dictator, although it may have seemed that way from time to time. But it should only have *seemed* that way.) At sixteen, a child should have the ability to make decisions for her life, *within reason.* For example, some things are not optional, like going to school, doing chores, and having respect for her parents, adults, and authority figures in general, as well as what time she has to be in the house at night. These are very basic rules of any household, regardless of the age of the child or whose house she lives in.

Now when I say sixteen-year-olds need to make decisions for themselves, that is not to say that Dad is not involved. Interestingly, when a teen's mother inquires, "Where are you going?" or "Who you are going with?" it is interpreted by the adolescent as "nagging." When a father inquires about (not demands) the same information, the teen actually flourishes from it. His interest increases a teen's self-esteem and social self-efficacy (belief in her own ability to succeed socially) and lessens the chances of delinquency in adolescence. This is versus a dad who seems to the child not to care.

However, there is a fine balance between allowing a teen to make decisions for herself and indicating to the child that Dad does not care. To show you care, a small amount of concern could be shown regarding such activities as what the teen did after school that day or what the teen and her friends are going to do that night.

Note too that inquiring about an adolescent's activities does not mean controlling what the child is doing. For example, our children, when they have reached sixteen, were required to let us know in some general sense where they were going. However, it was not necessarily to have to ask for permission. This might include going to a friend's house, depending on the circumstances. Who cares if a child says she is going to someone's home and she ends up at the mall across the street? The child needs to be home at a certain time, and if all goes well, she should have the freedom to make decisions for herself.

As you are learning, I do not feel there is a need to micromanage a child at age sixteen or older. However, it is very important at this stage to maintain a good relationship with the adolescent. Also, you'll want to do things together so that the family does not drift apart. Adolescents prepare to separate from their parents at about this age, but a child should want to spend time with her dad. If she does not want to spend time with him, then Dad has some work to do.

At age sixteen and older, our kids would still have to ask permission if they wanted to spend the night at a friend's house. They had to ask *before* going to the friend's house (but it could be the same day) and then only for nights that did not have school the next day. In other words, staying at the friend's house could not, under most circumstances, be without notice. This was an attempt to keep spontaneous and impulsive inappropriate behaviors from happening.

We would also have to know the friend our child was staying with. We did not necessarily have to know the parents of the friend, even though we did have to have the phone number and name of the parents. Plus, we generally did talk to the parents on the phone before allowing our children to spend the night at their house. We called the parents in this situation at least until our kids were seniors in high school.

Prior to age sixteen, we needed to know the parents too. A good rule (and there are always exceptions to the rule) about the parents of kids is that a good kid generally has good parents, and we generally knew the friends of our children. Even during adolescence, we kept very close watch over our children, but at the same time gave them the feeling of being independent. We cared enough about them to be involved in their lives. If kids do not want Dad to know the parents of their friends, then there is probably something wrong. That could be because Dad is overly controlling or there is something wrong with the friend or the friend's parents.

All of this is not to say that a dad should dictate the activities of the teen. Even in younger years, a child should be included in the decision process related to her activities (within reason and when age-appropriate, of course). But if Dad is too controlling, it signals to the teen (or a child at any age) that she is incompetent and incapable of making decisions for herself. In this scenario, a teen may very well become incompetent, as anyone would who is not allowed to practice a skill necessary for survival – in this case, to mature properly.

It is extremely difficult for some dads to allow their children to make decisions for themselves, especially when Dad, or Mom, has been making the decisions all along. If this is the case, a change in philosophy needs to be made. It is best to take small steps when changing parenting skills. Some things can be done all at once, like improving communication by making the decision not to yell at those we love. Other parenting changes might take a little longer to implement, as the parent might not be ready to relinquish control and the child may not be ready to accept the added responsibility just yet. However, depending on the problems that the child and the family might be experiencing, lessening control over the child might be the best course of action. More on this topic in the chapters on interventions.

SCHOOL WORK AND GRADES

Two big issues with this age group are schoolwork and grades. Generally, if there are behavioral problems in school, then there are behavioral problems at home and in other environments as well. Still it is more common for there to be more behavioral problems at home than outside the home. This is often due to a child's comfort level at home being greater than in other environments. However, for now, the discussion will be about issues with school.

Homework

One of the biggest issues with school is whether or not a child does her homework. If a child's grades are slipping, there is a pretty good chance the homework is not being done or not being turned in. *In regard to homework, the level of Dad's involvement is generally dependent on the age of the child.*

In the elementary school years, a dad, in cooperation with his wife, should actually be with the child as she is doing her homework. This will help her develop good learning and study skills. Naturally, this requires that Dad has good learning and study skills as well. In the event that Dad does not have these skills, this might be a good time to develop them – along with patience, a lot of patience.

As the child grows older (usually by the sixth grade), she begins to realize that homework is not optional and will generally do it without having to be reminded. At this point, the dad will still need to go over the homework with the child to ensure that it is done correctly. In seventh and eighth grade, the homework still needs to be checked, but only that it was done – not that it was done correctly. At this age, the child herself needs to be accountable for the quality of her work; however, Dad has to be available to help the child should the need arise. Help time should always be handled in a way that allows the child to feel comfortable enough to ask for it and that help should be given graciously by Dad.

By the time a child starts ninth grade, she should be able to be completely responsible for her schoolwork with little to no intervention from the parents. This is a hard one for many moms and dads. If the child is not quite ready at this stage, some help, especially with organizing and time-management, might be necessary. However, the more a parent does for a child at this stage, the less the child will do for herself. Grades may suffer in the beginning, but they should rebound, and the child will develop a sense of accomplishment and maturity by being able to do her work on her own.

Even at ninth grade and through the high school years, a dad should be available (at some point during the assignment) to help with questions and advice should the need arise. However, resist the temptation of getting too involved with schoolwork. Help, but do not do the work for the child – even if the homework is within your own field of work. For instance, when my children were in high school, I was a radar-systems engineer, and it was easy for me to get sucked into mathematical and science questions. What I had to learn was to have my child answer the question and then we would get into a discussion about it, which really helped them to understand the topic (and it really helped me to understand the topic as well!). If Dad is not familiar with the topic, this would be a good time to learn the topic so you can discuss it with your child. There are times when the child will be the teacher and you will become the student by asking her questions in an inquisitive manner about the topic. This will really help the child solidify her knowledge of a subject.

There are ways to help children find that learning is fun. For instance, this is not a time to try to show the children that Dad knows everything. Instead, it is simply a time to have a discussion with your child like you would with an adult, to honor your child's beliefs, knowledge, and positions on issues without judgment or condemnation. If Dad does not respect his child, who will? This respect is conveyed in everything a dad says and everything he does.

A parent's knowledge of certain areas can once again be challenged by high school courses that teenagers take. Working together and discussing issues and subjects can bring a dad and his children closer together. Recognizing that his child is becoming an adult, a dad allows her the freedom to voice her opinions and openly discuss issues. Remember that there are differences of opinion and then there are differences of fact. The opinion that the earth is flat does not make it flat.

On the other hand, the belief that one political candidate is better than another is an opinion, and it could certainly be discussed. However, a dad needs to keep in mind that the child's opinion, at least to the child, is important to her and should not be attacked.

An example of this comes from the last presidential election. Our youngest son Sammy took an interest in one of the candidates and he voiced his opinion with vigor. I had not decided who I was going to vote for as yet, and I asked him what he found so attractive about his candidate. My son had no realistic reason for his opinion – which certainly weakened his position. However, it was his opinion, and we discussed some of the issues facing the nation. During our discussion, I did not denigrate his opinion, even slightly, nor did I try to sway his opinion. As they develop emotionally, children need to be able to express their views – even if they oppose our own.

High school is a time when a child is in the beginning, middle, and end of adolescence. This is a time when a child matures very quickly. Think back to your own time in high school and remember the difference between the maturity level – physically, intellectually, and emotionally – between the freshmen and the seniors. They are miles apart.

The high school years are also a time when a child's emotional dysfunction can become very prevalent. All the issues of childhood that were suppressed have a tendency to manifest themselves in adolescence. If the relationship between a child and her dad is not worth much to her, there is a very good chance that she will come to believe that compliance with Dad's expectations at this age tends to be voluntary on her part. She may come to the realization that there may not be much that a parent can do to a child in terms of punishment at this age. A child can merely chose not to do what she is told, so compliance to the rules becomes voluntary, at least in her own mind.

If a child does not like or respect her dad, she may very well become oppositional and defiant. Adolescents learn very quickly that a parent's option for punishment become more voluntary on the part of the child. When a child has a poor or contentious relationship with her father, she may intentionally disobey in an act of defiance. This is a time when Dad has to apply all the things discussed in this book. Be patient, be kind, and realize that trying to force an adolescent into compliance will probably have disastrous results. It makes more sense for a dad to work on the relationship between himself and his child. Only when an adolescent cherishes that relationship, will she willfully comply.

SCHOOL IS IMPORTANT FOR MORE THAN GRADES

One thing that is *not optional* for teens is that they need to go to school, and this can very often be a point of contention. School is important for more reasons than grades. Adult social skills are being developed there. The ability to deal with difficult people, including peers, teachers, and parents, is being learned and hopefully mastered.

The principles delineated within this book about communication and relationships are all things that teens need to know and should be able to practice at home. That way, they will be prepared for school, social activities, and community involvement.

EARLY MATURATION OF TEENS

This might be a good time to mention that there is a population of adolescents who physically mature ahead of their peers. Early maturation involves physical development, but meanwhile their emotions and behaviors will more than likely be at the child's chronological age or younger. This can create significant problems for some teens, while being advantageous to others.

In general, boys who mature early tend to enjoy a more positive psychological adjustment overall, with better scholastic performance, better self-image, and greater popularity. On the other hand, these boys have a higher incidence of behavioral problems.

Girls with early maturation have mixed effects, including higher academic achievement and independence but lower self-esteem, poorer body image, and more conflict with parents. When early-maturing girls lower their academic achievement, they actually become more popular and have a more positive self-image. Note that the differences that come with early maturation in both boys and girls seem to disappear by the time the teen is a senior in high school.

Here's a problem to be aware of with early maturation. Once a behavior is learned and the child believes it is effective, the teen may continue to use the behavior even after a conflict is resolved. It is important for dad to be calm, consistent, caring, concerned, and understanding with a teen who is maturing early.

It is difficult for many teens who mature early to try to act like the age they appear to be. It is not unusual for adults, including fathers, to expect more from a teen who looks older than she is. Dad needs to help his child to just be a kid. Try not to be too concerned about what age she appears to be and allow the teen to just be the age she is.

JOBS ARE IMPORTANT FOR TEENS

High school is a time when a child is turning into a young adult. They are learning responsibilities, such as getting up on time, getting to school on time, and being able to do their schoolwork without being told (even though it is not unusual that a teen needs to be reminded). This is a time when teens often get a job and learn to drive a car. Both of these are big ego boosts, and big steps in the right direction in terms of being responsible and learning to be a self-governing adult. By the time they are sixteen years old, nearly any teen can reasonably handle working at a job for ten to fifteen hours a week without their grades suffering. That is, unless the child has a great deal of extracurricular activities that keep them too busy to work.

It is a good idea for a child who is sixteen or older to have a job. It is important for teens to have money of their own, and parents of teens over sixteen should probably not give the teen much money without the teen earning it. This is something that is gradual, and as the child grows older, she must increasingly do more chores to earn an allowance. The teen must understand that everyone in the house has chores to do and that at a certain age the allowance stops.

Children learn from modeled behavior. If the parent is responsible, hard-working, ethical, honest, and caring, there is a very good chance that the child will be once she achieves adolescence. Naturally, Dad needs to allow his child to do things for herself in order to develop these same traits. It is also a time when Dad has the lion's share of influence if he chooses to use it.

WHEN GRADES START TO DROP, TRY NOT TO OVERREACT – THERE IS USUALLY A REASON

There is no doubt that school and grades are important, but they should not be the focus of a dad's relationship with his child. Children, especially teens, get a great deal of self-esteem from doing well in their classes and in the social aspects of school. When teens do not do well in school, there is generally a reason. A sudden or slow and continuous drop in grades at any age is a sign that something is wrong. The child may be being bullied at school, abused at home or somewhere else, or suffering from an emotional or mental condition like depression.

How a dad approaches the topic of whether or not something is wrong and what it might be is extremely important. Often just being available is enough to let the child know she is not alone and no matter what the problem might be that she is loved by her dad. It is not uncommon when a child is being bullied at school, that the child does *not* want the parents to intervene. This can be difficult for some parents. Try to remember that this is a time for the teen to make decisions for herself. If she believes that she can handle it, let her handle it. It is important to let the child know that you are there for her, regardless of what the problem is.

When grades are dropping, it is very common for Dad to step in and make matters worse by overreacting. Once again, grades drop for a reason; the reason may be something that might seem completely insignificant to an adult but can cause a child a great deal of concern. Problems that a teen is having at school or elsewhere, including home, may have caused a decrease in her self-esteem. This may have caused her to become depressed, and with depression comes feelings of hopelessness and helplessness. Any additional pressure being applied to the child by Dad without a thorough understanding of the problem is unwise, and it can be harmful to the relationship between Dad and his child.

Another thing to understand is that a person, child or adult, who is depressed may have no difficulty doing the things they want to do. However, that person may find it nearly impossible to do the things that she is supposed to do. Partaking in things that makes a person feel better is not an indication that the child is lazy, does not care, or is not depressed.

It is not unusual for someone, adult or child, not to know what is wrong. Asking a depressed person "What is wrong?" or "Why are your grades dropping?" may not yield a reasonable answer. Over ten percent of high-school students are depressed. Depression *causes impaired memory and concentration.* That means a child suffering from depression *cannot* remember nor concentrate normally, and grades will likely drop as a direct result.

Depression can be so bad that some teens, as well as adults, cannot even get out of bed. This may not make sense to someone who has never been depressed, and it may not even make sense to the person who is depressed, in that there may not be an obvious reason for the depression. This topic will be discussed in more detail in Chapter 16, "Professional Interventions."

HIGH SCHOOL MAY NOT BE THAT BAD

If a child has been reared to understand the importance of school, then high school may not be too bad for the child and the dad. If a child has had difficulty with school up until high school, then high school can be downright miserable for her. It is important to understand that not all kids learn in the same environmental setting, or in the same way that other kids learn. There is a difference between a child who has been struggling with schoolwork all along and a child whose grades are recently dropping or plummeting. Regardless, it would not be a good idea to allow poor school-performance to have a negative effect on the child/dad relationship.

If a child needs help with her studies, give it to her. If a dad is incapable of giving the help his child needs, find the help that the child needs. Try to make learning a bonding experience. Kids will find the things that they do not want to do, or do not like to do, much easier to swallow if Dad helps them. Naturally, as the child grows older, these tasks should be done more and more independently. However, if the child needs help now with schoolwork, I would give it to her.

Adolescence is a critical time in a child's life. Be patient and kind, and take as much time as needed to help the child be successful. If the child is having difficulty in school, resist the feeling that in some way it is a reflection of Dad; don't let it affect *your* own self-esteem. There certainly are people who look at things from that perspective, and in some cases, they might be correct. However, if a dad is doing the best he can, that is all that can be asked for or expected. If that is all we can ask or expect from the dad, should we not extend that same consideration to our child?

Dad needs to do the best he can to keep his own ego out of child-rearing. The child is not an extension of her father. It is better to be a dad who is compassionate, understanding, and helpful than one who is demanding, demeaning, abusive, or short-tempered. It is important to be supportive and helpful. Rearing a child is not a race to the finish line, but more of a continual learning experience for both child and Dad.

Sometimes Dad feels that there is something wrong, but the child is not forthcoming as to why. Keep in mind that she may not know why. Or dad may not understand the problem once he has been informed. If the latter is the case, find someone who *can* help and who *can* understand. Start by asking the child's mother, and if together you cannot help the child, the need for a professional may be necessary. Chapter 16 discusses how a dad knows when treatment from a professional is needed.

SCHOOL IS IMPORTANT BUT IT IS NOT EVERYTHING

School is important but it is not so important as to damage the relationship between a child and her dad. For some children, school is a source of unbelievable stress. This stress can manifest itself in poor grades, social isolation, and behavioral problems at school and at home, drug use, delinquency, and an overall feeling of hopelessness. In this scenario, school may be too much for a child to effectively work through without help. At this point, it is imperative that Dad work with the school to devise a method that will satisfy the child's need for learning –

without damaging the relationship between the teen and her father. It is important to remember that no amount of failure outside the home will be made up by failed relationships inside the home.

As you have been reading, children do the best they can. If they are capable of doing well, they will excel. If the child's life has been full of chaos, instability, and inconsistency, then high school will probably be very difficult. As I mentioned earlier in this book, I spent a considerable amount of my childhood living in an orphanage, foster care, living with grandparents, and in a group home. By the time I got to high school, my mother had firmly implanted in my mind that school was a waste of time. After all, she had not finished high school and she was doing fine.

It amazed me, even while I was very young, that my mother actually believed that she was doing fine. Regardless, she had decided that my career path was to be a coffee-shop cook. I started down the path to fulfill that career when after the ninth grade I dropped out of school and worked as a dishwasher. One day it occurred to me that I was never going to be able to afford the things in life that I wanted. In order to get the things I needed and to be able to afford my newborn child – at sixteen years old – I was needed to get educated. Toward that end, I started community college at nineteen years old. I took one remedial class in math, and all the other classes during that first semester and all subsequent semesters were college-level courses. My grade point average remained above 3.5 for all my undergraduate studies.

I share this part of my life because it is important for some dads to realize that a child's fate is not set in high school. If a child does not do well in high school, she may do very well in college. Sometimes enrolling in college is the right move for a teen who is not getting along in high school. In California, there is a college/high-school program where juniors and seniors can attend community college while at the same time finishing their high-school curriculum. They still graduate with their high-school class.

High school is important but we need to understand that there is more to being successful in life than a high GPA. Just as important are social and communication skills. Studies have shown that high-school valedictorians (those are the high-school kids with the highest grades

183

throughout high school) do not do any better in life than the kids who get average grades. This is especially true when a child with average grades grows up with good social and communication skills. And where do children learn good social and communication skills? Children learn these skills at home and apply them to their outside relationships.

DON'T LET YOUR HOME BECOME A BATTLE ZONE
BECAUSE OF SCHOOL

School is important, but not so important that one's home should become a battle zone over poor school-performance. It is very difficult for some dads to separate their child's activities outside the home from the relationships inside the home. Teens can also be rebellious, oppositional, and defiant. It takes two to argue (however, it only takes one to yell and call names), and it takes at least two people for a power struggle to disrupt or even consume a household. When Dad does not engage in arguing or using "why" statements, degrading comments, sarcasm, and guilt trips, the home becomes much more calm. Most often, this also helps the grades go up or other inappropriate behaviors to decline.

DAD'S INFLUENCE ON ADOLESCENT SOCIAL SKILLS

Adolescence is a time when kids are learning to be adults. They practice being an adult; and they pretend that they are adults, all the while learning how to socialize in an adult world. Those teens who have had a solid foundation in terms of social and communicative skills are at an advantage over teens who have not. However, it is never too late to learn appropriate social and communication skills.

A dad's influence on social skills, communication, and a sense of self-efficacy in adolescence is significant in the teen's life. By this age, a child's social skills are significantly influenced by how nurturing or how protective a dad is. Overprotective fathers do not let a child make decisions for herself. This may be out of fear that she will fail, or that he will lose control of her, or maybe out of fear that she will be successful and no longer need to rely on her dad. Regardless, fathers who are overprotective are afraid of something. Overprotectiveness creates self-esteem problems and social problems for children. Dads have significantly more influence on a child's social skills and social competency *in adolescence* than anyone else in the family. This includes daughters as well as sons.

In most cases, a dad can help a child navigate her way through adolescence while at the same time helping her improve her academic performance – without engaging in any of the negative reactions described above. There might come a time when Dad has to allow his child to sink or swim. That time may very well be when school performance makes the home environment uncomfortable for *any* of the family members. Again I say, "*Any* of the family members" because sludge flows downhill. In a home where there is a lot of chaos, it is often the youngest child who is affected the most – regardless of who is the problem child. If it is the youngest child who is the biggest problem, there is a reason for that, and a review of previous chapters may be necessary.

There is something important that teens may not realize during this difficult stage – this is that they have a life too, separate from their family. In fact, the life they are living is *theirs,* and they need to take that seriously. Meanwhile, it is difficult for some dads to allow their children to be responsible for themselves. So know that some adolescents need to be reminded that "This is *your* life"; succeed or fail, "it is *your* life." Some kids will take that to mean that they can do with it as they please, and in some regard that is correct. Other teens will realize that living with Mom and Dad is temporary, and entering an adult world unprepared is very scary.

In the end, being irresponsible hurts the one who is being irresponsible (that includes adults and dads who are irresponsible). In addition, living with an irresponsible person is difficult for everyone around him or her. When Dad models the desired behavior and allows his teen to make decisions for herself, even when dad may not agree with her 100%, the child begins to realize that she is becoming an adult. She will also start to realize that her behavior has ramifications on her and those around her. If she loves and cherishes those around her, her decisions will probably be more reasonable.

DECISIONS NEEDS TO BE WITHIN CERTAIN GUIDELINES

Most children who have been raised with age-appropriate responsibilities have little difficulty making the transition to adolescence and then to the developmental stage of young adult. When I suggest that teens in high school make as many decisions for themselves as possible, it is important that these decisions are within certain guidelines. These guidelines should have been established long before the child reaches adolescence. Families have rules, and those rules often do not go away, regardless of the age of the child. For example, a family that does not allow smoking in their home would expect the child not to smoke in their home – regardless of the age of the child. Even when a child reaches eighteen years old, she needs to be aware that she still needs to follow the house rules. There is a monumental difference between allowing a child to be responsible for her life and her being able to do as she pleases.

There are also differences between the privileges that a sixteen-year-old has and a seventeen-year-old has – just as there are differences between the privileges that a seventeen-year-old has and the privileges that an eighteen-year-old has. By the time a child is sixteen years old, she should know what is expected of her, and should be doing that. Occasionally she may need reminders.

A RECAP

Adolescence can easily be the most difficult stage of development for both the child and Dad. This a time when a child becomes an adult and that transition is difficult, even under the best of circumstances. A dad who is patient and kind, allows his child to take on increasingly more responsibility and authority over her life, and is responsive to his child's needs will have much fewer problems navigating through adolescence.

WHAT'S NEXT?

In Chapter 13, I will be discussing the issues that families might have when the marriage is experiencing trouble. We will also look at the impact of divorce, and how a dad can be there for his kids. I encourage dads to use their influence to make the marriage work and keep the family together.

KEY CHAPTER POINTS

1. Adolescence is the stage of emotional development in which the attribute of *identity* versus *role confusion* needs to be resolved.
2. Adolescence *should* be the most difficult time of a person's life. (Not that anybody wants to make it that way, it is just the nature of it.)
3. When the proper groundwork is laid ahead of time, the problems in this stage are less frequent and of less magnitude.
4. When the child turns sixteen years old, the father should become more of an advisor. There is a fine balance in allowing teens to make decisions for themselves while at the same time showing that Dad cares about them and their activities.
5. If Dad is too controlling, it signals to the teen (or a child of any age) that the child is incompetent and incapable of making decisions for herself.
6. By the time a child starts the ninth grade, she should be able to be completely responsible for her schoolwork with little to no intervention from the parents.
7. It is imperative that Dad respect his teen's beliefs, knowledge, and positions on issues without judgment or condemnation. If Dad does not respect his child, who will?
8. Teens often come to the realization that compliance to their parents' directives is voluntary.
9. When a child is having problems, any additional pressure from Dad to perform better in school will undoubtedly make matters worse, at least between the child and her dad.
10. Over 10% of teens suffer from depression. Depression causes impaired memory and concentration, which means that a depressed person *cannot* remember or concentrate as well, and grades most often will suffer.

11. School is important, but it is not so important as to damage the relationship between a child and her dad.

12. If a child's life has been full of chaos, instability, and inconsistency, then high school will probably be very difficult for the child, academically and socially.

13. School is important, but not so important that the home should become a battle zone over poor school performance.

14. There is a monumental difference between allowing a child to be responsible for her life and her being able to do as she pleases.

13

Broken Families

There are many families – where both parents live together with their children – that behave in a manner that seems to be broken. The parents argue constantly, yell at each other and the kids, and those who live in the home seem to believe that this is normal. The majority of this book is written for those types of families, but not only those families. It is also for families that just need a few things to think about that might help the parents relate better with each other and also with their children.

This particular chapter is focused more on the families that are no longer intact. The parents are separated with a divorce imminent, in process, or already completed. Chapter 13 is focused on the father being the non-custodial parent. In cases where the father is the custodial parent, most of the information in this chapter is still relevant – except that the father would put himself in the position of the custodial parent and the child's mother would be in the position of the non-custodial parent. However, in terms of being a stepparent, it is important to understand that there are major differences between the influence of a stepfather and a stepmother. The influence of a stepfather will be discussed in more detail in the Chapter 14.

GOING THROUGH A DIVORCE IS HARD ON EVERYONE INCLUDING THE KIDS

The divorce rate of first marriages in this country is at or above 60%. So it is not uncommon that a child will experience divorce. This does not even *sound* good – that a *child* would *have* to experience divorce. Divorce is devastating to adults, and we often get very wrapped up in the conflict, the property settlement, which parent the kids will live with, when Dad gets to see his kids, and so on. It's easy to lose sight of the fact that the kids are going through the same issues. However, the kids have virtually no say in the divorce, who gets the kids, and where they are going to live, etc. Most kids would rather have the parents work things out.

Even in homes where the parents are arguing, the majority of kids would still like to have, and still need, the security of two loving parents. Just because the parents have failed in their relationship (and there might be very good reasons) does not mean that the children should have to suffer for it. Would it not be better for the parents to honor their commitments to each other and the children, and do whatever they need to do to make the marriage work?

Most children of divorce do not want to leave the family home, move to a different town, go to a different school, have to acquire new friends, and have to learn how to live with parents who spend more time denigrating each other than worrying about what is really important. What should be important to parents is raising their children and modeling how to make relationships work, even when the marriage is having problems.

The child of divorce is often the one whose wishes and needs are completely discounted. The parents might be in such pain themselves that they cannot see the child's stress and anxiety over the current state of the household, nor his fear of what the future might hold. It is very common for parents of divorce to believe, at least tacitly, that the child is in favor of the divorce as well.

This book is not about blame, but about solutions. Before a man divorces his wife, he should think long and hard. In divorce, it is most likely you will lose most of your possessions, your home and family, and

191

the identity of being a father and a husband. Also know that the majority of mothers will remarry within the next couple of years. When that happens, someone else will be spending a whole lot more time with your kids than you will be, assuming that the children reside with the mother. You also get absolutely NO say in who that individual is (neither do the kids in most cases), how their new stepfather behaves in general, whether or not he knows anything about raising children, or how he treats *your* children.

THE INFAMOUS TRIAL SEPARATION

This chapter is for families that have not been able to work things through and have separated. A separation usually comes before a divorce. For our purposes, the term separation and divorce are synonymous. However, there are times when parents have a "trial separation." A trial separation is, in my opinion, a coward's way of saying that he or she wants to date other people, and if everything else fails, we can get back together. Kids do not need their parents to "try" a separation; what they need is for their parents to try harder to make the marriage work.

Regardless, there are times when all the hard work and effort does not maintain a marriage. However, a dad should always do whatever he can to use his influence in the family dynamic to mend the damage that can cause a divorce. No one has more influence in a family than Dad. Keep in mind that it takes two to make a relationship successful, and there are times when, even with the best of husbands, his good behavior is not enough. What I am hoping is that after reading this book, a husband/father will have the tools to improve the relationships within his realm of influence and make the possibility of divorce much less.

When a divorce is imminent, in process, or completed, it is imperative to spend extra time with the children and help them come to terms with the changes. There are times when the divorce is so devastating to children that it is difficult for them to recover. Other children seem to take it with a grain of salt. Both situations are *very* sad. When the situation is difficult for the child, the problems become obvious. However, in the case of the child who appears to be doing well, the truth is that he may very well be hiding his true feelings. Or the family home may have been so disturbing to the child that the change in the family dynamic is a relief.

CHILDREN'S AGE DIFFERENCES AND DIVORCE

The age of the child plays a significant factor as to how well he will adjust to the changes in the family dynamic. The younger the children are at the time of the divorce, the more difficult it is for them. Young children do not understand what is going on, and they have not developed the necessary cognitive abilities to think through something this complicated. They have a tendency to live only in the present, and the present might be very uncomfortable for them. Children before the age of five years old do not like big changes to their daily routine. Some young children have difficulty even sleeping in a bed that is not theirs, much less living in a different home and without one of the parents.

Preschoolers are very likely to develop behavioral problems. These may include feelings of anger and hurt, and they may revert back to more infantile behaviors like bed-wetting, tantrums, and fears. Preschoolers also do not have social support outside of the home, and the parents are often not emotionally available to help the child through this period. Additionally, young children often blame themselves for the divorce, and they use nonsensical thinking like "If I had put my toys away, Daddy would not have left." This puts quite a burden on a young child. Too often it is the case that Dad forgets that the children are having a difficult time as well. He may not be there to help the child, may be incapable, or lacks the necessary skills to help. This may very well be because the dad does not have much to give at this point, due to his own emotional dysfunction.

Overall, teenage children handle the stressors of a divorce better than younger ones. These kids are old enough to understand, and they usually do not hold themselves responsible for their parents' actions. Teenage children are often more in tune with the status of the parental relationship than the parents are, and they may very well have already surmised that a divorce was coming. Adolescents might try to act as mediators between the parents in an effort to keep the family together.

Additionally, teenagers often have their own social support, aside from the family, and they seek comfort there. Teens often turn to their friends for advice, but that should not take the place of their father. Dad is most often the person a child seeks when he is having a problem; he wants to know Dad's view on things and respects his advice. If a child is going elsewhere for advice and support, there is some *blending* that needs to be done (more on this in the next chapter). Blending is the joining of two households or may be the integration of a single family.

The children that are in the middle (between young children and adolescence; *five to thirteen years old*) also have a difficult time with divorce. They are old enough to understand what is going on to some degree. However, they are not yet old enough to realize that Dad's leaving is not their fault, and therefore they might become more insecure. This is due to the fact that children generalize behaviors. They may come to believe that "if Dad stopped loving Mom, then Dad may stop loving me as well." They can also be under the false conception that they could help patch things up.

Many school-age children believe that the divorce is because of them. They feel that they are responsible for making amends so that the family will stay together. Some children try to fix the parental relationship, while others choose sides in an effort to gain support from one or both parents. It is important to remember that the children, in most cases, are in extreme pain and turmoil before, during, and after the divorce. It is also important to remember that when parents divorce, it is *never* the children's fault. Therefore it is never acceptable to even remotely allude to that thought, much less say it. The emotional damage of comments that parents make when going through difficult times can be life-changing to a child. This is true even after the parents have moved on with their individual lives and are past the pain of the divorce. The child may never forget the things that parents say when they are upset.

CHILDREN'S GENDER AND THE EFFECTS OF DIVORCE

There is also a difference in a child's gender and how well he or she deals with the parents' divorce. Girls, for the most part, fare better than boys during and after a divorce. Boys often start to exhibit behavioral problems even before a divorce is imminent. This is more than likely due to the chaos within the home, as well as the lack of paternal modeling that is so important in raising a male child. When a father is not appropriately involved early in a child's life, the chances of good outcomes diminish. When a father is no longer residing in the family home, the boys often suffer the most. This might manifest itself in delinquent behaviors, poor school performance, drug use, and oppositional/defiant behaviors at home, school, and within the community.

It is important to reiterate that if the father/child relationship is poor or contentious, then the absence of the father might actually benefit the child. It is a smart man who knows when he is doing more harm than good and makes the necessary effort to change. Naturally, if a father cannot change to benefit his children, it would be best that he be gone from his children's lives. Of course, that would not exclude him from being financially responsible for his children.

AFTER THE DIVORCE

In the best of cases, a non-custodial father will be able to maintain a *decent* relationship with his kids. In order for a father to be a *good* dad, he still needs to maintain a good relationship with the child's mother, at least in regard to the children. That becomes increasingly difficult to do when you are divorced and married to other people. When a father is demoted to a non-custodial parent, his influence drops precipitously. It is hard to maintain a high degree of influence when Dad is not living with the kids. On the other hand, the child's new stepfather will have a high degree of influence – good or bad.

The majority of non-custodial fathers decrease their visitation and other contact with their children within two years after the divorce. Over half of fathers have virtually no contact with the children at all after two years. The fathers who do have contact have it inconsistently with decreasing frequency. It is important for a father to have a schedule of visitation and then stick to it. In this manner, the children have more security and consistency, along with being able to plan for the visit.

It is important that children have an ongoing relationship with their father. However, keep in mind what is best for the child. If a father's visitation schedule is inconsistent, it will cause further trust issues between the child and the father. Make sure you do what you say you'll do, whether that is being there to pick up the children or taking them somewhere. Also be on time. There is little more frustrating to a child than having a father who is not able to keep his word.

With the decreased participation of the father in his children's lives, it becomes apparent how that new dynamic would affect the emotional connectedness in the family. His level of emotional connectedness to his kids will be low when the relationship with them is dependent upon their mother. When the relationship between the father and mother is severed, a father with low emotional depth and poor emotional connectedness to his children will either stop seeing his children entirely or see his children in an effort to maintain some control over their mother.

When a father develops an emotional connection to his children, separate from the emotional connection he has with his wife, a father will in all likelihood continue to have contact with his kids. This man will not try to use the children as a means to control his estranged wife, and he will be able to maintain a higher level of influence with his children. If a father cannot do this, he needs to apply the principles of this book and work on his emotional connectedness with his children. If a man cannot develop an emotional connectedness with his children, this pattern will most likely repeat itself in the father's next relationship.

Very often when a man remarries, his new wife has custody of her children and the man becomes a stepfather. How much more difficult will it be to form a relationship with someone else's children if a man cannot form a meaningful relationship with his own children? It will be virtually impossible.

SPLITTING THE KIDS

Sometimes parents, or the court, come up with the concept of sharing the kids. In most cases, this does not work very well. This is when the kids live part-time at Mom's and part-time at Dad's, dividing up the time equally in a 50/50 split. This is the court's (as well as a bunch of do-gooders') idea of equality for the parents and what is best for the children. Having the children's lives literally torn in two by living in two separate residences cannot be a good thing for children. This is one good example of why it is not a good idea to let a court make decisions for you and your family. It is best to work things out between yourselves. Naturally, there are exceptions to the rule, but try to work things out with the children's mother, and do not let a court do it.

When parents split the children in this way, in most cases the children's lives become more chaotic, and problems will most likely be intensified. Children of all ages need a place that they can call home; that is where they live. They can go visit the other parent's home. Even if parents have the financial resources to duplicate everything a child possesses, it is not a good idea to split the kids' time because the parents could not work things out.

When the time is split, the children have a tendency to "run" to the parent who they have the least problems with. It is not unusual for parents to become engulfed in a manipulation by the children, especially teenage children. Additionally, when parents split the kids' time and the parents are not on the same page with child-rearing practices, discipline, and ways of punishment, some pretty severe problems might occur. This would include problems with the children, but also conflict between the parents. Children need consistency; they needed it when their parents were married and they need it now that their parents are divorced. It would be a shame to continue the same type of conflict after a divorce because the parents are trying to share the kids.

Kids generally love both of their parents, so make the best decisions for the *child*. One parent should have the lion's share of custody, with the non-custodial parent having very liberal visitation. Even then, the child needs to feel that he belongs in both homes and within both family dynamics, even though his formal place of residence is at one of the homes.

I am hoping that by now it is becoming obvious how difficult divorce is for the children. I am also hoping it is becoming obvious that what might seem to be in the best interest of the father is not necessarily in the best interest of the child. Dad needs to be aware of what is best for his children and that may not seem fair to Dad. To a child, there is not much that's fair about a divorce and the child is the one who has to be considered first.

MAKE NO COMMENTS ABOUT THE CHILD'S MOTHER

Understanding that there is an emotional connection between a child and her parents – both Mom and Dad – it becomes clear that any derogatory comment from one parent about the child's other parent would be viewed by the child as a comment about the child. The child will internalize the statement. For example, if Dad says to his child, "Your mother is a …" the child interprets that as Dad telling the child, "*You* are a …" It is a sad state of affairs when a dad sinks so low as to impugn a child's mother regardless of what the mother may have done. It would be best to say nothing about her at all to the child.

It is imperative that Dad resist any temptation to berate the mother in his children's presence. This includes when a child is in the other room or is asleep. It is amazing how well a child can hear, and kids are often not asleep when they are supposed to be. Making negative comments about a child's mother is one of the most damaging behaviors a dad can engage in. Any benefit the dad may feel that he is achieving by talking poorly about his estranged wife would be a lie. Any derogatory comments made about a child's mother – even if it were true – will only damage the child/father relationship, and it may very well turn the child against his father.

KIDS SHOULD NOT BE USED AS LEVERAGE

When parents are not getting along, it is not unusual for one or both of them to use the children as a bargaining chip or as leverage against the other parent. It is important for Dad to always protect his children, even from his own comments about the child's mother. Try to keep in the forefront of your mind that the woman who is on the other side is still the child's mother. That child still loves her just as he still loves his father.

Using a child for leverage includes behaviors such as keeping a child from the other parent or the father not allowing his child to go on a school outing with his friends to an amusement park because it's scheduled during his visitation time. (Dad can simply make other arrangements for his visitation time with the kids.) Children are not possessions, and therefore they should not be treated like one. Dad needs to remain cooperative with his visitation schedule, even if his estranged wife is not. Dad gains nothing by being uncooperative, and ultimately non-cooperation only hurts the child.

Being a non-custodial father means that Dad needs to make the best use of the time he has with his kids. Sitting around watching television might be enough for some children, and it can be fun if Dad takes the time to interact with his kids in the process. For other kids, this type of interaction is painful, and they require more active activities. These can include going to the park, taking a hike, walking around the mall, or going to the movies.

Spending time with the kids does not have to cost a lot of money. Often the most fun time kids have with their dad costs no money at all. Money is often tight during and after a divorce, so Dad might not have much of it to spend. The fact that money is tight or the reasons why money is tight should not be discussed with the children or blamed on the children's mother. Children are not capable of dealing with the stress of financial problems.

It is important to remember that the children are having difficulty with the current situation. So, when Dad has visitation, he should spend that time with his kids. Too many times I have heard of the non-custodial parent taking the kids and dropping them off at Grandma's house or another relative's house while Dad goes to work or – are you ready for this one? – he goes to his girlfriend's house. This is not to say that a father does not have the legal right to bring his kids to his mother's home while he goes and does something else. However, it is important to understand that just because a person has "a right" to do something does not make it the "right" thing to do. Still, it is perfectly all right to bring the kids to visit Grandma – while Dad visits there too – as this might be the only time she gets to see them.

When Dad does not spend time with his children during visitation, it is damaging to the kids and his relationship with them. Also, using a child in some way during Dad's visitation to do emotional harm to the children's mother only damages the emotional well-being of the child and the relationship between the child and his father. An example of this might be when a father's visitation falls on a weekend that is important to the child's mother and the father enforces his visitation in an attempt to annoy her. In all likelihood, this type of behavior will only draw the child closer to his mother, and the child will want to stop going with his father. This is something a dad would never want to have happen.

Additionally, the kids most likely do not have many of their belongings at Grandma's home, and they might not have much at Dad's house either. Dad needs to understand that seeing their father may not be a reward in itself for the children. So have some fun things planned to do with them.

CHILDREN WILL TELL THEIR MOTHER EVERYTHING

When Dad has visitation, it is important to be careful what information is disclosed within earshot of the kids. Children do not keep secrets very well, and it would be a mistake to believe they will not tell their mother everything that happened. This is actually what parents and kids do in good relationships – communicate in an open and honest manner with each other. Dad should not be engaging in any activity that a child would have to keep secret. It is too much to ask that a child keep portions of his life locked up inside. It is sad to think that a child would have to separate and compartmentalize his own life because his parents separated the family life.

People cannot keep secrets; they have to tell at least one person. Then that person has to tell at least one other person. Well, children are no different. Plus, the further the secret gets from the source, the less secret it becomes. Within a very short period of time, it seems that entire world knows the secret. Therefore, it is best not to keep secrets, or at least, not to ask one's children to keep secrets.

BEING PUNISHED AT DAD'S HOUSE

Punishment gets to be a sticky subject when Dad does not have custody of the kids and only sees them periodically. I suggest that if a child is in trouble at Mom's house, then leave the trouble at Mom's house. It does little good to have a child be punished at a home where no problem occurred. The same would be true if a child gets in trouble while visiting Dad. Depending upon the trouble, he would not be punished for it at Mom's house. There are exceptions to this rule. However, for the most part, a non-custodial father does not want to put added stress on his relationship with his children because of something that happened at someone else's home.

This is a topic that should be discussed with the child's mother. That way, it will not be a surprise to her when your child is not grounded or punished when with Dad. Parents need to be able to discuss issues with each other as they pertain to the children in a calm, consistent, caring, and concerned manner. If they cannot – and Dad may not be the problem – there needs to be some soul-searching. Remember that you are trying to do what is best for the child, not what is best for the parent.

It would also be unwise to allow a child to believe that Dad's house is a safe haven from the rules at his primary residence. However, under most circumstances, punishments should be kept at the home in which the infraction occurred.

There should be very few opportunities for a child to get into trouble when he is at Dad's house for a visit. One reason is that Dad should be with him most of the time. There will be times when Dad needs to help his children with some of the tasks that might normally be accomplished at the children's primary residence, like homework, especially if grades are dropping.

It is important to remember that a child is not emotionally equipped to deal with the stress of divorce. It is not uncommon, that when a child's grades start to drop, behavioral problems arise too. During a divorce, the parents often lose sight of their children's emotional turmoil, and then they punish them for the behavioral changes, which were the result of the parents' actions. This only makes matters worse.

BRINGING PROBLEMS FROM ONE RELATIONSHIP INTO THE NEXT

This is a good time to address that whatever problems a man (this holds true for women as well, but this book is about men) has in a marriage, he will also have in the next marriage (or relationship) – if those problems are not resolved. The resolution is usually done through psychotherapy – individual and couples therapy. There are times when the marriage is not salvageable. In such cases, the parents should seek counseling together and/or individually so that their divorce causes as little pain to the children as possible.

Most of us have heard at some time that we keep "making the same mistakes" when it comes to picking a partner. This is more often true than not because we are still the same person. We are still attracted to the same things, and no matter how hard we try, we most often find the exact same type of person that we just left. They just have a different name. Even when one goes far out of his way to find someone entirely different, it is very concerning to realize a few months or years down the road that you found "the exact same person." Only when someone makes changes within himself can he find a mate who is more emotionally healthy.

This is due to the principle that people are attracted to certain attributes of a person – physically, intellectually, and emotionally. All of these attributes are important, and generally they match up fairly well. For example, a very intelligent person will generally find someone who is also very intelligent. However, the most important of these attributes is how well we match up emotionally. If we, as men, have a level of emotional wellness, we will be attracted to a female who has a similar level of emotional wellness. On the other hand, whatever level of emotional dysfunction we have, we will be attracted to a female with a similar level of emotional dysfunction. Failures in relationships are due to emotional dysfunction, and it would be a mistake to blame a failed relationship entirely on the other person.

Let's say that the attraction a man has to a woman is significant enough that he marries her and wants to spend the rest of his life with her. It is a sure bet that his emotional level of functioning is similar to hers. And is it any wonder that problems might come up when two people try to establish a life together, and their emotional level of functioning has been stifled in the adolescent stage or at a previous stage of emotional development?

(I feel that I must add a disclaimer, and that would be about when one of the participants of the marriage has a psychiatric disorder. In such cases, there might be long periods of time when things go near perfectly, only to become intolerable at other times. The same holds true for parents who engage in substance abuse/dependency and alcoholism.)

NEW SIGNIFICANT OTHERS

It is unfortunate that, all too often, Dad has a new girlfriend during or shortly after the divorce. It is very abusive for a father of a child to cheat on the child's mother and carry on a relationship with another woman while being married. It is more acceptable to find a girlfriend after the divorce is completed. However, even in these cases, do not include the children in the relationship for a while. I understand that children are a big part of a relationship, but it creates significant turmoil in a child's life to see his father with, and showing affection to, someone other than the child's mother.

This would be a good time to show respect for one's children and not include a significant other in the child's life. *Wait* until *the children* have acclimated to the new situation. It is asking quite a bit to include a new parental figure into a child's life before the child is safe and secure in a residence, adjusted to a new school if necessary, and has had time to come to terms with the changes in the family dynamic.

If there is another woman involved in Dad's life, and the dad is not the custodial parent, it is much easier to segregate his dating life from the life his enjoys with his children. Of course, it is not unusual for a man to want to include his new romance in the life of his children. Still, it would be best to keep the time a father has with his children –with just his children. The children should not have to share their time with a woman who, at least initially, they are likely to resent. It is also not fair to ask a child how they feel about Dad's new flame. A child will generally not know what he is feeling and say he's okay with it when he is not. This holds true for both boys and girls.

A dad has a tendency to believe that his children are as happy as he is when he finds that new significant other. All too often children are introduced to the new girlfriend, and the kids are expected to be okay with it. Most of the time, they are not. Introducing the girlfriend as a family member like an "aunt" is not a smart covert way of hiding the fact that Dad has replaced his child's mother with someone else. Plus the child has not met her until now, and does a father really want his child to believe he is having sex with a family member?

Introducing the woman to the kids as Dad's new "friend" does not work well either. Children are usually too smart to buy that one, especially if Dad's new *friend* spends the night. This is the type of behavior that causes a lack of trust between the child and the father. And this is a time when the child's trust for his father is already being put to the test.

During such a critical transitional period, Dad *does not want to fail* his children. Dad needs to remain calm, consistent, caring, and concerned for the well-being of his children. Be considerate of the child and his love for his mother by not bringing another woman into the family dynamic just yet. Keep your personal life personal and away from the kids.

When a family is impacted by divorce, it takes time for children to understand what is happening and acclimate to it. It takes more time for a child to come to terms with Dad showing affection to a woman other than his mother. This is an area where Dad can show how much he cares for his children and put their needs before his own.

REMAINING AN ACTIVE DAD
DURING AND AFTER THE DIVORCE

Divorce is one of the most difficult transitions a child goes through. It is difficult for everyone involved, and Dad needs to keep in mind that his children have virtually no say in anything that is going on. They are forced to do whatever their parents want them to do and to go wherever their parents want them to go. Plus, they are expected to *like* it. This is a period of a child's life when he especially needs a dad who is calm, consistent, caring, and concerned for his children – always.

It is important for a father to understand what a child is going through and be responsible for *his* own actions. When a father/husband conducts himself as described herein, then his children have a good chance of getting through this difficult time without long-lasting detrimental outcomes.

All that said, in the majority of marriages, there is a good possibility that a husband possesses the influence to keep a marriage together – if he chooses to exercise that influence. Most women are very caring, loving, forgiving, and understanding. That is not to say all women, but these are the personality traits that women are born with; they are innate. Men need to learn these traits. When a man behaves toward his wife in a manner that is explained in this book, there is a very good possibility that the marriage will not only survive, but flourish. It has been my experience that if a husband does what a good husband is supposed to do, most marriages will remain intact.

We can always find someone to blame for our behaviors. It is a little bit harder to look in the mirror and come to the realization that "I could have done better." There is no better time to learn this than now. If the divorce is complete, with no chance of reconciliation, this is when Dad needs to apply the principles of this book to his children. At the very least, he will be better equipped to enter into and be successful in an intimate relationship when the time comes. More importantly, he will be building and repairing the relationship with his children *now*. Dad can still apply these principles to his estranged wife as well, in that it is important to remember that your ex-wife is still your children's mother.

WHAT'S NEXT?

In the next chapter, I continue the discussion about families that have not been able to stay together. Chapter 14 discusses the process of joining two families into one. Additionally, we'll look at how the non-custodial father needs to be able to cooperate with his children's new stepfather. You'll also see that the stepfather needs to learn how to develop influence with his new stepchildren. Furthermore, it is also very important for a divorced father to continue to use the principles from this book, even when he no longer lives with the children and their mother. The advice in Chapter 14 is also helpful for helping Dads who want to create a stronger bond in families that are still together.

KEY CHAPTER POINTS

1. Even in homes where the parents are arguing, the majority of kids would still like to have, and need, the security of two loving parents.
2. What should be important to parents is raising their children and modeling how to make relationships work, even when their marriage is having problems.
3. When a divorce is imminent, in process, or completed, it is imperative to spend extra time with the children and help them come to terms with the changes.
4. The age of a child is a significant factor in how well he/she will adjust to the changes in the family dynamic. The younger the child, the more difficult a divorce will be, and they often blame themselves.
5. When a father is no longer residing in the family home, the boys often suffer the most. This might manifest itself in delinquent behaviors, poor school performance, drug use, and oppositional/defiant behaviors at home, at school, and within the community.
6. What might seem to be in the best interest of the father may not be in the best interest of the child.
7. Making negative comments about the child's other parent is one of the most damaging behaviors a divorced parent can engage in.
8. Children of divorce will tell their mother everything.
9. If a child is in trouble at Mom's house, leave the trouble at the mother's house.
10. People are attracted to intimate partners whose emotional level of function/dysfunction is similar.

11. Keep any new girlfriends away from the children until you know the relationship is serious. And then, introduce them *only* after the children have had a chance to acclimate to their new life after the divorce.
12. It would be best to apply the principles of this book to your wife and children and not get divorced.

14

Family Blending

This chapter discusses some of the issues that many families experience in one form or another. Some families act as a loose collection of individuals and not as a family. It is necessary in all families that the family functions like a family. I refer to the process of getting a family to act as a family as *family blending*. If the biological father has not been actively involved in his children's lives, it may be very helpful to approach improving these relationships as if he were a new entity. Walk softly, try not to make changes too quickly with the children, but do what has been discussed so far. Whether the family dynamic is of the original parents or a family with a stepparent, this chapter is meant to provide useful information about improving new and/or existing relationships with one's children or stepchildren.

BLENDED FAMILIES AND STEPFATHERS

In this chapter, I will cover the many issues that being a stepfather brings into a household and how a *good enough* stepfather can become a stepdad. However, there is a great deal of information in this section that is very beneficial to every dad, and I suggest that both stepdads and biological dads read the entire chapter. Still, keep in mind that stepfathers have certain issues that biological fathers may not have and vice versa.

I will discuss how to initiate a relationship with a new stepchild and how to improve a relationship with a new or existing stepchild. We will see that these same techniques are effective in improving the relationship between a biological dad and his children.

To begin this chapter, I feel it is necessary to state that it is an honorable man who can love someone else's children as his own. It will become obvious that the connection between the stepfather and his new bride is paramount to the relationships that a man develops with his stepchildren. There is an innate connection between a mother and her children. When a man establishes an emotional connection with his wife, it makes establishing an emotional connection with her children much easier. That is not to say, however, that there will not be problems for the stepfather in establishing relationships with his stepchildren.

One of the most difficult achievements a man can accomplish is to successfully blend two families. Research shows that 60% of second marriages end in divorce, due to a failure of successfully blending the children of one or both spouses into the new family dynamic. Research also indicates that a stepfather, in most circumstances, has nearly the same influence as a biological father, and, in some instances, even more influence (positive or negative). Due to this influence, there are several factors to consider when blending families. In addition, all of the information in this book that discusses how a man can be a good dad applies to being a good stepdad.

In most situations, the biological father already has a relationship established with the child – regardless of the quality of that relationship. In some cases, however, it might actually be easier to begin a new relationship with the child as the stepfather than to repair a damaged relationship between a father and child.

A child always wants to have a good relationship with her dad. Even in cases where a child does not acknowledge the need for this relationship, internally that relationship is still desired. It may often be the case in blended families that a biological father still has contact with his children and maintains an ongoing relationship. The objective of a stepdad is not to take the place of a biological father. Instead, it is to augment the child's life with a good role model on how to have successful relationships and to build a relationship based on trust, love, and understanding.

THE BIOLOGICAL FATHER MAY HAVE DROPPED OUT
OF THE CHILD'S LIFE

It is also not unusual for the biological father to have, more or less, dropped completely out of a child's life by the time the mother remarries. Research shows that the majority of fathers, once divorced, all but cease visitation with their biological children within two years after the divorce is final. It is also not unusual that once the mother of the children remarries, the biological father decides to reunite with his children. Whether you are the biological father or the stepfather, this period is an excellent opportunity for a man to practice all of the skills that we have discussed so far.

It is important for the new stepdad not to forget that, in most cases, stepchildren also have biological fathers (whether that father has a relationship with the child or not). The bad news for the biological father is that if the children do not reside with him, he may lose a great deal of influence with his kids. And by the same token, a stepfather can become a good stepdad and the influence that he develops with his new spouse and stepchildren can be just as influential as if he were the biological dad.

This does not mean the children have to make a choice between one or the other father. It does mean that if both dads wish to be relevant in the child's life, there should, at least on some level, be agreement as to the best way to rear the children and then, of course, act that way. It would be a mistake for two fathers to try to influence the same child by utilizing differing parenting methods. As you read earlier, the same holds true for a dad and mom who are married and in a committed relationship. Utilizing differing parenting skills, philosophies, and means of discipline to raise the kids just will not work. As a stepdad, it *may* mean that *you* have to be more reasonable, understanding, calm, and consistent than the biological non-custodial father.

Biological fathers have a really difficult time (which translates into "get really upset") taking advice from their ex-wife's new husband. Remember that people get divorced for a reason; if the ex-husband is the reason for the divorce, you may need to become a specialist on dealing with difficult people. On the other hand, if the ex-husband is *not* reason for the divorce, that could very likely mean that *you* married the reason for the divorce and, once again, you may need to become a specialist on dealing with difficult people. Regardless, as the stepdad, you will need to understand and be able to apply the principles in this book very quickly to your new bride and her children, as well as your own children.

NEW STEPFATHERS WITHOUT CHILDREN OF THEIR OWN

A new stepfather who does not have any children of his own brings a whole new set of issues and concerns to the table. It would be best not to try to parent someone else's children until you figure a few things out. This could take a whole different book, but start with the principles contained herein and remember to apply them to your new bride. Practice these principles with her, *listen* to *her* feedback, and *then* apply the principles to the children. Until you have actually had a successful relationship with a child, try not to consider yourself a dad and try not to expect to be treated like one. Being a dad is a lot of work, well worth the effort, but work just the same.

Just because a guy marries a kid's mom does not make that individual a specialist on child rearing. Neither does the fact that a guy was once a kid himself make him qualified to be a dad. Take it slow, and be patient, consistent, and calm – always calm. This would also be one of those times where one should walk lightly with the biological father if the biological father maintains a relationship with his children. They are his kids and he probably knows them better than you do. You might be able to learn something from him.

KIDS ARE EMOTIONALLY CONNECTED TO THEIR PARENTS

When considering the non-custodial parent, you must never forget that a child is emotionally connected to her parents, whether the parent resides with the child or not. It is not unusual for a child to disregard or even forget about the problems that existed between her and her father, or her mother and father, and remember only the good attributes of the father. It is also not unusual for children – especially teenagers – to defend the non-custodial parent with a great deal of gusto, even if their

212

relationship had been poor or contentious. The child would interpret any derogatory comments made about the biological father as a derogatory comment made about her. This is one reason a child may very well defend her biological father, even if it makes no sense to do so. If there is one cardinal rule about blended families – and this is a good rule of thumb regardless – it is to NEVER SAY ANYTHING NEGATIVE ABOUT A CHILD'S PARENT(S). This includes your new bride, the child's mother.

"YOU ARE NOT MY DAD!"

During a relationship with stepchildren, a significantly high percentage of stepdads at some point have heard the phrase, "You're not my dad!" In most cases, this is merely another way of saying, "I don't like the power you have over me." Rather than being offended by the truth (because you are not her dad, but a stepdad, even though you may be the only father she has even known), one should realize that this relationship is in need of some additional blending or repair. This might be an opportunity to calmly remind the child, "Even though I am not your biological father, I love you as if you were my own child," and then proceed from there. Keep in mind that regardless of the pedigree of the child, if the home you are living in is yours and your wife's, the people who co-reside within that house are under certain obligations to abide by the rules of the house. This is true regardless of the child's age.

IF ALL GOES WELL

If all goes well, it takes about two years for the relationship between a new stepfather and his new stepchildren to become well established. What I mean by this is that the child cherishes the relationship she has obtained with her new stepfather, and that will be the basis of the relationship. If the new stepfather tries to step into the role of biological dad in the beginning of the relationship, the children will often be resistant. This is more likely when the children are in their teenage years, becoming more challenging at the age of fourteen and up. Generally, the younger the children are at the time the family is blended, the more accepting and cooperative they are. On the other hand, younger children have a more difficult time with change, inconsistencies, and chaos.

Additionally, when the children are younger, boys generally have a more difficult time with the transition than do girls – with this trend reversing in the later teen years. It would be a good idea to sit down with one's prospective spouse well before planning a life together, to ensure that the emotional and psychological well-being of the children has been thoroughly discussed.

WHAT'S IN IT FOR THE KIDS?

It would be a mistake to believe that children are as happy about getting a new stepfather as you are about getting a new wife. (My assumption is that you are happy about getting a new wife!) All too often in a blended family, the new wife has custody of her children, and the new stepfather has visitation rights to his own children, who are probably living with their mother. In this scenario, the stepfather is a new authority figure in the home with his new wife and her children.

Even in the case of children who desperately want a dad in their life, they may still resist having a new stepfather living in the same home, telling them what to do, and showing public affection toward their mother. It is very easy to be so happy with your new spouse that both of you lose sight of an important fact – that the children may not see much benefit to them in this new way of life.

It is important that the children experience a similar level of joy that the parents are experiencing being newly married. It can be very frustrating for children to see their mother (or father) in a happy new relationship while they feel left out. Remember that they have gone through the separation and divorce, and all the sadness and chaos that can bring. The children need to feel as if they too have something to gain in this new marriage. They need to be happy in this new blended family, even if the only change is the addition of a stepfather. Any change to the family dynamic can have significant impact on the family as a whole.

CHILDREN'S CONCERNS ARE RARELY CONSIDERED

The children of a blended family are often not considered when the new parents decide to marry. In fact, it is almost universal that the children's wishes, concerns, fears, and needs are *not* considered and *rarely discussed* with the children.

In addition, there needs to be something in this new relationship for the children beyond the philosophical position that they are getting a "new" or "better" father. The children, in all likelihood, still love their biological father very much, regardless of the actual relationship they had with him when their parents were married. The children may be very resistant to the idea of a new father figure in their life.

For example, when Carla and I first got married, I was aware that the children were nowhere near as happy about the marriage as my new wife and I were. Carla's daughter Nicole was nearly eighteen-years-old, and she had difficulty with the idea of a new stepfather. There had been problems between her and her previous stepfather, and Nicole admitted to her mother that she had difficulty allowing herself to get emotionally close to me. Carla's son Sammy was about to turn eleven, and I knew that if our relationship were not something that he cherished, my influence on him would be based on fear and punishment. These are two things that no relationship should ever be based upon.

I was aware that it would take time for the relationship between the children and me to develop. My new stepdaughter, although having a problem allowing herself to get emotionally close to me, was always well behaved and polite. Allowing Nicole to voice her concerns and giving time for our relationship to develop made a world of difference to her. However, Sammy's behavior was such that I had difficulty initiating a father-son relationship. He had behaviors that were contrary to how I felt a young man should behave. I was also aware that the responsibility to develop the relationship between Sammy and myself was *entirely* mine.

This was certainly not the case with the eighteen-year-old daughter Nicole. Note that the older a child is, the more responsibility she has in developing a relationship with a stepdad, and the larger her role in whether or not the relationship is successful. But until about sixteen years old, the responsibility of initiating, developing, and maintaining a relationship between a stepfather and his stepchild is largely the stepfather's.

There are cases within intact families where the biological father has not previously had a good relationship with his children. It would also be his responsibility to initiate and foster the relationship with his own children. When children become adults, they can do things to improve the relationship with Dad. However, it is very difficult, if not impossible, for most children to be responsible for the relationship they have with their father. Later, as the children grow older, move out of the family home, and start a family of their own, they now have more influence over the relationship they have with either parent.

In our case, Sammy did not see any benefit for him whatsoever with his mother re-marrying. She had been single for eight years with Sammy being the center of attention for his mother and his older sister. Sammy was able to manipulate and control both his mother and sister with great ease. Neither of them expected Sammy to do anything for himself. To a man such as myself, who has a great deal of respect for women, I found his behavior to be completely unacceptable.

It would then be easy to see the conflict I had within *myself*. I too was previously married, and I have six boys of my own (all of whom were either away at college or graduated college and living independently, at that time). All of them have great respect for their mother and for women in general. As they were growing up, my six sons were brought up with the understanding that they do as their mother says. I knew when Carla and I decided to marry that the relationship with Sammy was going to take a lot of effort on *my* part.

AMUSEMENT PARK DAD OR HARD ASS

I did not want to start off the relationship with Sammy with me being a amusement park type of stepdad who just has fun with the child without acting like a father. I also knew it would damage our relationship if I came down on Sammy with harsh discipline and trying to change his behaviors too quickly. This would have had a counter-productive effect on his behavior and on our relationship. Additionally, if I came down hard on Sammy, his mother would probably rush to his defense, and that would have caused friction between my wife and me. So I decided that I would have to integrate *myself* into *Sammy's* life.

Sammy had always enjoyed a pretty good relationship with his mother. He would talk to her from the time he got in the car after school till the time she put him to bed at night. He would talk about the most ridiculous things one could possibly imagine. However, when I was with them, he said virtually nothing. I knew that if I could not get him to talk to me, my influence over him would be minimal.

When I was present, Sammy was a perfect angel. Yet I was not so naïve to believe that my sudden presence in the home was enough to make Sammy behave well when he was not at home or if I was not with him.

As you have read, a child's behavior can be significantly influenced when a dad is not around by the value the child places on the relationship he has with his father. If that relationship is something the child cherishes, the child will do the best he can to make Dad proud of him. I had not yet reached that status with Sammy.

Now, if we analyze the family dynamic, it is easy to see that the mere addition of another person actually changes everything. I had to devise a way to initiate a relationship with Sammy that he could become vested in, and such that *he* was willing to participate. I started off by going to *his* baseball games and taking an interest in *his* studies, mostly helping him with *his* homework – although schoolwork should never be the center of any relationship with a child. Nonetheless, children often gain a great deal of self-esteem by doing well in school. Additionally, it gave Sammy a chance to show me what he was doing and what he knew about the subjects he was studying.

At ages seven to twelve years old, it is very common for a child to believe that he is "the best" at everything he does. This is perfectly normal, and if the child did not believe that he were the "best at everything," there's a good possibility that he would not try anything new. Nor would he continue with something that he is not really good at doing.

217

This reminds me of the time one of my boys got his first Nintendo system. It was when Nintendo first came out, and my son was about eight years old. He had never played the game before in his life. He was playing *Mario Brothers,* and as he sat in the living room playing the game, he looked back at me as I watched him play. He said, "Did you know I was this good at this?"

Children in pre-adolescence (ages seven to twelve) also have a very difficult time understanding how other people feel and the effect that they have on the feelings of others, as well as on other people's behaviors. Sammy felt that everything he did was brilliant and/or funny, and it was certainly not my place or intention to tell him otherwise. It is a good thing for a child his age to have inflated estimations of his ability and of himself.

Going to my new son's baseball games was easy; I like baseball games. I like being with Sammy's mother and sister, and we all had a good time. But going to a baseball game in and of itself does not *make* a relationship. My wife and I knew when we got married that in order for the relationship between Sammy and me to develop, he and I would need to spend time together. This meant that if he were in his room watching TV or playing video games, he would not be with me working on our relationship. We disconnected the TV and Internet connection in his room.

What I found to be effective in getting Sammy to talk to me was that we would watch TV together, very often a show that *he* preferred. During the commercials, I would mute the sound and ask him what *he* thought about the show or what *he* thought was going to happen next. He would come out with some far fetched and unusual scenarios. However, I needed to remember that what makes sense to an eleven-year-old will probably not make much sense to a forty-seven-year-old, and it was my job to merely listen and encourage him to talk.

Meanwhile, there were certain programs that we did not allow to be watched in our home. This would include programming like MTV, and I would never encourage or endorse any of the "reality"-based programs that have become so popular, like *Real Housewives* or some of the other nonsensical trash that is currently being aired on television. Keep in

218

mind that children *learn* behaviors, and they have a difficult time distinguishing inappropriate behavior if it is being modeled to them. Television is a very powerful model of behavior.

One of the programs we would watch was the series *Lost* when it first came out. The initial season was quite interesting, and it kept you wondering what was going to happen next. Sammy had multiple theories on what was taking place on that island, and often his theories turned out to be much more plausible than the actual plot of the series. Additionally, by watching a program like *Lost*, he was able to see its inconsistencies. That way, he managed to recognize that the basics of the program were not real. Like, where are all these people getting food from? He was also able to discuss the illogical behaviors of the people on the show, which started some good discussions about how people should act in general. I tried not to apply Sammy's comments to himself, or his own behaviors, but allowed Sammy to come to these conclusions for himself.

I was also to learn that Sammy enjoyed playing chess. He had been playing chess with his uncle, whose house he would go to after school waiting for his mother to pick him up. So Sammy and I started to play one or two games of chess a day, after his homework was done. He turned out to be a pretty good chess player, but again children this age think they are the best at everything they do. So when I offered to spot him my queen (in other words, I would play him without my queen), Sammy said that he could beat me even with my queen in play. I suggested, "Well, let's play without my queen for now and then see how it goes."

Now I take no enjoyment in beating an eleven-year-old at anything, which is why I spotted him my queen. On the other hand, even though I still took it easy on him, I would not merely allow him to win. Not at chess. Chess is a game that takes skill, it takes planning, and it takes strategies that need to be learned. He would not learn these attributes if I allowed him to win without earning it.

As I said, Sammy turned out to be a pretty good chess player, and these games really improved our relationship as well as his chess skills (planning and strategies). It was during these games that our relationship took a turn. Up until this point, Sammy really did not trust me, and I

219

imagined that he had no reason to do so. I was aware that trust takes time to *earn,* even for Dad. When I would tell him something, Sammy would listen to me, but he trusted his own feelings and his own intellect more than he trusted mine. In fact, he trusted his own instincts beyond what *anyone* else told him, and therefore it would be a mistake for me to take his lack of trust in me personally.

As I played chess with Sammy, I would advise him, "If you make that move, you will lose your (whatever the piece might be) in the next three moves." Sammy would generally make the move regardless, ultimately losing the piece I had forewarned him about. This went on for weeks. It would have been very easy for me to give him more information as to what piece he would lose, how he was going to lose it, or what he could do about it. However, my intentions were to try to get him to trust me to the point that he would ask. And the day came when he asked, "How?"

That one word, that one question, of asking, "How?" started to change our relationship. He started to see that what I said had validity, it had credibility, and that I was willing to, and wanted to, help him to succeed. It also showed him that I cared more about him than I did about winning a game. It was not long before Sammy was able to beat me at chess. This was done because, as we played, I taught him how to beat me, how to be a better player. He began to trust me with regard to chess, and if we recall that children generalize behaviors, he began to trust me in other areas of his life as well.

DADS AND STEPDADS HAVE INFLUENCE
IN SOCIAL SITUATIONS

One of the first areas beyond chess where Sammy was able to exhibit trust in me and my advice/opinions was in social situations. It may seem unusual that dads have significant influence in teaching children to be more social, but it is true. Sammy had some fairly significant social problems. One of the reasons was that Sammy was under the mistaken impression that he was funny. Now, what might seem funny to a bunch of fourth graders was not necessarily funny to older children and adults.

One of the easiest things to teach Sammy was that he had to remember who his audience was and where he happened to be while he was being funny. Being a clown in class is not acceptable, though similar behavior may be completely acceptable on the playground. I knew that it would damage our relationship and our communication if, when he told me a joke, or acted like a goofball, I acted derogatory or condemning toward him. I would generally let him know that what he said would be funny to his friends, or say something like "I bet your friends liked that."

As our relationship grew, he and I both appreciated the relationship more and more, and Sammy's behavior in all areas improved, including at school. This evolved to the point where we *enjoyed* spending time together. For example, there were times when my wife went away for the weekend with a group of her friends, and she would ask Sammy if he wanted to spend the weekend with his cousins. Sammy would generally answer, "No, I think I'll just stay at home with Dad."

That does not mean that there were no problems. There are always problems when raising children, but the relationship was coming along nicely. This type of relationship building is something that needs to be done with all of our children, whether we are the biological father or the stepfather.

My stepdaughter Nicole and I developed a very good relationship with little effort on my part. She turned eighteen shortly after Carla and I were married. Because of Nicole's age, I just acted like a dad ordinarily would with an eighteen-year-old daughter, and she flourished with that. At this point, both of my stepchildren (and I do not refer to them as "stepchildren" but my own children; nor do they refer to me as their "stepdad" but Dad) are grown and on their own, and both are doing wonderfully. I could not be more proud of them if they were my biological children. Stepfathers have as much or nearly as much influence as a biological father – if he chooses to exercise it.

ALWAYS DO WHAT IS BEST FOR THE CHILDREN

It is important when working on improving the relationships with our children – whether they are our biological children or our stepkids – that we do what is best for the children. When raising a child, there is a window of opportunity that, should it close, is lost. Dads need to be Dad when a child is doing well, having troubles, is not pleasant to be around, or does everything in her power to make life miserable for everyone around. Children will test our resolve, our patience, and our love for them. One day they will leave the house to live on their own; a dad's job is to see that they are prepared.

WHAT'S NEXT?

In the next chapter, I will be discussing areas of being a dad that can be difficult. Every child needs to learn what to do to be successful. Much of the teaching is done by modeling the desired behavior, but other behaviors need to be taught directly, like tying shoes. Major topics that will be covered are discipline and punishments and how to understand the difference between them and when to use them.

KEY CHAPTER POINTS

1. One of the most difficult achievements a man can accomplish is to successfully blend two families.
2. A child always wants to have a good relationship with her dad.
3. Even when the biological father does not reside with the child, he still may retain a great deal of influence over the child depending upon the relationship between the child and father and the new family dynamic.
4. Children should not have to make a choice between their biological father and their stepfather. There really is room for both to have a role in the children's lives.
5. It would be a mistake for two fathers to try to influence the same child by utilizing differing parenting strategies.
6. Being a stepfather may mean that you have to be more reasonable, more understanding, calmer, and more consistent than the biological non-custodial father.
7. Just because a man marries a child's mom does not make him a specialist on child-rearing.
8. When considering the non-custodial parent, it is best to remember that the child is emotionally connected to both parents, whether a parent resides with the child or not.
9. It is not unusual for children – especially teenagers – to defend the non-custodial parent with a great deal of gusto, even if their relationship had been poor or contentious. Don't let this take you by surprise.
10. A child might interpret *any* derogatory remark made about her parent as a derogatory comment made about the child.
11. Never, ever, say anything derogatory about a child's parents. If you want to marry a woman with children, you must accept this as part of the deal.

12. In blending families, it takes about two years for the new relationships between the stepfather and his stepchildren to become established.
13. It would be a good idea to sit down with one's prospective spouse well before planning a life together to ensure that the emotional and psychological well-being of the children has been thoroughly discussed.
14. It is important in a blended family that the children experience the same level of joy that the parents experience being newly married.
15. The children in a newly blended family need to feel as if they too have something to gain in this new marriage. It is often assumed that because the mother and new stepfather are happy, the children should be happy as well.
16. The addition of any person to the family dynamic can have a significant effect on all members of the family.

15

Interventions, Discipline & Punishment

This chapter was placed toward the back of the book for a reason. My hope is that once the earlier chapters are read, a dad will have a better idea of why his kids behave as they do and being using his influence to initiate appropriate behaviors and effect change to negative behavior. Still, there will be times, even when a dad does everything he is supposed to do, that a child misbehaves. Chapter 15 is designed to help a dad know the difference between interventions, discipline, and punishments and understand what might be appropriate and useful. Always remember that everything a father does for and to his children is to help them, even when that is very difficult to keep in mind.

The way I describe *intervention* may be new to you. In my approach to parenting, an intervention is any interaction used to help a child and may include discipline and punishments. The majority of interventions are to teach or help a child. An example of a simple intervention is helping a child put on his clothes. A more complex intervention would be helping a child with an interpersonal problem with a friend. Understand that there are times when a child has greater needs than a parent might be prepared for, and that is when a professional intervention is call for – such as from a physician, mental health specialist, or educational consultant. The next chapter, Chapter 16, will address profession interventions in more detail.

This chapter is intended to help Dad understand some of the standard and appropriate interventions, disciplines, and punishments that can help the child develop in a healthy way. At the same time, these steps can help maintain, and even improve, the relationship Dad has with his children.

DISCIPLINE – AN ACT OF CORRECTING

It is imperative to know that the term *discipline* for our purposes means "to correct," and not "to punish." There are times when a child may need to be punished, and it should only be after sufficient and effective discipline has been employed. For example, in the story from Chapter 11 about one of my boys sanding the wrong car, punishment would have been completely inappropriate. It would also have been damaging to the child and the relationship between him and his dad (me). My four-year-old son did not know that he was doing anything wrong. Therefore, redirecting him to sand the proper car, and increasing my supervision over him, was the appropriate intervention. It was an intervention because instruction was given and an increase in supervision was employed.

The younger the child, the less he understands. Dad must lead by example and remember what a child is capable of. It is imperative to ensure that the child, regardless of the age, understands what is being conveyed when Dad punishes him. A non-verbal child (one who does not understand words) will not respond to any punishment in a positive way in that he does not understand what is going on. Most often, he does not understand what he did wrong or what is expected of him. Yelling at or spanking a young child will in all probability have long-term detrimental effects on him.

Talking to a young child is invaluable. It teaches a child the things that he needs to know. Young children (*one to three years old*) understand words that are spoken by others before they learn how to use them. Regardless of whether a child can cognitively understand what is being said, children need to be spoken to in a calm, confirming, validating way. For a non-verbal child, the tone of voice the father uses is often more telling and convincing than what is being said.

If a child is not informed of what is expected of him, or if the behavior has not been modeled to him, he will not know what is expected. A young child who is overly punished will learn to be hopeless (hopelessness is a key component of depression), doubt his own abilities, and may in all likelihood develop delinquency problems or depression. Children of all ages need to have a feeling (but not necessarily a conscious awareness) that they have some degree of influence over their environment. This environment includes the home, parents, and any other occupants. This influence might be something as simple as causing dad to smile when he calls the child's name, or picks him up when he falls down and talks to him in a calm, reassuring tone.

The older a child becomes, the more aware he is of his environment and what influence he possesses. Many children can anticipate the effect their behavior might have on their father and either confide in him or keep things from him.

Young children do not understand punishments like timeouts. A stern "no" is much more effective when a child is doing something that he knows he should not be doing. A stern "no" is enough to let a child up to two or three years old understand that a behavior is unacceptable. Talking to a young child in a calm, consistent, and loving way is a very effective way to extinguish a behavior that the parent does not want. On the other hand, it would be best to supervise young children so that they do not get into things that they should not.

A key way to help a child understand what is acceptable and what is not is through *consistency*. I have discussed consistency throughout this book, and I am hoping that the reader will understand that in child rearing there is little that is more influential – *good or bad* – than consistency. Allowing a child to engage in a behavior that is improper for any length of time is reinforcing that behavior. The longer a behavior is reinforced, the longer and more difficult it will be for the child, as well as the parent, to extinguish that behavior.

As a child grows older, he will eventually (usually by five years) understand the link between the cause-and-effect of an unacceptable behavior and a punishment. At that point, *timeouts* can be effective. A timeout is a short period of time when the child is separated from the activities of the home and from those he loves. This might be sitting in the corner, which would be a more serious timeout than going to one's room or sitting on one's bed. A timeout, as with any punishment, should be because of a serious infraction and it should not be used very often. A child being punished often is an indication that Dad needs to improve his supervision of the child, and that improved supervision will help the child to make better decisions.

Sometimes a child learns he can do as he pleases because Dad is not watching. In all likelihood, he will grow to exhibit the same undesired behaviors as he gets older. Dad needs to be an active participant throughout his child's life, and he helps his child learn what is appropriate or not appropriate from an early age. In this way, the child will learn that compliance is a way to be accepted by his dad and delinquent behaviors will be decreased.

Again, it is important to understand that if a child is constantly in need of punishment, there is a parenting issue that needs to be addressed. Children who are modeled appropriate behaviors, taught appropriate behaviors, and supervised properly are seldom in need of being punished. When a child needs to be punished, it is generally because of a parenting problem. A child should not be held responsible for the shortcomings of his dad.

This is also very age-dependent, with younger children needing more supervision and instruction than older children. The modeling, instruction, and supervision are essential at an early age. Youngsters learn to be responsible, and then there is an increase in autonomy as they grow older. When punishment is used, the age of the child should also be considered before a punishment is rendered, and the punishment should be appropriate for the child's age. Punishments should also be brief and to the point.

The length or intensity of any punishment is extremely important. Punishment needs to be effective, but not so punitive that it demoralizes the child. For example, a five-year-old can handle a five-minute timeout. A six-year-old could handle a six-minute time out. However, it is always best to do what Dad can do to supervise young children and assist them in making good decisions so that punishment is not necessary.

As the child grows older, the behaviors may become more drastic in terms of non-compliance. This is when having the parenting skills to effectively deal with non-compliance becomes essential. Each child is different, and a very important thing to remember is if a punishment is not working with that child, stop using it. *More of the same* is often not effective, and it only demoralizes the child, instills hopelessness, and damages the relationship between the child and Dad. This is a time for a father to utilize all of his parenting skills, and that gives him the opportunity to be a Dad. Remember, kids do the best that they can, and no child likes to be the focus of punishment.

There are very few children who, from well-thought-out plans of their own, exhibit patterns of misbehaving, do not follow rules, and are disruptive. Misbehaving is generally a result of learned behaviors, lack of self-control, and issues with immediate gratification. Meanwhile, there are children who are generally taught from an early age to delay gratification for non-essential wants, like a new toy or waiting to have dessert until after dinner. These children are much better behaved, patient, and compliant to rules without having to be constantly punished. If discipline (i.e., being corrected) is consistent, age-appropriate, and compassionate, the child grows up being much more compliant, with rules, not only at home, but at school and within the community as well.

Let's say Dad finds himself in a situation where the child is getting older (this could be as early as four-years-old, or teenage years) and showing signs of defiance and a general disregard for rules. In this situation, more of the same types of punishment will only make matters worse. Additionally, a dad has to live with himself and be at peace in his own mind about his actions toward his child being appropriate – in terms of what is *best for the child*. If we allow our child's defiance to become a personal issue affecting our own self-esteem, then we have already lost.

On a related note, dad should not allow his behavior toward his children to be personal or feel that he always has to be right or always needs to win. As children grow older, the seemingly blind obedience that a child had when he was eight years old gives way to a person who can make decisions for himself. Now it seems that a reasonable explanation is needed with direction for behavior. This is not to say that a child should not do as he is told merely because he is told to do so. On the other hand, what dad wants his child to grow up to be a robot? What Dad does not want his child to be able to think for himself and be able to see when something is wrong? We want our children to have the assertiveness to stand up for themselves and, possibly, even someone else.

If more defiance and disregard for rules appear, this is a time when having reasonable explanations for expectations and behaviors becomes very important. However, if a six-year-old wants to do something and he is told "no," he might not be able to understand the reasons why, and it may *not* be absolutely necessary to explain the reasons why. This would be the case when a child is too young to reason for himself. On the other hand, a fifteen-year-old deserves a well-thought-out explanation.

This is also a time when the philosophies that Dad and his wife have thought out and modeled to their children become very important. For example, your fifteen-year-old daughter does not want to go to church. The philosophy has always been that "this family goes to church," and also a point along the lines of "because that is what we do." This may be a cause for an argument from an adolescent, but it is hard to argue with the philosophy that, as a family, we go to church.

What if philosophies and expectations of behaviors have not been established at this point? Then now would be a good time to sit down with your wife and write some down. They will evolve over time but now would be a good time to start. It is also important to realize that the argument that "this is what we do" does not work if Dad does not do it himself. For example, in a home where using foul language is not permitted, it would be difficult for a child to adhere to that rule when Dad does not adhere to it. Further more, the excuses that "I'm older" and "I'm your father" do not work that well, and they are hypocritical. Model the desired behavior as children and adolescents can see through hypocrisy a mile away.

It may appear that, from time to time, the child wins, and it might even seem that the child got away with something. This might be a good time to rethink the way we are looking at things. Realize that flexibility, along with appropriateness, makes a significant difference in future behaviors for children. It is hard to disobey someone you respect, love, and enjoy being with. Dad wins when, after all of the arguments are over and all the battles are finished, his child leaves the nest and goes out into the world prepared and able.

PUNISHMENT SHOULD HAVE SOME CONNECTION
TO THE BEHAVIOR

This next section is an area that is extremely important. A child needs to be able to realize that there is some correlation between the inappropriate behavior and the punishment for the behavior. For example, an eight-year-old was riding his bicycle without a helmet. The first time, his parents merely told him to put on a helmet (an intervention), and they asked the child if there was a reason he was not wearing the helmet (notice the parents did not use the word "why"). In such a situation, there may very well be a reason that the child is not wearing his helmet, such as the helmet is the wrong size or it hurts to wear the helmet. If this is the case, the problem should be rectified. The child should also be reminded that he is never to ride his bicycle without a helmet (discipline). Remember, if a child is *allowed* to ride his bike without a helmet today, to the child, it is acceptable to ride his bike again tomorrow without his helmet.

The child rode his bike without a helmet again. This time, he was warned that if it happened again, there would be a consequence (more discipline). Up until this point, the situation was handled properly. However, the boy rode his bike a third time without a helmet, and then the parents sent him to his room for a twenty-four-hour timeout (punishment). He was only allowed out of his room to go to the bathroom and to eat. *Ouch!*

There was absolutely no correlation between being exiled to his room for any length of time – much less twenty-four hours – and riding a bicycle without a helmet. Most of those reading this book have probably already figured out the appropriate punishment in this example. It should be for the child to lose the privilege of riding his bicycle for a period of time. The first punishment – not necessarily the first occurrence – might be for one day. The next time, it might be two days and so forth. If the problem continued, then the child might need to lose the privilege for quite some time. The rationale for being severe in this case is that it is a safety issue to ride a bicycle without a helmet. In this case, the child did indeed crash his bike, and he needed to go to the hospital for twelve stitches to his forehead as he was not wearing a helmet..

The moral to this story? Reinforced behaviors are more likely to be repeated, and punishments that are not correlated to the behavior have little effect on changing the behavior.

PROBLEMS AT SCHOOL

This is an area where Dad needs to remain calm, and it often requires some creative thinking. As you learned earlier, kids who misbehave at school generally misbehave at home as well. When the home is inconsistent, and unacceptable or inappropriate behaviors are randomly disciplined, a child will often be a behavioral problem at school. Dad may have gotten into the habit of telling his child numerous times to do something or stop doing something before the child complies. However, a schoolteacher expects a child to do as he is told *every time* he is told and *when* he is told. Can you imagine a classroom of thirty eight-year-olds who all have to be told two or three times to do something?

Regardless, it is difficult to punish a child at home for something that he did or did not do at school. Depending on the age of the child, he may not be able to form a correlation between his behavior at school and the punishment at home. The best way to ensure that a child is well behaved at school is to be active in your child's behavior at home. Ensure that when the child is told to do something or not to do something, he complies. Anything that is important enough to have a child do, or not do, is important enough to ensure the child complied.

It might be best to work with the school and the child's teacher to collaboratively devise expectations, rewards, and punishment for the child. Then again, some kids have to have the two environments completely segregated, in that the child cannot correlate the two. For example, I was asked to assess an eight-year-old boy who had just had a

232

temper tantrum in his classroom. He had been grounded for three days at home for misbehaving at school, and if he did not get into trouble this day, the boy would be able to play video games with his older sister when he got home. He had promised his sister that he would play with her today. As the day progressed, the stress of not misbehaving became too much for him, and he became agitated and disrupted the class. The teacher, who knew nothing about his promise to his sister or of the child being grounded at home, told the boy that she was going to call the child's mother. He freaked out and tore the classroom apart. As a result, the police were called.

It was subsequent to this that I was called in to assess the child. The child's father arrived before me, and the boy was perfectly calm with his father sitting next to him along with the school principal and the child's teacher. When the child explained why he had gotten so upset, it made a lot of sense. The parents seemed to be doing the best they could with a very difficult child (the boy had already been diagnosed with Bipolar Disorder). The father stated that the child was "fairly well behaved at home" but that he was grounded for his behavior at school. Together, the team came to the realization that the longer the child was in class, the more agitated he became – making it almost certain that he would not get through the day without some type of problem.

This child had behaved for two complete days, which was very hard for him, and he became more stressed because he promised his sister that he would play video games with her. Together, Dad and I devised a plan to help improve the child's behavior at home and at school. We decided that his video game time – one hour a day, or two with another player – would be delayed up to three hours if he misbehaved. If the behavior warranted it, he would lose his video game privilege for that day. He would start over again the next day without any punishment being carried over from the previous day. The reason for this was that this child could not correlate the punishment with the behavior. They were in two different environments, and the punishment was delayed from the behavior. Therefore it made matters worse.

Because the team noticed that the boy had more problems later in the day, the teacher and principal suggested that he be put on an abbreviated school-day. He would come to school at the normal time but then go home at lunchtime rather than complete the rest of the school-day. This worked out well in that the child's mother was home during the day. His time at school was then slowly increased as the year progressed, and his behavior control improved.

Up to this point, the child had misbehaved virtually every day, and he had temper tantrums in the classroom at least once a week. After this assessment and collaborative effort with the school and the parents – all of whom had good follow-through with the child – the boy did not have a temper tantrum for the next three months, which is when I stopped following the case. I do not know what happened after that, but it was clear that our behavioral remedy was the proper approach for this particular child. It is also important to understand that this was a team approach with the school principal, the boy's teacher, the father, and myself. It seems that no one person, or one environment, would have been successful in remedying this problem and being of help to the boy.

As children grow older, the length of punishment can increase. However, I find it counter-productive to ground a child for more than three days at a time, with younger children only being grounded for a couple of hours or one day. Even then, there should be some way for the child to become ungrounded. Sometimes as a child becomes a teenager, the child may be grounded for three days and have to perform some task, before he is ungrounded. If he does not perform the task, then he remains grounded until the task is completed. This too can be counter-productive if the child refuses to do the task. In such a case, I would do the task with him. This usually works for a child who is being defiant. I know it seems that in this case the child is running the show, but it only *seems* that way. Dad has just got the child to do what he was supposed to do, but with help. Often, pulling weeds or raking leaves is much more enjoyable for the child when Dad is working with him. Plus, this shows that the child would like to spend more time with Dad, and that is a good thing.

There are times when a child merely refuses to do anything. That is a time when Dad has to stop and think what is best for the child and the rest of the family. Allowing a teenage child to make poor decisions has natural consequences. For instance, if a child who is on the football team in school refuses to do his homework or study for class, his grades will drop. He may very likely be removed from the football team as well. That was his choice, and he can blame no one but himself.

For children of any age, it is best not to have a one-size-fits-all type of punishment. I prefer having punishment on three levels. *Level One* is for something that is not very serious but warrants a punishment. In this case, we would limit our child from going to friends' houses (although friends could still come to our house), reduce media access, and limit his television viewing to only educational channels.

Level Two would include Level One restrictions as well as losing all video game and computer usage for three days. Regardless, we did not allow unlimited use of video games and no Internet without supervision under most normal circumstances. In both of these areas, the child might be allowed to reduce the restrictions by doing additional work around the house.

Level Three is for more serious issues, and the child would have no media at all, except for the five educational channels on television, no friends over to the house, and have to complete some work around the house or elsewhere. Children need to have something to keep them busy, and television is one way of doing that. The educational channels help the child learn. The only problem is that the kids start to like the educational channels, and they watch them even when they are not grounded!

I know this does not sound like that harsh a punishment compared to what some kids experience. However, when you have a good relationship with your child, being grounded at all is painful for him, and our intentions were not to punish the child. Instead, our aim was to help him learn that there are consequences for one's actions. Punishment is meant to help the child. Punishment is not meant to make Dad feel like he won or that Dad got even with the child for messing up. When the child knows that his dad is upset with him because the child needed to be grounded, very often he feels very bad, and that is enough to bring about change in his behavior without strict, inappropriate, and ineffective punishments. It is all about the relationship Dad and his children enjoy that is important.

It is important that kids have things to do to keep them busy. When a child is grounded or his daily activities have been interrupted, something needs to fill that void. The old "read a book" usually is not realistic, unless the child is used to reading in the first place. If reading is used as a means of punishment, the child will, in all likelihood, correlate reading with punishment and not want to read at all. Therefore, it is best that the child who is grounded be given things he can do, preferably with his dad.

I DO NOT LIKE TO BE GROUNDED

As our kids were growing up, I did not like to ground them. The reason is that when a child is grounded, it seems that the entire house is grounded, and I do not like to be grounded. It is acceptable that, even during Level Three punishment, the grounded child be allowed to accompany the rest of the family on outings and such. The only other way to handle it would be to leave someone at home to babysit, and that would not be fair to that person. I would also not ostracize the grounded child from the rest of the family or what the family was doing, like watching TV; he could watch what we were watching.

Another thing that I refused to do was to follow my kids around. I know parents who follow their adolescent kids to see if they "violate" the rules or to ensure that the child is where he is supposed to be. I have counseled parents who were really upset because their daughter continued to disobey the rules. For example, the child was given permission to go to a specific friend's house and then the child went across the street to talk to another friend without prior consent. This is a power struggle, and there is no need to be that controlling over an adolescent child, especially in high school.

As I explained earlier in the book, I also do not expect more from my kids than I do from myself. For example, if I were grounded and my parents went out to dinner without me, I would probably not only watch television but watch whatever I wanted. I refuse to do crazy things like take the TV power cord or cable, or see if the TV is warm when I get back from dinner. To avoid all of this, my wife and I just tell the grounded child that while we are out for the evening he can watch whatever he wants on television. He is also told that when we get back home, he is grounded from watching TV again.

Note that a child does not have to be grounded or otherwise punished by the parents every time he disobeys. Earlier in this chapter, I mentioned natural consequences. Well, when a child gets in trouble outside the home, the natural consequences of his actions may very well be sufficient. Let's say that a child gets in trouble for talking in class, and he has to sit out recess when a child would normally play with the other kids. That punishment, which was done at school, is appropriate and no further punishment is needed at home. In this case, the punishment is correlated with the misbehavior, which was at school. Otherwise, the child will feel as if he is being punished twice for the same offense. Plus, he will, in all likelihood, avoid telling his parents anything about his school day, and the child may even avoid going home.

We want our kids to feel that they can talk to us without us overreacting. We do not need to punish a child for everything he does wherever he does it. In the above example, the school was much better equipped to correlate the punishment for the child with the environment than a parent could. Being punished at home does not correlate, in a child's mind, to talking too much in the classroom.

Some kids are more difficult than other kids. If a child continues to have problems, then different interventions need to be devised. Kids do the best they can. When they do something well, show them that you noticed it and that you appreciate it. As dads, we want to be able to acknowledge that our child did something right. This helps us to avoid power struggles when the child does do something wrong.

We do not want to start a power struggle in our home. If punishments were too punitive when a child was young, there could be some very serious consequences for the parents as the child becomes an adolescent. If you find yourself in that situation, this would be a good time to be patient and kind. Kids do not respond immediately to changes in parenting skills, so this is a time to be really patient with them.

TELEVISION, COMPUTERS & VIDEO GAMES

It is generally easier to control a behavior that has not been allowed to get out of control in the first place. As you read earlier in the book, children learn, not only by experiencing things for themselves, but also *vicariously*, that is, by watching and listening to others. Vicarious learning is very active while listening and viewing media, such as television (even the commercials), movies, Internet, and video games.

One of the great psychological researchers, Albert Bandura, stated, "It has been shown that both children and adults acquire attitudes, emotional responses, and new styles of conduct through filmed and televised modeling." Children learn a great many things from film and television. Too often, television and other forms of entertainment are used as babysitters. It is far too easy to just turn on the television or sit a child in front of a video game or computer than to interact with them.

Used in moderation, all of these items are acceptable. However, it is very important to monitor what a child is listening to and watching. An infant has no idea what is being televised; however, he is learning from every program. Additionally, when a child is asleep, they can still hear and may still be able to process that information. It is very important to protect children from adult-type programming. In media today, even advertisements can be very influential for developing children's minds. This would also include violence, real or implied.

For example, infants up to about twelve months cannot differentiate between media and reality. I was recently at an R-rated (for violence and gore) movie, and a couple in the row ahead of us had an infant with them who cried for most of the movie. Could you imagine what was going on in that child's mind, believing that everything she was seeing and hearing was real?

In addition, *computers* are wonderful ways of learning; however, they are also powerful ways of learning things that dads do not want their children to know just yet. Being traumatized is always just one click away on a computer that is connected to the Internet. I used to raise exotic birds such as cockatoos, macaws, toucans, etc. I was also interested in breeding monkeys. Shortly after the Internet was connected in my home, I did a search for monkey breeders. What a surprise that

238

was. Can you imagine the type of search results that came up? And, of course, I had to check out some of the sites. Would one expect a child not to be as inquisitive?

It is a good idea to keep a computer with Internet access in a public room or in a room that the kids are not supposed to be in without adult supervision. Many kids go through childhood and even through high school without unfettered access to the Internet, and they grow up to be perfectly normal. On the other hand, when children are given ample supervision and are brought up with respect and responsibility, Internet access may be a useful tool. However, I would still keep the computer in a common room.

Video games can be a source of great enjoyment as well as a source of great discomfort. Once a privilege is given to a child, it is difficult to take it away. Such is the case with video games, cell phones, and text messaging. Video games can cause severe problems within a home, and careful consideration should be made when purchasing a system as well as the individual games. There is absolutely nothing to be gained by giving a child violent games, or games that model maladaptive behaviors. If there are behaviors on the video games that Dad does not want his children to engage in, don't buy the video game.

In our house, the rule for video games was very simple; no one can die. This did not include *Mario Brothers* and *Donkey Kong* and games such as that. But there was no shooting of guns at humans or any animals. There are plenty of games that can be played where there is no or very little violence, like a football game. Video games and television programs where people beat each other up, like kickboxing or wrestling, were not allowed either in our home. I have personally listened to dozens of horror stories of adolescents who were admitted to the hospital for being a "danger to others" due to moves that were learned by watching wrestling and kickboxing and trying them out on their younger siblings.

If it is necessary that kids watch wrestling, make sure that Dad is watching it with them. Dad should explain what is going on and the inappropriateness of trying the moves on someone. Additionally, there is absolutely nothing good to be gained by allowing a child of any age to watch kickboxing or full contact fighting.

CELL PHONES

It seems that almost every child today has a cell phone. They can be a useful tool or a nightmare for Dad. Generally, like television, movies, and the Internet, cell phones, when used appropriately and for their intended purpose, can be very useful and help a family communicate with each other. However, giving a child a cell phone can be a huge mistake. When communication between Dad and a child is already strained or insufficient, a cell phone may make matters worse.

A cell phone can keep a child, as well as adults, from communicating with other face-to-face. Telephonic communication does not allow one the ability to read and interpret non-verbal communication, and they can limit communicative growth in children. Additionally, the cell phone can become a source of entertainment, immediate gratification, and a means for becoming over-stimulated. Young children have difficulty with impulse control already, and children need to learn to delay gratification. It is also very difficult for someone who is constantly stimulated to be in a state without stimulation.

It is often best that children be limited in their cell phone usage, and then to allow use only for specific reasons and with specific individuals. Too much of any activity is not good for a child. Once the child has been exposed to using media of this type, it is very difficult to take it away. It is best not to give children unfettered access to items, such as cell phones or the Internet, which would be considered for adult use to begin with. A cell phone may not be considered an adult tool to some, but it gives a child the sense that they are acting like adults. This *may* be good, but using a cell phone as a source of entertainment, and without supervision, may be a source of conflict in the near future.

Dad should model good cell-phone etiquette, and here is an important thing for a father to consider. When he is with his children, limit the time spent talking on a cell phone to anyone else, except the children's mother, and even then, only on topics that are okay for the children to overhear. It is the wrong move to be talking on a cell phone to someone else on the kids' time with Dad. This sends a sad message to the children that they are not important (it sends the same sad message to one's wife). Dad needs to be present when he is with his kids, and there are few instances when a phone call should interrupt that time together.

And what if a phone call needs to be made or the phone rings and needs to be answered? It is a good idea to ask the child, "Do you mind if I take this?" or "I'm sorry to interrupt our time but I must briefly take this." In this way, it shows the child that Dad is considerate of his child's feelings and respects his child's opinion and time. The phone is not more important than your time together. These same principles work well while associating with adults.

CONSTANT ENTERTAINMENT

We live in a world of being bombarded with constant entertainment. What happened to the days of taking a trip in the car and looking out the window? What happened to spending that time talking to one another or playing games with each other, like finding all the letters of the alphabet on the road signs and license plates? When children are constantly entertained, they may lose the ability to interact in live social environments. This may cause kids to become socially inept or awkward.

Some road trips seem to take forever, and young children may have a difficult time sitting still for long periods of time. This is something that should be considered before embarking on a trip of any length. Young children have a poor concept of time, and if a trip is going to take a very long time, then some sort of entertainment may be necessary. However, the older a child gets, the less entertainment is needed. A good rule of thumb is that no media is necessary if a trip in the car takes less than one hour. This would include DVDs, video games, cell phones, and even MP3 players. Listening to music is usually a good way to pass the time, but what if each family member in the car is listening to something different? If that is the case, the family is not being together in the present. Listening to a music system in the car is a good way for Dad to monitor what his kids are listening to and a good way to expose the kids to Dad's music and vice versa.

MUSIC

This chapter will end with a short note about music. It is very influential, so be careful what you allow your children to listen to regarding music. It is *so* influential that music is one of the key means of worshipping God. The lyrics of songs stay in our head, and they are played over and over again – even long after the music-playing device has been shut off.

Anyone who has ever been to Disneyland and gone on the ride It's a Small World understands how a tune can play over and over and remain in one's head. The more one tries to get the song out of one's consciousness, the more it sticks around. The most effective way to rid one's self of a tune is to replace it with a different song or a different train of thought.

When my wife Carla and I go to Disneyland, she loves to go on the It's a Small World ride. Immediately afterwards, I like to go on the Pirates of the Caribbean ride because I can tolerate the lyrics from "Yo ho, It's a pirate's life for me" much better than from the tune "It's a Small World (After All)."

Music can be used to motivate and inspire. It can also influence one's mood very quickly, especially if one is depressed or angry. Listening to depressing music when one is depressed can easily make the depression worse. Additionally, when one is angry, listening to angry music may make a person more easily agitated. Lyrics that are obscene or abusive have a tendency to make it easier to adopt those feelings, philosophies, and behaviors.

LOVE GENEROUSLY, PUNISH RELUCTANTLY

Nothing can ever take the place of a Dad who is in the present with his kids and takes a genuine interest in their lives. When Dad is actively involved with a child's life, that life gets easier as well as Dad's. The best way to solve a behavioral problem with a child is not to let it occur in the first place. Practice the strategies of this book, be patient and kind, be in the present, and love each other. When punishment needs to be handed out, do it sparingly and reluctantly. When a dad loves his children, he does not want to see them hurt, especially by Dad. Just be a dad by just loving each other.

WHAT'S NEXT?

In the next chapter, I will address some issues that affect families in a very serious way. I will discuss mental issues and mental disorders of childhood. We will also look at how to know when it's time to seek a professional intervention with a physician or a mental health professional.

KEY CHAPTER POINTS

1. An intervention is any interaction that is used to help a child.
2. The term "discipline" means to instruct or correct and not specifically to punish.
3. The younger a child is, the less he understands, and punishments may do more harm than good.
4. A non-verbal child will not respond to punishment in a positive way. He does not understand what is going on and most often does not understand what he did wrong or what is expected of him.
5. It is always best for Dad to do what he can to guide his children so that punishment will not be necessary.
6. Frequent punishment of a child is often an indication that Dad needs to improve his supervision of the child and that he should help this child make better decisions.
7. A key way to help a child understand what is acceptable and what is not is through *consistency*.
8. Punishments should be brief and to the point.
9. If a punishment is not working, stop using it. More of the same is often not effective, and it only demoralizes the child, instills hopelessness, and damages the relationship between the child and his dad.
10. A child needs to be able to realize that there is some correlation between the inappropriate behavior and the punishment for the behavior. Punishments that are not correlated to the behavior have little effect on changing the behavior.
11. Anything that is important enough to have a child do is important enough to ensure that the child complied.
12. Computers are wonderful ways of learning. They are also powerful ways of learning things that dads do not want their children to know just yet.

13. There is absolutely nothing to be gained by giving a child violent games, or games that model maladaptive behaviors.

14. It is often best that children be limited in their cell phone usage and then to allow use only for specific reasons and with specific individuals.

15. The best way to solve a behavioral problem with a child is not to let it occur in the first place.

16

Professional Interventions

I feel it is important to begin this section by explaining that most parents do not consider the possibility that their child may have a psychiatric problem. More often than not, changes in a child's behavior, changes in mood, and changes in thought processes are considered to be issues of behavior – such as being oppositional, delinquency, or using drugs – rather than a mental issue. One of the reasons for this line of thinking is that, more often than not, such changes in a child are issues related to the environment as well as the internal issues that most kids go through. However, there are times when there is a psychiatric issue that needs a professional intervention. The purpose of this chapter is to help dads understand when it is time to call for such help. Most mental health interventions start with a visit to one's primary care physician.

SOME BACKGROUND

The majority of childhood mental disorders have a genetic basis. This is not to say that one parent necessarily needs to have a disorder in order for the child to have it. A genetic predisposition for a mental disorder would not only apply to a child's parents but also to extended family. It could be that a grandparent, aunt, uncle, or cousin has a disorder. It is possible that one could have the genetics for a disorder but not manifest symptoms. Additionally, the more distantly related the relative (who has the mental disorder) is from a child, the more the chances of a diagnosable disorder decline. On the other hand, if a parent has a diagnosable disorder, the greater the chances are that the child could have the same or a different disorder.

It is not yet clearly understood how a parent (or other relative) who has one disorder may have children (or another type of related child) who have a different disorder. However, this is common. For example, a parent who has bipolar disorder may have a child who has schizophrenia, an obsessive-compulsive disorder, or an anxiety disorder.

The prevalence of young children who meet criteria for at least one disorder is actually quite high. Nearly 20% of children between the ages of two and five have a diagnosable disorder. Twenty-one percent of children between the ages of nine and seventeen meet criteria for a diagnosable disorder. This would be at least minimal impairment in one or more domains of functioning at home, school, or social situations.

For a diagnosis to be made, there must be a fairly severe functional impairment in one or more of those domains. Most people have some behaviors that could be considered diagnosable. However, if there is not a fairly severe impairment in one or more of the domains of home, school, or social situations, the behavior may not warrant a diagnosis and subsequent treatment.

For example, a person may have a phobia (an exaggerated fear) of snakes (which is a very common fear and has credibility in certain situations). A fear of snakes, in itself, is not necessarily a disorder. However, if the person is confined to the home or unable to go outside because of that fear, this could constitute a diagnosable condition. The reason is that the phobia is impairing the person's functionality in at least one or more domains.

Disorders are not evenly distributed between boys and girls. Boys are more likely, sometimes much more likely, than girls to be diagnosed with a disorder that affects the child's mental capacity, mood, or behaviors. While some childhood disorders diminish with age, there are others that continue into adulthood. *It is important to note that the father of a child with a disorder will need to have additional help for himself to learn how to help his child develop as normally as possible.* It would be a mistake to believe that any parent would know how, without training and a great deal of patience, to parent a special needs child. In these cases, Dad needs to seek assistance on how to help his child develop into a self-governing adult. The sooner this help is acquired, the easier it will be to help the child and the better the outcome will be.

THE MORE COMMON CHILDHOOD DISORDERS

Below is a list of some of the more common disorders in children and adolescents. This list is by no means inclusive. If a child is experiencing abnormal behavior, it is best to take her to her physician as soon as possible.

- **Autism.** This disorder is *not* very common, and it includes a spectrum of illnesses. Approximately two to five children out of 10,000 are affected. Approximately 70% of those with autism have some degree of mental retardation. There are cases of *high functioning autism*, such as Asperger's Disorder, whereby the child is very intelligent but exhibits social issues. However, keep in mind that not every child who has social problems has a disorder.
- **Mental Retardation.** This condition affects about 1% of the overall population, with less than three children out of 100,000 having *severe* mental retardation. The majority of children with mental retardation have a *mild* form of the disorder, and they can grow up to have normal lives. It is imperative to have the issue diagnosed as soon as possible and to involve the child's school to help the child develop intellectually to her fullest potential.
- **Attention-Deficit / Hyperactivity (ADD / ADHD).** ADD/ADHD has a prevalence of approximately 9% of school-aged children. The disorder is the most commonly and frequently diagnosed disorder of childhood, and it is very common in the school-age populations. Among school-age children, boys have a higher rate of ADD/ADHD than girls, by a margin of four to one. Younger children exhibit more symptoms

than older children, with symptoms declining as the child ages. (ADD/ADHD will be discussed in more detail later in this chapter.)

- **Anxiety, Disruptive, and Mood Disorders.** Children and adolescents between the ages of nine and seventeen have prevalence rates of 13% for anxiety disorders, 10% for disruptive disorders, and 6% for mood disorders. It is also common that disorders overlap, and a person may have more than one disorder at a time. For example, someone may have an anxiety disorder as well as another disorder, such as depression or ADD/ADHD.

- **Adult Mental Illnesses (including Bipolar Disorder and Schizophrenia).** Some of the predominantly adult mental illnesses, such as Bipolar Disorder and Schizophrenia, can manifest in children and adolescents. These are severe mental illnesses, and they generally do not appear in male children until late adolescence or the early twenties, and later in life for females. However, there are instances where children and adolescents are symptomatic. "Symptoms" of these types of disorders can easily be suggestive of drug usage. A simple drug screening kit can be obtained from most pharmacies to rule out that possibility very quickly. Regardless, it is best to have the child evaluated by a physician as soon as possible, especially if there is a family history of mental illness.

As stated above, the majority of *severe* mental disorders do not manifest symptoms until a person is in the late teens or early twenties. There are childhood disorders that are diagnosed at a very young age, such as Autism, Attention-Deficit Disorder (ADD), and Attention-Deficit Hyperactive Disorder (ADHD). The latter two are often misdiagnosed and treated with medication when a behavioral intervention is what is needed. Again, when I state that there is a need for a *behavioral intervention,* my intention is that the child *may* need a psychotherapist. In addition, Dad will *definitely* need to see a psychotherapist. It is naïve to think that just sending a child to a psychotherapist is enough. Dad needs to go too, to learn parenting skills that will help the child. (It would be best if both parents see a psychotherapist but it is imperative that Dad go.)

In addition, holding a child completely responsible for the problems she manifests would be misguided. Her behavior problems may, in all likelihood, be a family dynamic issue. When a child is taken to a psychotherapist, it is imperative for Dad to become aware of the underlying motivations of the child's behaviors. These motivations may be environmental in nature, an area that Dad has significant influence over. The more a dad knows about how to help his child develop, the better it will be for the child and the entire family.

Engaging the services of a child psychiatrist is imperative in the event that a child needs to be prescribed medication related to the disorder. Whenever a child is taking psychotropic medications (any medication for behavior or mood), a psychotherapist is a must. For example, if a child is suffering from an anxiety disorder, all of the anti-anxiety medication in the world will not solve the underlying cause of the child's anxiety. A long-term solution to the anxiety would be treatment with a psychotherapist. If a child is taking psychotropic medications, Dad should be seeing a psychotherapist as well – if for no other reason than to learn how best to help his child.

It is not unusual when a child is having psychiatric problems that a lot of stress is placed on the parents. The parents have a tendency to argue with each other, which can only make matters worse. It is wise to take a family systems approach to treatment when a family member is having a psychiatric problem. In this way, the entire family is working together to help the child. That is not to say that the other children need to go to psychotherapy – even though it may become necessary. However, the parents will need a great deal of assistance.

NATURE VERSUS NURTURE

There is often a debate in the media about the way in which a child develops behaviors and personality. Is this a product of the child's environment or the child's genetics? There is no need for a debate. There is ample research to confirm that a child's psychological development is a product of *both* environment and genetics. This is aside from issues like Down syndrome or other genetic issues that a child is born with (which has nothing to do with the environment). The point is that, even in cases of genetic abnormalities, the environment plays a major role on personality development and the severity of current and future behavioral problems.

ADD/ADHD

ADHD can be a result of a genetic predisposition for ADHD and/or environmental issues. The environmental issues may be some that have been previously discussed in this book. If ADHD in a specific child is a result of a chemical imbalance in the brain, then medication can be very helpful. In fact, a behavioral intervention without medication will in all likelihood be counterproductive and very frustrating for the child, Dad, other members of the family, and people outside the home. The diagnostic criteria for ADHD is that the symptoms must be in at least two environments. These two environments are usually home *and* school.

It is not unusual for some parents not to notice that their child has difficulty with concentration or hyperactivity while at home. I am reminded of a friend who told me that the school psychologist for her eight-year-old had asked that she have her son "diagnosed." His behavior at school was indicative of ADHD; however, his parents stated that they did not see any behavioral problems at home. We were sitting in a bowling alley during this conversation, and the child was clearly hyperactive with poor attention and concentration. His parents needed to tell him the same thing more than three times before he would comply, and then only because his parents got upset with him.

When this child had a question, he would have to ask his parents at least three times before they would acknowledge him. Their answer was usually for the child to "be quiet." Being in the presence of this family dynamic was very uncomfortable for me. The mother of the child asked my opinion of whether or not her son had ADHD. I suggested that she do as the school psychologist requested and have the boy formally diagnosed by a psychologist or a psychiatrist. It was clear to me that there were ADHD-type symptoms. It was also clear that there was a lack of parenting skills, and it seemed likely that the child's behavior was learned.

In this case, even if the parents took the child to a child psychiatrist, and a prescription was written for medication (which certainly might have had a positive effect on the boy's attention span and reduce his hyperactivity), there would still need to be changes in the family dynamic. To believe that the child would be able to take some pills and this problem would be solved – a problem that the parents did not even acknowledge – would be naïve. It is also very difficult to treat a child for a diagnosable mental condition, when the parents do not see the behavior as a problem.

Approximately 5% of children in the United States are *diagnosed* with ADD or ADHD, with the majority of them being boys. (Approximately 9% of children have the disorder but not all are diagnosed.) The diagnosis is often mistakenly made while their real problem is inadequate sleep, family conflicts, inadequate parenting skills, allergies, or other problems unrelated to brain development. Additionally, most children outgrow ADD and ADHD symptoms and behaviors by the time they are in their senior year of high school. However, it is important to note that if the problem is not biological, but environmental, the symptoms may continue for decades after the child becomes an adult. The sooner a professional intervention is made, the better the outcome will be.

Other problems that children might have include *impulse control issues*. This often resembles ADHD but might resemble something more like a temper tantrum. The difference in determining if a child is just having a bad day or having a disorder, in simple terms, is a matter of intensity, frequency, and duration of the outburst. If there are others in the home who exhibit similar behaviors, it would not be unreasonable to believe that the child is mimicking that behavior. It is up to the father to lead by example and model the desired behavior.

REASON'S FOR CONCERN? CONSULT A PHYSICIAN

As mentioned previously, there are examples of children's mental issues that would be a challenge for any parent – regardless of their willingness to help. In fact, there are children who display symptoms of some very debilitating mental illnesses, such as Obsessive/Compulsive Disorder, Bipolar Disorder, Psychotic Disorder, and Schizophrenia. Once again, it is important to emphasize that parents and other family members are generally the last ones to believe, or even consider, that a family member has a serious mental disorder. Often parents believe that their child is using drugs. This accounts for the kid's "strange behavior," or inability to focus, concentrate, and having difficulty with mood regulation. Again, if there is enough reason for concern, consult with a physician.

The ability to regulate one's own mood is something that should be learned within the first four years of life. If a child has not learned this, it can be very challenging to handle. This is when Dad needs to take a deep breath and practice the principles within this book. The first principle is always to be patient and kind. Children learn from their parents. When Dad acts in a manner that depicts patience and kindness, the children will usually follow suit.

OPPOSITIONAL/DEFIANCE

One of the most difficult behavioral issues in children is that of the oppositional/defiant (ODD) child. This goes beyond the behaviors of a child not doing something she was told to do. The ODD child seems to go out of her way to be defiant, even when there is no apparent reason. ODD children are generally a problem at home, but they can also exhibit similar behaviors at school and in the community. This type of child can be a challenge for any parent.

The symptoms and behaviors of ODD usually are present in a child prior to the age of eight years old. The prevalence rate is between 2% and 16%, and this disorder is more prevalent in boys than in girls. ODD is also more prevalent in families where at least one of the parents has a history of mental illness or substance abuse. It is also more common in households where there is serious marital discord.

Oppositional/defiant behavior can be a result of many issues, with the first being behavioral modeling. The most effective treatment for this type of disorder is prevention. Children learn from watching the behavior of others and then they generalize behaviors that are similar or *seem* to work for the child. If a behavior is successful, the child (or adult) will continue to use it. Once a behavior ceases to be successful, it is generally stopped; in other words, it is extinguished.

The ODD behaviors of a child may seem voluntary, and it is important for parents to know that not all children who show these signs are behaving this way by choice. Some children have extreme problems self-regulating their mood. Symptoms of *mood dysregulation*, that is when a person has difficulty monitoring and handling their moods, can appear very similar to a child who is being oppositional/defiant.

On the other hand, children can be very insightful with conscious or subconscious knowledge. A child knows that if she throws a big enough fit, a parent will eventually give in. This is especially true when the child is in public, but it can also be a strategy that works at home. There are children who seem to "torment" their parents, and their aim appears to be to wear Mom and Dad down to the point that it is easier to give in than to enforce boundaries. It may be painful for a while, but giving in is *not* a good approach. As you learned earlier in the book, it would be best to decide ahead of time if Dad is going to give in and do so without the child acting out. In this way, the child's outburst is not being reinforced, and hopefully there will become a disconnect in the child's mind between the acting out behavior and getting her way. On the other hand, if the answer is "no" – and there should be a good reason for that answer – then the answer needs to remain "no."

Keep in mind that an answer does not need to be given right away. It is perfectly acceptable to think about it for a while and discuss it with one's wife before deciding what to do. It is also acceptable to change an answer once Dad has had some time to think it through or talk about it with his wife. Kids need to know that their parents are reasonable.

However, when Dad is trying to change a behavior that has been intermittently reinforced, it is best to decide first what the answer is going to be and then *stick to it*.

As you've been reading in this book, inconsistently reinforced behaviors are the most difficult type of behavior to change (slot machines use this philosophy to get players to continue to play). If a child acts out to get her way, she will continue to act out to get her way. The more she acts out, the better chance she believes that Dad will tire of the behavior and give in to her demands. It only reinforces the behavior of acting out if dad first says "no" and continues to say "no" but eventually gives in. In this case, the child will continue to escalate the emotional intensity until Dad gives in.

When the well-thought-out decision is that Dad will not give in, then prepare for the worst and do not give in. This is a time when a well-thought-out plan needs to be in place *prior* to the child acting out. Dad needs to know what he is going to do and be prepared for it. This is one of those situations where most parents will *not* know how to extinguish these types of behaviors. Dad may need to seek guidance from a professional psychotherapist who is familiar with this type of problem.

Not all children who act out with oppositional/defiant behaviors have a disorder. One of the reasons that children, and especially teenagers, become oppositional/defiant, besides being adolescents, is that they are trying to establish their own identity and autonomy. Younger children may merely be trying to get their way. Trying to be patient and kind with a child who is oppositional/defiant can be very difficult, maybe even impossible. The older the child is, the more difficult it can be to stay calm and patient with an oppositional/defiant child.

Working with this type of child will call upon all of Dad's parenting skills and patience. Even then, the child may not respond as Dad would like her to, and if she does respond, it may not be right away. When Dad makes changes to how he acts and reacts toward his children, as well as other family members, the children will probably not follow suit as quickly as one would like. Another reason that some children are oppositional/defiant is that they might be suffering from depression.

DEPRESSION

One of the most common psychological issues that teenagers face is depression. In the United States, approximately 9% of adolescents, ages twelve through seventeen, have experienced a major depressive episode in the past year. (The prevalence of depression for children under the age of ten years is less than three percent.) Nearly two-thirds of those who are depressed contemplate suicide, with 10-15% making a suicide attempt. In addition, gender appears to play a significant role in depression in young adults, with twice as many females experiencing depression than males. However, this is not the case with adolescents, whereby adolescent males experience similar rates of depression as adolescent females.

The diagnostic criteria for *Major Depressive Disorder* is depressed mood, change in appetite, sleep disturbance, fatigue or loss of energy, diminished interest in activities that usually are considered pleasurable, poor concentration, impaired memory, feelings of hopelessness, social withdrawal, indecisiveness, and low self-esteem. In a *Major Depressive Disorder*, these symptoms are severe, dramatic, and much more functionally impairing than in a *Dysthymic Disorder* (a general feeling of being sad or "down in the dumps" for more days than not), with adolescence being the most frequent age of onset for a *Major Depressive Disorder*.

Though listed above, the symptoms of depression vary from person to person. Still, there are criteria that are common to most individuals with depression. The most common symptom of depression is hopelessness. In addition to the aforementioned symptoms, depression in adolescence is often accompanied by symptoms of school phobia, poor school performance, truancy, asocial behavior (that is, social isolation), antisocial behavior (that is, delinquency), sexual promiscuity, oppositional behavior towards parents and authority figures, and running away.

While these are the symptoms that define depression, the causes of depression may be various and complex. Studying adolescent depression is more difficult, due to frequent mood swings normally occurring at that age. Research has explored the relationship between children and their

256

dad, and it has found that the quality of the parental relationship may have a significant influence on depressive symptoms in adolescents. In fact, research indicates that this relationship can have a significant influence on a child's overall emotional well-being, including depression, self-esteem, self-efficacy, and social skills.

Furthermore, studies that included the relationship between Dad and his children have found that when fathers were emotionally disengaged with their children, there were greater depressive symptoms and behavioral problems for the adolescents. This is also the case when a dad is emotionally disengaged with the child's mother as well. When a Dad is emotionally disengaged with the child and/or the child's mother, the child is at greater risk for major depression.

As would be expected, the children of a dad with a positive level of engagement with his children have less depressive symptoms and fewer behavioral problems. In addition, a father's disengagement has an additive effect on a child when he is both emotionally and physically absent from his child's life. This leads to the child having feelings of emotional alienation and abandonment, as well as disappointment and disillusionment in this paternal relationship.

Depression can be a very serious problem for some adolescents. Suicide, as a key example, is the second leading cause of death among adolescents. Among adolescents, suicidal ideations (thoughts of considering suicide) and suicide attempts are the dominant reason of adolescent psychiatric hospitalization for this age group. Studies show depression as the most common precursor to suicide, and there are many risk factors that are social in nature. Adolescents often conceal their symptoms of depression, and they have a tendency to be more action-oriented than adults. What may seem insignificant to an adult may seem insurmountable to an adolescent.

Adolescent depression usually stems from one of two main origins. Adolescents become depressed due to difficulties in maintaining a positive self-view (self-esteem), or they develop a fear of being abandoned. Some of the precipitating events of adolescent depression include family problems, separation or divorce of parents, *parental* substance abuse, discord with peer(s), problems at school with peers and/or school grades, and any other event that may lower the child's self-esteem.

MEDICATION

Many parents become apprehensive about the possibility of starting their child on psychotropic medications, such as antidepressants or a stimulant for ADD or ADHD. It is important to understand that not everyone who is depressed needs to take an antidepressant. However, if the level of depression is severe enough that it impairs a child's ability to concentrate, the child's normal activities are impaired, and her grades at school are suffering, then it might be time to consult one's primary-care physician.

Many parents research medications on the Internet and become frightened of their side effects. When a child's development is impaired due to behavioral or emotional issues, the potential side-effects are viewed as less concerning. Every medication has side effects, most of which the majority of users do not experience. Look at the warnings on any over-the-counter medication, like cough syrup or even eye drops. The side effects are staggering. It would be best to consult one's primary-care physician or one's pharmacist before taking any medication. If side effects develop, report it to your doctor.

I was asked to consult with a family whose ten-year-old child was a major behavioral problem at home, at school, and within the community. I went to the child's home and witnessed his inability to sit still, follow instructions, or focus on anything for more than a couple of seconds. After a short period of time, and talking with the child's parents, it became obvious that the young boy had Bipolar Disorder. The child had been under the care of a psychiatrist for the past couple of years, and he was on medication for this disorder. The parents were so nervous about the long-term ramifications of the side-effects, they would not allow the psychiatrist to raise the dose of the medications.

The boy's parents were very well educated and financially stable. They had two other children who seemed to be suffering greatly due to the behaviors of their older brother. The parents were often arguing and blaming each other for the child's behavior. My suggestion was to allow the psychiatrist to treat the child as she saw fit. After a consult with the child's psychiatrist, the parents agreed to a higher dosage.

I returned to the house one week later to check on the family's progress. The young boy sat at the table with his parents and me for thirty minutes without interrupting or displaying any type of inappropriate behavior. The parents were ecstatic with the progress their child had made. The school was also very grateful. This had been going on for nearly three years before the parents allowed the psychiatrist to effectively treat their child. This was due to the parents' concern about things they had read on the Internet, and they naively had feared for the child's well-being. The child now has a chance to develop normally and live a normal life. Hopefully, the chaos brought about by the oldest son's disorder was not too damaging to the emotional well-being of the younger two sons. Only time will tell.

As mentioned earlier in the chapter, it is also very important to understand that children virtually *never* need to go to see a psychotherapist without the parents seeing a psychotherapist as well. Children do not develop in a vacuum. The problems that children develop are the result of specific or general environmental or genetic issues. If there are problems with the child beyond normal developmental issues that Dad does not know how to effectively handle, sending a child to treatment is futile without Dad going as well.

FINAL THOUGHT

Again I must emphasize that whenever a child is in treatment, whether it be with medication or psychotherapy or both, Dad needs to seek his own psychotherapist. Psychotherapy can be beneficial for Dad in an attempt to help his child. If Dad cannot be calm, consistent, caring, concerned, and nurturing, he may be in need of some help to become so. Holding the child solely responsible for the chaos in the home, even though he may be the identified patient, would be naïve. This could very likely cause issues with the other children in the home as well as put quite a strain on a marriage.

It is important for Dad to be able to realize when a child is having problems beyond those that are normal for her age group. This is not to say that Dad needs to be paranoid about his child's emotional well-being and run her to the doctor every time something comes up. However, when a pattern of behavior emerges, or the behaviors seem bizarre or inappropriate for the age of the child, it is best to seek professional help. The best place to start is with one's family (or primary-care) physician.

WHAT'S NEXT?

The next chapter was one that was difficult to write. It addresses behaviors that are inappropriate in a household where children are being raised.

KEY CHAPTER POINTS

1. Most parents do not consider the possibility that their child may have a psychiatric problem.
2. The majority of childhood mental disorders have a genetic basis.
3. The prevalence of young children who meet criteria for at least one disorder is nearly 20% of those between the ages of two and five.
4. In order for a diagnosis to be made, there must be fairly severe functional impairment in one or more of the domains of home, school, or social situations.
5. Mental disorders of children are not evenly distributed between males and females, with boys being more likely to have a mental condition.
6. Holding a child completely responsible for the problems she manifests would be misguided when her behavior problems may be a family dynamic issue.
7. It is not unusual, when a child is having psychiatric problems, that a lot of stress is placed on the parents, and the parents have a tendency to argue with each other, which can only make matters worse.
8. Even in cases of genetic abnormalities, the environment plays a major role on personality development and the severity of current and future behavioral problems.
9. Attention Deficit/Hyperactivity Disorder (ADD/ADHD) has a prevalence of approximately 9% of school-aged children, with boys having a higher rate than girls by four to one within this age group.
10. Oppositional/defiant behavior (ODD) can be a result of many issues, with the first being behavioral modeling.
11. One of the most common psychological issues that teenagers face is depression, with the most common symptom of depression being hopelessness.

12. Studies have found that when fathers were emotionally disengaged from their children, there were greater depressive symptoms and behavioral problems for the adolescents.
13. Most mental health interventions start with a visit to one's primary care physician.
14. It is very important to understand that children virtually never need to go to see a psychotherapist without the father seeing a psychotherapist as well.

17

Inappropriate Paternal Behaviors

This was a very uncomfortable chapter to write, and it will also be for many of you to read. A great deal of thought went into whether or not the chapter should be included in the book. However, I have learned that if something cannot be hidden, it is best to shine a light on it. It would be a mistake to believe that the behaviors in this chapter do not occur, and in the homes where they are occurring, it is important to discuss it and make a concerted effort to change.

WHEN IT'S MORE THAN TIME FOR A CHANGE

This chapter is written for men. This is a chapter that was not written to make the reader feel good. In fact, after reading this chapter, one might feel worse. For example, we have all said or done things that we wish we had not. However, the topics discussed in this chapter go beyond the normal miscommunications, arguing, name-calling, or occasional alcohol use that might go on in nearly any home. The topics in Chapter 17 are the behaviors of human suffering that make life uncomfortable for not only the person who partakes in such behaviors, but also those around him.

I must also point out that while certain types of inappropriate behavior (such as alcoholism or domestic violence) are taking place, the children often *seem* to be faring well. However, it is not unusual that children start to exhibit emotional and behavioral problems *after* the parents' inappropriate behavior seems to be under control.

It is important for Dad to remember that the children have been through a difficult time. This would be a good time to utilize the techniques delineated within this book. Keep in mind that when Dad stops an inappropriate behavior that has been occurring for years, the children may be skeptical that the behavior is really changed. This is especially true if the behavior has been stopped before, only to reappear.

It is important to continue to reassure the child that you are making every effort to change. This would be a good time to practice the conversation with your wife and then have it with your children. Remember that love is patient, love is kind. Dad usually starts to feel good about his newfound freedom from bondage, and he must be patient and kind to his children in order for them to feel free as well.

Once again, this chapter is written for men. The majority of men do all the things that are expected of a man except for minor issues and behaviors as previously discussed in this book. Most men are decent and caring, as well as law-abiding citizens. A very small percentage of men participate in the behaviors articulated in this chapter. When they do, men cause a significant amount of damage to their family, their community, and to themselves.

The problems discussed in this chapter may not be strictly masculine problems. However, they are significantly more male-based than female-based. For example, the majority of alcoholics are male. The majority of crimes in this country are perpetrated by males. The majority of sexual abuse and serious physical abuse to children in this country are by males. While it is true that women engage in all of the behaviors delineated in this chapter, it is about these issues and the influence that men have on their families. Of course, it is also true that women have a great deal of influence on their families. But when these types of behaviors are being perpetrated in a home by the mother, the father of the home has the influence to help rectify the problems. In most cases, a father has much more influence than anyone else within a home.

This chapter is not intended to spark a debate about all the good things that most men do for their family, their community, and for humankind in general. A good man who is a good husband and a good father may feel the need to skip over this chapter. However, even for those men, it is probably a good idea to see what some families have to live with on a daily basis. This helps to understand why others act the way they do. Additionally, there is information in this chapter that every family needs to know. Inappropriate behavior in someone else's home does affect those who come to visit. For instance, a father's children may be subject to some of the ills of this chapter while visiting other children's homes or even a relative's home. The first inappropriate behavior discussed in this chapter is the angry person.

ANGRY PEOPLE

Angry people tend to express themselves in angry ways. Angry people also live a lie. This is not a discussion about people who get angry every so often, but about those who are angry most of the time, or even all the time with those who they are supposed to love. This is also about those dads who, when they get angry, behave in a manner that frightens their children, their wives, and others around Dad.

Angry people are often very sensitive people, easily hurt, and quick to feel insulted. They lack self-esteem, misinterpret the intentions of others, and are fearful most of the time because anger *is* fear. The angriest man you have ever known is trying to hide the scared little boy inside, afraid that others will see him for the person he knows that he is. And that person, in his own eyes, is worthless, unheard with the belief that no one cares about him because he is not worth caring about. That is the lie, and an angry person will go to great lengths to protect that lie, and to keep others from seeing what he knows to be the truth.

Angry people do not always act angry, even though they may be angry inside. For instance, let's take the person who constantly yells and screams, ridicules and demeans at home. In contrast, he may appear to be calm and courteous at work, in the community, or in social situations. On the other hand, a person who acts out aggressively in the community is usually a tyrant at home with his own family. These types of people often go well out of their way to prove to the entire world that they are not angry, but their families know the truth.

Angry people are those who break things, throw things, and punch things, and they can be so full of rage that they cannot see straight let alone be calm, reasonable, or restrained. Angry people also blame their behaviors on others, making their family feel as if they are the problem. An angry father might correlate his angry outbursts at home as a problem with his family when the problem is the father.

Recognizing that You Have an Anger Issue

One can tell when they have a problem with anger. This is by coming to the realization that they do not have control over the problem, instead the problem has control over them. A test for anger problems would be for the individual to try to go seven days without getting angry. If that fails, break it down into smaller steps and try to go twenty-four hours without being angry. If that fails, break it down to even smaller steps, and try not to get angry before lunch. Most people can go weeks, months, and even years without being angry. This is not to say that people do not get upset. It is a far cry from being upset to being angry.

When one is upset, he can still talk and think about a problem. He can still listen to others about the problem, and he can still find workable solutions in a manner that is not degrading or demeaning to those around him.

When a man gets angry, reason no longer applies, and the damage that is done to a father's children can be devastating. For example, you're driving down the freeway and somebody cuts you off. That could upset most people, who might think to themselves, "What an idiot!" Few people in this situation, being cut off in traffic, tend to think to themselves, "Oh that poor man, he must have some sort of a medical emergency." So in this situation, it would be very normal to be upset (remember that anger is fear and being upset is at the bottom end of the anger spectrum). It would be just as normal to "drop it" as soon as it occurred and get on with life.

An angry person does not "drop it." Instead, he starts to do things that are inappropriate, irrational, and stupid. For example, a freeway accident near my home was recently covered on the news. It occurred while the motorists were driving down a steep grade. According to the report, a motorcyclist pulled in front of a motorhome, which was traveling at sixty-five miles an hour, and then the biker slammed on the brakes of the motorcycle.

It was assumed by the investigators that the person driving the motorhome in some way angered the motorcyclist. Those who witnessed the accident were not able to determine what the motorhome driver could have possibly done to annoy the motorcyclist. No one was able to ask the motorcyclist himself why he pulled in front of a motorhome, on the freeway, going sixty-five miles an hour, downhill, and slammed on the brakes. This was due to the fact that the driver of the motorhome was not able to stop it, and the motorhome ran over the motorcyclist, killing him instantly.

The motorcyclist is an example of an angry person, irrational, out-of-control, and doing things that are clearly inappropriate. Angry people often misinterpret the actions of others as hostile when that is not the intent. Life-changing events may occur when an angry person acts upon those misinterpretations in violent ways. However, people are able to distinguish when they are getting upset and are capable of change.

Learning New Responses to Anger

When a person gets angry, his body goes through very specific physiological changes. His heart rate increases, he starts to sweat or becomes clammy, his muscles tense up, and he starts to say and do things that he feels little control over. Once we learn what those changes are, we are able to monitor those changes, understand that we are starting to get upset, and take measures to stop from getting angry. It is easier to monitor one's physiological symptoms and take steps to calm oneself *before* going into a rage. This works not only for the rageaholic but also for nearly anyone who has ever been upset.

There are few people who have raised children that have not been very, very upset. It is also not unusual for people who are in a relationship to get upset at some point with their partner. Being able to monitor one's own physiological changes, having the ability to determine that you are becoming upset, and taking steps to change your responses are a benefit to everyone in the family dynamic.

Angry people also have a tendency to perseverate about (or dwell upon) the reason they are angry to the point that it can become an obsession. They often cannot let go of the reason that they are angry, even though the reason may be irrational. Meanwhile, in the majority of cases, when someone says something that annoys or hurts another person, the speaker is usually not aware that what they said was annoying or hurtful. Additionally, the majority of hurtful comments were not intended to be hurtful, and when it is pointed out, the person will usually be very apologetic. Angry people have a difficult time accepting an apology. They will virtually never give an apology, and they often blame the other person, regardless of whose fault it was.

It is not unusual for angry people to come from angry families where no one listens until the yelling starts. When we remember that behaviors are learned, it becomes easy to see that in a house where there is a lot of yelling, children may not respond until yelled at. If a child learns by repeated modeling that he does not have to obey until Dad starts to yell, he will very likely not obey until Dad does yell. This reinforces the belief of the angry father that he must yell and be angry before anyone will listen to him. So the child continues to disobey until his father yells and screams, and the father continues to believe that his son will not obey unless he yells and screams. The father may also believe that the child does not listen to him because he is not worth listening to. This makes the father feel more worthless and yell all the more.

Angry people try to solve problems using anger, and they often get their way. However, rarely does a problem actually get resolved by anger. The brain does not operate well when it is agitated, and the function of reasoning does not work well when the brain is subjected to anger. So solving problems when one is annoyed is not an easy feat to accomplish. It is nearly impossible when a person is angry.

It may appear that an angry person gets his way or wins an argument. However, the reality is that people who are not angry usually do not want to be embarrassed or abused and often give in to appease the angry person. I remember a staff sergeant (rank E5) in the Air Force who was angry. He yelled all the time and was quite intimidating if crossed. This was before the time of computers, and the pay record for each member of the Air Force at the base was in a folder in that location's payroll office. If the folder was not there, you did not get paid. Well, there was something wrong with the angry sergeant's paycheck one day, and he went to the payroll office and "tore up the little one-striper (rank E2)" in the payroll office. This angry person was listened to and assured that his problem would be resolved. Even so, the angry sergeant did not get paid again for months. An exhaustive search was made for the sergeant's pay record, which was eventually discovered at a US military airbase payroll office in Turkey!

This was an example whereby an angry person thought his anger had got him what he wanted. In reality, his outburst created a huge problem for him, and it seems that the "little one-striper" won the day. An additional note about this staff sergeant is that he was sent to a psychiatric hospital for evaluation as ordered by our commanding officer. The sergeant was discharged, against his will, from the military due to his anger problems.

It is important to understand that there might be a very good reason why someone is angry, especially from the angry person's point of view. However, the angry person needs to understand that his anger is like a cancer to those around him. It could be compared to spraying anger around like spray paint, squirting over onto everyone within earshot. For example, I worked with an elderly man who was one of the few remaining victims of polio, and he had to walk using crutches. One of my co-workers once made the comment that "he is so angry." The person she was talking to responded by saying, "Wouldn't you be?" The reality of it is that he certainly had been dealt a bad hand. However, that is no reason to make other people miserable. People have a great deal more respect for those who overcome adversity with a fighting spirit rather than a fighting mouth. Remember what a man says has a great deal of influence. A person who has control over his mouth has control over all of his behaviors.

SUBSTANCE ABUSE PROBLEMS

Many angry people have problems that go beyond anger. It is not uncommon for angry people to have substance abuse issues, along with other addictive behaviors. In terms of substance abuse, it will undoubtedly make an angry person angrier. There are no street drugs (marijuana, cocaine, methamphetamine, alcohol, PCP, speed, LSD, heroin, etc.) that will make a person less angry. Agitation is also a side effect of mood-altering legal medications such as sedatives or antianxiety medications (Valium, Xanax, Klonopin, Ativan, etc.) and painkillers (Vicodin, Norco, Oxycodin, Morphine, etc.). Using medications that were developed and manufactured for medical purposes, in most cases, would not be considered substance abuse when using them as prescribed. On the other hand, any substance that is illegal would be considered substance abuse.

Substance abuse is one of the foremost causes of emotional dysfunction within a family. It is nearly impossible to be reared in an environment of addiction or substance abuse and not suffer from the effects. Substance abuse creates instability, inconsistency, chaos, and abuse in a family, regardless of which family member is abusing the substance.

Parents who abuse substances have a significant influence on whether their children will use substances. Children have a tendency to generalize behaviors. For example, if a parent smokes cigarettes, children, usually adolescents, generalize that behavior to believe that smoking marijuana is also acceptable. They may also generalize the behaviors to the smoking of any substance, including cocaine and heroin.

The children of parents who drink alcohol often generalize that behavior to the use of cocaine and marijuana. Parents may excuse their own substance use with excuses like they are old enough, or they are using a legal substance. Adolescents often do not buy into those excuses, and they rationalize in their minds that their own substance use is justified. I have had countless cases of adolescents who were admitted to the hospital for making suicidal statements after an argument with one or both parents about the child's marijuana usage just to learn that at least one of the parents had been smoking marijuana at home in front of the children. The overwhelming excuse was that the parent had a marijuana card. Adolescent children are much more sophisticated than that and will not buy into such an excuse. This is the same with expecting a child to wait until he is eighteen years old to start smoking cigarettes or twenty-one years old to start consuming alcohol when the parents are using these.

It is difficult for a parent to keep his child from a behavior in which the parent engages, regardless of the age of the child or the frequency of the behavior. A parent does not need to be an alcoholic to imprint the use of alcohol on his teenage child. The rule of thumb on these types of issues is if a father does not want his child to engage in a behavior, then the father should not engage in the behavior himself.

(We would have to exclude sex with one's wife from this category; however, children should *never* see or hear his parents having sex. This can become a problem in the case where a parent is living with a person, and the couple is not married. It is difficult to ask a child to abstain from sex with someone other than a spouse if the parent is having sex with someone other than his spouse.)

When a father abuses substance(s) (including prescribed drugs), the amount of damage he does to his family can be long lasting and far reaching. The type of abuse that often accompanies substance use is physical, verbal, neglect, or a combination of the three. Even in cases where the parent is a "functioning addict" (including alcohol, drugs, or other addictions), whereby the father seems to the outside world to function normally, the home-life is generally very chaotic and abusive by nature.

Statistics indicate that 75% of domestic violence is from a person who abuses alcohol or drugs. This violence in the home, whether specifically directed at a child as well or not, is extremely damaging to the children who witness spousal abuse by their fathers. Male children who *witness* domestic violence are seven times more likely to abuse their own wives. They are also six times more likely to sexually abuse their own children than fathers who were brought up in a home without domestic violence.

An example of the functioning addict is a case where the father goes to work every day, pays the bills, and does everything he is supposed to do in order to maintain his job and income. Then he comes home from work, sits in front of the television, and drinks beer until he becomes intoxicated. In this example, the father is not physically or verbally abusive; he merely drinks himself into a coma every night. However, his wife and children live in the home, and this father is there physically but is not emotionally available to his family. This would be a case of a father who neglects his children, which can be as damaging as physical and verbal abuse.

The above example is from real life, and this man's wife and children were very angry. In fact the fifteen-year-old son was finally hospitalized because he could no longer accept his father's neglectful behavior. The father could not see that his drinking was a problem; after all, he did everything he thought a husband/father was supposed to do. He worked, and did a very good job of providing the necessities for his family.

The issue in this case is that the father, who has significant influence, was sitting in the living room watching television every night, as well as all weekend, and the children could not access him. His wife was ready to leave him, and his son was homicidal and hospitalized for wanting to kill his father.

This may seem like an extreme reaction from the child. However, living with a father who remained unavailable and uninvolved while his family was in a state of dysfunction finally became too much for the son. The boy's mother tried her best to be both parents while the father sat and watched television while drinking, avoiding any interaction at all with the family. The father's response was "She's the one who wanted the children." He saw no problem with his behavior.

In this particular case, the family had to accept the fact that the father was not going to change. They also could not allow the failure of their father to become a failure for themselves. The children had to make the conscious choice to understand that they needed to take responsibility for their own lives, without any positive input from their father, and get on with life. This would include doing well in school, obeying the rules, getting a job when they were old enough, and not following the example of their father, which was to start drinking, or using any substances at all.

Unfortunately, it is not unusual for addictions to overlap. Many men who have a substance abuse problem also have a problem with sex addiction in some form or another. The most used form of sex addiction is pornography.

PORNOGRAPHY

It seems that the more permissive our society becomes, the more desensitized we become to sex. What two married people do in the privacy of their bedroom is between them; however, when there are children in the house, certain precautions must be taken. When parents have a cavalier attitude about sex, children have a tendency to generalize those attitudes and become cavalier as well. Children of any age should *never* be subjected to any unwanted sexual pressure, including pornography, or movies with sexual content.

A child who is not ready to deal with the stressors of sex when he or she is exposed to it (via pornography, or physical sex in general before the person is emotionally ready) can develop severe problems. The younger the child, the more stress that is placed upon the child. Infants and toddlers cannot tell the difference between movies, pictures and reality. This not only applies to pornography but to movies that have violence in them as well.

Therefore, infants and toddlers cannot tell the difference between behaviors such as anger and sex when being perpetrated (even consensually) upon someone else, as in a movie, or the same being perpetrated upon them. Just as a child cannot emotionally differentiate between anger or violence being perpetrated toward a parent or sibling, young children have difficulty differentiating violence or sex in a movie and real life. This is called *vicarious abuse*. Can you imagine how you would feel if you witnessed a murder, a rape, or other violence? It just might have a negative effect on you. That is how vicarious abuse is perceived by young children. Later in life, a child, an adolescent, or even an adult might display symptoms of being abused themselves when the abuse was perpetrated upon them vicariously.

The private viewing of pornography by a father in and of itself may not be detrimental to the well-being of his family. However, when pornography, or any other behavior, takes significant time away from the family, it becomes a problem.

With the advent of the Internet, a wide array of data, information, and viewing content is available without ever leaving one's home. One study indicates that 25 million Americans spend up to ten hours a week viewing Internet pornography. Another 4 to 5 million Americans spend over eleven hours a week viewing Internet pornography. In a 2003 survey, 47% of families surveyed said that pornography is a problem in their home. This is either from the parents viewing pornography or from trying to keep the children from viewing pornographic sites. By the time of this writing, I am certain that the problem is much worse.

Additionally, nine out of ten children between the ages of eight and sixteen have viewed pornography on the Internet, with most of the viewings being *unintentional*. However, once a child is exposed to pornography, curiosity may continue to bring the child back. This includes female children as well as male children. Children model behaviors, especially those of their parents, but from other persons as well. The media is a significant source of modeling for children and adults alike.

As mentioned earlier, as my children were growing up, I made it a point not to allow them Internet access without it being in my office or in a public room of the house. Use of e-mail, Facebook, or other social media uses was permitted only in moderation and for specific purposes. We tried to keep our children very busy with activities so that there was not a lot of time to get into trouble or have cyber-relationships. There is ample evidence that children who communicate in methods that are not face-to-face have diminished social and communication skills. This is true for adults as well.

There is a serious problem in this country with cyber-networking between children and sexual predators. When one does not know with whom one is communicating, this makes it very easy for predators to befriend a socially isolative or awkward child. While I was working at a psychiatric hospital, at least once a week a child was admitted due to issues with a cyber-stalker or being bullied online.

The world is not safe for children, and adults as well, who are not aware and do not take seriously the dangers that are a fact of life. This is not to advocate being overprotective of our children. Instead it's about being able to educate our children about being safe and being able to read your own body signals. If something feels wrong or dangerous, it probably is wrong or dangerous. Children need to be educated that there are some very bad people out there. The horrors that children see at the movies and on television do actually occur in real life.

It would be a mistake to try to keep our children from the knowledge of such things. There is a fine line between educating a child about dangerous people and occurrences and terrorizing them to be afraid of everyone or of trying new things. The majority of children grow up without serious complication from outside the home. Open, honest, and caring communication will generally be enough to help children make good decisions about their safety as they mature. Being a dad who is accessible, calm, caring, consistent, and concerned will foster good relationships with his children. It will encourage them to trust him and what he tells them. In this type of parenting, a child trusts his dad and often that is enough to keep the child from making bad decisions.

CHILD ABUSE

As a dad, we want to lift our children up. We do not want to demoralize them with punishments that are unreasonable, painful, or abusive by their nature. That's right, some behaviors toward a child are abusive by their very nature, such as a lack in any of these areas – love, nurturing, and physical attention like holding and hugging. (This type of parental behavior is considered neglect.) Other behaviors are abusive by the action itself and its nature, such as yelling, arguing, name-calling, derogatory comments, corporal punishment, and any type of assault.

As briefly discussed early in the book, when a parent strikes a child, the parent has come to the realization that they do not know what else to do. It would be a sad situation for a parent's first line of punishment to be to strike a child. Therefore, I assume that it is a last resort.

There might come a time when a spanking seems to be the only alternative. If so, do it sparingly and with regret. Never hit a child in anger, but calm yourself and think it through. Try to understand what message you are trying to send to the child and determine if a spanking is the way to convey that. Additionally, different states have different laws in regard to corporal punishment (i.e., a physical form of punishment), and it would be best to understand what those laws are before using it.

BEYOND CORPORAL PUNISHMENT

Any other form of physical action toward a child is abuse. If a spanking leaves a mark or a welt, then the spanking was abusive as well. Naturally, one might not know how hard to spank a child if they do not do this regularly. Yet this is an area where there should be very little practice. It would be best to re-read this book and apply the principles before resorting to striking a child.

Other forms of physical abuse or neglect would include having a child do an excess amount of work, or stand for more than a few minutes in the corner. Sitting in the corner for too long is also damaging to the child. Not allowing a child to eat, sleep, go to the bathroom, or come in the house if the weather is bad are all forms of abuse.

Any punishment that harms the child – like having the child hold his arms out, hold a burning match, do extensive exercises (beyond what he is capable of), or restraining the child yourself with cords or belts would also be considered abuse. Not giving a child the necessities of life would be considered neglect. Neglect can be as damaging as physical abuse. It is always best to try to understand why a child is behaving the way he is and to use a behavioral intervention. That way your response should not be damaging to the relationship you have as Dad with the child.

SEXUAL ABUSE

Some things are so inherently wrong that it does not need to be stated. When any adult becomes sexually excited from a child, it is time for that adult to remove himself from children and seek immediate help. The damage that is done by an adult having any sexual contact with a child is devastating to that child, most often for the rest of the child's life.

If your child has been sexually abused, it is imperative to get the child to a psychotherapist immediately and to keep them in therapy for as long as it takes. There are times when a child does not want to talk about the abuse, and that is all right. Should the child stop therapy and have problems later on, get the child back to therapy immediately. It is also important to understand that the effects of sexual abuse may very well manifest themselves in behaviors that have nothing to do with the trauma. When a child has been sexually abused, be aware that the child's *normal emotional development has been altered, and it is hard to say with any degree of accuracy what the long-term ramifications will be.*

If the child starts to behave differently, seems depressed, grades start to drop, becomes unusually argumentative, or becomes aggressive towards siblings, parents, or peers, Dad should get the child – male or female – to a psychotherapist immediately. There are also age-appropriate support groups for children who have been abused. *It is imperative that the abuse not be made public* for reasons I will discuss shortly.

I categorize sexual abusers into two categories, *opportunists* and *predators*. The opportunists generally prey upon children within their own home or family. These are children who might not have been otherwise available to the abuser. This would include children who come over to the home to play, spend the night, or go on outings with the abuser and his family.

· The predator is one who seeks out children, entices them, and even abducts them. Predators are most likely opportunists as well, and no child is safe from this type of person. The predator works on improving his ability to abuse children, and he knows, instinctively, who is a candidate. For the pedophile (that is a sexual abuser who preys upon *pre-pubescent* children), young children are especially vulnerable. Most young children do not have the ability to resist this type of predator, who often entices with toys, games, and candy. They also tell children lies, such as that their parent is hurt or that their parent sent them to pick up the child. Young children most often do not know how to say "no" to an adult, and it is very important that children be made aware that not all adults are safe.

For example, when I was five years old, both of my parents were in prison. My siblings and I lived with our paternal grandparents. My grandmother would warn me not to get into a car with a stranger as "they do terrible things to little boys." She never said what those terrible things were, but it was enough to ensure that I did not get into a car with strangers or even talk to someone I did not know. She also told me that these "bad people" would try to get me into their car by offering me candy. Thank God she told me these things. In kindergarten, as I was walking home alone one afternoon, a man in a car parked on the street asked me if I would like a ride home. I told him I was almost home and "no thanks." He slid over to the passenger side and opened the car door. Again he asked if I would like a ride and told me to get in. I said that I just lived down the street. He then asked me if I wanted some candy. At this point, I remembered what my grandmother had said and I screamed as loud as I could as I ran down the block.

To this day, it concerns me to think about what might have happened if my grandmother had not warned me about strangers. As I mentioned, she never said what these people might do, but this experience was enough to scare me to the point that I never walked home alone again. The sad part was that I was too afraid to tell anyone about what had happened. I have made it a point to let my children know that they tell me anything. Note that in warning children about such possibilities, role-playing protective behavior can be useful, as we do not want a child to have to figure out what he/she would do in a given situation. It is best to know ahead of time what the child is to do and have practiced it.

Children who have been sexually abused have a six times greater chance of being re-abused by another perpetrator than someone who has not been abused. This sounds counter-intuitive, as one might believe that if someone has been abused that person would be more sensitive to signs of being abused. Unfortunately, this is not the case. It is well documented that children who have been abused are, more often than not, abused again, even as adults.

In one study, adolescent girls were asked to watch a video and to turn it off when they felt the situation was dangerous. The video being watched was as if the person was walking down a city sidewalk and came upon a dark alleyway. The girls in the study who had not been sexually abused stopped the tape as soon as the dark alleyway approached on the screen.

The majority of the girls who had been sexually abused did not stop the video and continued down the dark alleyway. They also did not stop the video when they saw a man in the shadows of the alley. They finally stopped the video when they saw a knife in the man's hand. There is not a good explanation for this phenomenon, except issues with boundaries and possibly a sense of desensitization. The data indicates that predators understand this, and they use it to their advantage.

This makes it very important for children not to divulge such information to the masses, but only to people who are safe. Once other family members, neighbors, friends, and the other children at school find out what has happened, the news spreads very quickly. Special care must be taken to ensure that the child is not re-victimized by someone else. The mindset of the abuser is simply that the child has been abused already, what difference does it make if she/he is abused again?

If you learn that your child has been the victim of sexual abuse, believe her or him. Most children do not lie about such things. In fact, it is very difficult for most children to report such things – especially if it is a family member. Do not minimize the behavior of the perpetrator no matter how much you would like to believe that it is all a big mistake. Not believing or minimizing the child's experience only re-victimizes the child and will destroy the child/father relationship.

If you learn that your child was abused, it is imperative that the child be taken to therapy as soon as possible. Children who have been abused and subjected to sex at an early age may very well sexually abuse other children. This may not be in an attempt to harm the other child, but sex is a learned behavior. Once a child has been subjected to sex, it is very difficult to stop that behavior.

Most children who were molested as a child do not become child molesters. However, most child molesters were molested as a child. The best treatment to keep the child from becoming a molester himself/herself is psychotherapy. The sooner the intervention, the better the results.

Keep your children safe. Know who their friends are and know their parents. Do not let a child spend the night at a friend's house unless you are very sure that the child knows what to do if something should happen, even by another child. Be more cautious with daughters, but remember that boys are sexually abused as well. Also, more often than not, boys will *not* talk about it. On the other hand, try not to be paranoid. But if you feel something is not quite right (and you may be wrong), go with your gut instinct just the same. It is better to be safe than sorry.

NOT BEING MARRIED TO A CHILD'S MOTHER

A note to men who are not married, by choice, to their child's mother. You are already too selfish, immature, and irresponsible to be a good father. This would be a good time to either grow up and do the right thing or be gone from the child's life. It is probably for the best that you stay away from the child and the mother to allow her to find a man who can be a dad. But know that this does not relinquish a man from his financial responsibilities for the child.

When a man is not married to his child's mother, he is demoted to "Mom's boyfriend," and never achieves full dad status. I have acquaintances who have been together for decades and have children together but never married. The mother will inevitably introduce the child's father as "my boyfriend." Most adults will assume that you are not the biological father and merely "Mom's boyfriend." Additionally, any respect that you had from acquaintances prior to learning that you are not married to your children's mother has all just been lost. There is a gigantic difference between being "Mom's boyfriend" and a husband.

Realize that being married to a child's mother is crucial to the well-being of the child and to the parental relationship. If a man cannot make a commitment to the mother of his child, how can he make a commitment to her child – much less be a dad? If a man cannot make a commitment to his child's mother, how could he possibly be able to experience the intimacy that comes with being married and expect to emulate the intimacy and security to his child?

When two people marry and make a commitment for life, the intimacy between the two increases significantly. Those who are not married may not understand this, but there is a huge difference between being married and just co-habitating. This difference is manifested within your children. How would it feel if a child introduced his father as "my mom's boyfriend"? Hundreds of times I have heard adolescents say, "My parents aren't married – they just live together." It makes the child feel out of place and insecure in the family dynamic, and once again, it also reduces the father to nothing more than "Mom's boyfriend."

There is a connotation that goes along with a man who fathers children, lives with the children's mother, but does not marry her. Often, and I have yet to figure out why, the mother of the child gives the child the father's last name, or even names the child after the father. A man who does not marry the child's mother should not have the child named after him. Who in their right mind wants to be branded with a name of the man who did not have the decency to marry his mother? In addition, all too often, the parents separate, and the child is left with a name different from his mother's. When these unmarried parents separate, the child is then left with a name that reminds the mother every single day of the man that she, in all likelihood, despises. This just might put some additional stress on the child and the mother/child relationship.

Unfortunately, the decision to have a child is not always a planned event. When this occurs, there is little that can be done but to man up and do what has to be done. Children will change your life. If a man is not ready for that, it is best not to have children. The only way to ensure that a man does not father a child is to not have sex. Any male old enough to ejaculate can sire a child but it takes a man to be a dad. If one is not man enough to be a good father, it is best to leave the task to someone who is.

KEY CHAPTER POINTS

1. Keep in mind that when a dad stops an inappropriate behavior that has been occurring for years, the children may be skeptical that the behavior is really changed. This is especially true if the behavior has been stopped before, only to reappear.

2. One can tell when they have a problem. This is by coming to the realization that they do not have control over the problem, instead the problem has control over them.

3. When a dad changes, he usually starts to feel good about his newfound freedom from bondage, and he must be patient and kind to his children in order for them to feel free as well.

4. Anger is fear. The angriest man you have ever knew is afraid that others will see him for the unworthy person he believes he is.

5. When a man gets angry, reason no longer applies, and the damage that is done to a father's children who witness an angry dad can be devastating.

6. Angry people often misinterpret the actions of others as hostile when that is not the intent. When an angry person acts upon those misinterpretations in violent ways, life-changing events may occur.

7. People have a great deal more respect for those who overcome adversity with a fighting spirit rather than a fighting mouth.

8. It is nearly impossible to be reared in an environment of addiction or substance abuse and not suffer from the effects. In many cases, this is true even after the addiction has ceased.

9. It is difficult for Dad to keep his child from a behavior in which Dad engages, regardless of the age of the child and regardless of the frequency of the behavior.

10. Male children who witness domestic violence are seven times more likely to abuse their own wives. They are also six times more likely to sexually abuse their own children.

11. Forty-seven percent of families surveyed reported that pornography is a problem in their home. This includes the parents viewing pornography or trying to keep the children from viewing pornography. Also, 90% of children between the ages of eight and sixteen have viewed pornography on the Internet, with most of these viewings being *unintentional*.

12. Children who communicate in methods that are not face-to-face have diminished social and communication skills. This is also true for adults.

13. Children who have been sexually abused have a six times greater chance of being re-abused by another perpetrator than someone who has not been abused.

14. Most children who were molested as a child do not become child molesters. However, most child molesters were molested as a child.

15. If a man cannot make a commitment to a child's mother, how can he make a commitment to the child?

16. While certain types of inappropriate behavior (such as alcoholism or domestic violence) are taking place, the children often *seem* to be faring well. However, it is not unusual that children start to exhibit emotional and behavioral problems *after* the parents' inappropriate behavior seems to be under control.

18

A Final Note

It is never too late to be a good father. Regardless of how old a man's children are, the principles contained in these pages will help improve any relationship a man has. I do not know a single father who does not look back at being a parent without some degree of regret. That regret does not have to continue, and any contention between a man and his children can be turned around into a healthy relationship. It is much easier to apologize for things that did not go right than it is to make excuses for them.

My first son was born when his mother and I were sixteen years old. Twenty-one months later, after I had been in the Air Force for over a year, we had twin boys. Six months later, I was transferred overseas and she and I drifted apart. She remarried and eventually moved with the three boys from California to Minnesota. My eldest son now lives near me in California but the twins set up their lives in Minnesota. They come out to visit, and my wife Carla and I go out there to visit them.

Last year, during one of the twins' trips to California, we all went to Laughlin, Nevada for the weekend. Carla rode with her brother in his truck, and the three boys and I drove in my truck. On the way out there, they were talking about their stepfather who had passed over twenty years ago. They were joking about the way that they were disciplined and how punitive he could be. When things settled down, I apologized to them for being treated that way. One of the twins said, "It's not your fault, Dad."

I responded by saying, "I apologize just the same."

"You don't need to apologize, you weren't even there."

"That's what I'm apologizing for. Not being there."

Regret can be a horrible thing. Try not to let it eat you up. Make no excuses but explain how stupid you have been; apologize and get on with being a dad. Regardless of how old a child is, he or she still wants to have a good relationship with his or her father.

As I wrote earlier, there will be times when a father's love is not enough to keep a marriage and a family together. Those are times when a man needs to continue to do the right thing and be calm, consistent, caring, and concerned.

Being a father is full-time job. One that must be integrated with a man's worklife, hobbies, friends, aspirations, and his family. A father must put his wants and needs second to those of his wife and his children. A husband/father's love and the way that he interacts and treats his wife and children have the influence to overcome significant obstacles. A husband has the influence to keep a marriage from coming apart in that women are naturally born to care and love for their loved ones. When a husband satisfies his wife's needs, she will, in all likelihood, respond in a manner in which her husband will really appreciate.

THE MOST CHALLENGING THING A MAN WILL EVER DO

As I've noted a number of times in this book, being a good father can be the most challenging thing a man will ever do. Meanwhile, his influence over those who love him is far-reaching and everlasting. A dad is someone who his children should be able to come to when things are going well and when they are not. A dad is someone who a child should feel secure and safe with and be able to tell him her most secret thoughts without fear. A dad who loves his child and shows it in the way that he behaves toward his wife and children will have a positive influence on his family more so than anyone else.

Just Be a Dad

The secret of being a good dad is to be all the things that you have just read about. The only caveat is that you cannot just read the words and so deceive yourself that you're done; do what the book says. I know you love your family. Now go and act like it. Always remember, love is patient... love is kind.

References

Ainsworth, M. (1989) "Attachments beyond infancy." *American Psychologist, 44*, 709-716.

Ainsworth, M., Blehar, M., Waters, E. & Wall, S. (1978) *Patterns of attachment: A psychological study of the strange situation.* Hillsdale, NJ: Lawrence Erlbaum Associates.

Aldous, J. & Mulligan, G.M. (2002) "Fathers' childcare and children's behavior problems: A longitudinal study." *Journal of Family Issues, 23*, 624-647.

Allen, J.P., Marsh, P., McFarland, C., McElhaney, K.B., Land, D.J., Jodi, K.M. & Peck, S. (2002) "Attachment and autonomy as predictors of the development of social skills and delinquency during mid-adolescence." *Journal of Consulting and Clinical Psychology, 70,* 56-66.

Amato, P.R. (1994) "Father-child relations, mother-child relations, and offspring: Psychological well-being in early adulthood." *Journal of Marriage and the Family, 56*, 1031-1041.

Amato, P.R. (1998) "More than money? Men's contributions to their children's lives." In A. Booth & A.C. Crouter (Eds.) *Men in families: When do they get involved? What difference does it make?* Mahwah, NJ: Lawrence Erlbaum Associates.

Amato, P.R. & Booth, A. (2001) "The legacy of parents' marital discord: Consequences for children's marital quality." *Journal of Personality and Social Psychology, 81*, 627-638.

Andrews, J.A., Hops, H., Ary, D., Tildesley, C. & Harris, J. (1993) "Parental influence on early adolescent substance use: Specific and nonspecific effects." *Journal of Early Adolescence, 13,* 285-310.

Arbona, C. & Power, T.G. (2003) "Parental attachment, self-esteem, and antisocial behaviors among African American, European American, and Mexican American adolescents." *Journal of Counseling Psychology, 50*, 40-51.

Armsden, G.C. & Greenberg, M.T. (1987) "The Inventory of Parent and Peer attachment: Individual differences and their relationship to psychological well-being in adolescence." *Journal of Youth and Adolescence, 16,* 427-454.

Arnett, J.J. (2000) "Emerging adulthood: A theory of development from the late teens through the twenties." *American Psychologist, 55,* 469-480.

Bandura, A. (1977) *Social learning theory.* Upper Saddle River, NJ: Prentice Hall.

Bandura, A. (1982) "Self-efficacy mechanisms in human agency." *American Psychologist, 37,* 122-147.

Belsky, J. (1998) "Paternal influence and children's well-being: Limits of, and new directions for, understanding." In A. Booth & A.C. Crouter (Eds.), *Men in families* (pp. 279-293). Mahwah, NJ: Erlbaum.

Bendell-Estroff, D.B., Shiota, L., Monseratt, L., Hill, L. & Del La Rosa L. (2008, August) *Family issues: Conduct disordered and conduct exemplary fourth grade boys.* Poster session presented at the meeting of the American Psychological Association Conference, Boston, MA.

Ben-Zur, H. (2003) "Happy adolescents: The link between subjective well-being, internal resources and parental factors." *Journal of Youth and Adolescence, 32,* 67-79.

Berger, K.S. (2001) *The developing person through the life span.* (5th ed.). New York: Worth.

Biller, H.B. (1993) *Fathers and families: Paternal factors in child development.* Westport, CT: Auburn House.

Bowlby, J. (1958) "The nature of the child's tie to his mother." *International Journal of Psychoanalysis, 39,* 350-373.

Bowlby, J. (1988) *A secure base: Parent-child attachment and healthy human development.* New York: Basic Books.

Brody, G.H., Moore, K. & Glei, D. (1994) "Family processes during adolescence as predictors of parent-young adult attitude similarity: A six-year longitudinal analysis." *Family Relations, 43,* 369-373.

Buchanan, C.M., Maccoby, R.E. & Dornbusch, S.M. (1996) *Adolescents after divorce.* Cambridge, MA: Harvard University Press.

Buist, K.L., Deković, M., Meeus, W.H. & Van Aken, M.A.G.
(2004) "Attachment in adolescence: A social relations model analysis." *Journal of Adolescent Research, 19*, 826-850.

Cave, G.A. (2010) "Maternal and paternal differential attachment associations and inpatient adolescent psychological well-being." *UMI/ProQuest.*

Coleman, P. (2003) "Perceptions of parent-child attachment, social self-efficacy, and peer relationships in middle childhood." *Infant and Child Development, 12*, 351-368.

Coleman, P. & Watson, A. (2000) "Infant attachment as a dynamic system." *Human Development, 43*, 295-314.

Coley, R.L. (1998) "Children's socialization experiences and functioning in single-mother households: The importance of fathers and other men." *Child Development, 69*, 219-230.

Coley, R.L. (2001) "(In)visible men: Emerging research on low-income, unmarried, and minority fathers." *American Psychologist, 56,* 743-753.

Cooksey, E.C. & Fondell, M.M. (1996) "Spending time with his kids: Effect of family structure on father's and children's lives." *Journal of Marriage and the Family, 58*, 693-707.

Cozzarelli, C., Karafa, J.A., Collins, N.L. & Tagler, M.J. (2003) "Stability and change in adult attachment styles: Associations with personal vulnerabilities, life events, and global construals of self and others." *Journal of Social & Clinical Psychology, 22,* 315-346.

Crockett, L.J., Eggebeen, D.J. & Hawkins, A.J. (1993) "Father's presence and young children's behavioral and cognitive adjustment." *Family Relations, 14*, 355-377.

Davies, P.T., Myers, R.L., Cummings, E.M. & Heindel, S.
(1999) "Adult conflict history and children's subsequent responses to conflict: An experimental test." *Journal of Family Psychology, 13*, 610-628.

Deković, M. (1999) "Risk and protective factors in the development of problem behavior during adolescence." *Journal of Youth and Adolescence, 28*, 667-684.

Deković, M. & Meeus, W. (1997) "Peer relations in adolescence: Effects of parenting and adolescents' self-concept." *Journal of Adolescence, 20*, 163-176.

DeWolff, M.S. & van Ijzendoorn, M.H. (1997) "Sensitivity and attachment: A meta-analysis on parental antecedents of infant attachment." *Child Development, 68,* 571-591.

Ducharme, J., Doyle, A.B. & Markiewicz, D. (2002) "Attachment security with mother and father: Associations with adolescents' reports of interpersonal behavior with parents and peers." *Journal of Social & Personal Relationships, 19,* 203-231.

Elkind, D. (2001) "The Hurried Child." (3rd Edition) Cambridge, MA. Perseus Publishing.

Engels, R.C.M.E., Finkenauer, C., Meeus, W. & Deković, M. (2001) "Parental attachment and adolescents' emotional adjustment: The associations with social skills and relational competence." *Journal of Counseling Psychology, 48,* 428-439.

Erikson, E.H. (1982) *The life cycle completed.* New York: W.W. Norton.

Forehand, R. & Nousiainen, S. (1993) "Maternal and paternal Parenting." *Critical Dimensions in Adolescent Functioning, 7,* 213-221.

Furstenberg, F.F., Jr., Morgan, S.P. & Allison, P.D. (1987). "Paternal participation and children's well-being after marital dissolution." *American Sociological Review, 52,* 695-701.

Goleman, D. (1995). Emotional Intelligence. NY. Bantam.

Gomez, R. & McLaren, S. (2007) "The inter-relations of mother and father attachment, self-esteem and aggression during late adolescence." *Aggressive Behavior, 33,* 160-169.

Gottman, J.M. (1997) "Raising an emotionally healthy child. NY. Simon & Schuster.

Gottman, J.M. (1998) "Toward a process model of men in marriages and families." In A. Booth & A.C. Crouter (Eds.), *Men in families: When do they get involved? What difference does it make?* (pp. 149-192). Mahwah, NJ: Erlbaum.

Harper, S.E. & Fine, M.A. (2006) "The effects of involved nonresidential fathers' distress, parenting behaviors, inter-parental conflict, and the quality of father-child relationships on children's well-being." *Fathering, 4,* 286-299.

Hayashi, B.M. & Strickland, B.R. (1998) "Long-term effects of parental divorce on love relationships: Divorce as attachment disruption." *Journal of Social and Personal Relationships, 15,* 23-38.

Hazan, C. & Shaver, P. (1987) "Romantic love conceptualized as an attachment process." *Journal of Personality and Social Psychology, 52,* 511-524.

Hoffman, M.A., Ushpiz, V. & Levy-Shiff, R. (1988) "Social support and self-esteem in adolescence." *Journal of Youth and Adolescence, 17,* 307-316.

Horesh, N. & Apter, A. (2006) "Self-disclosure, depression, anxiety, and suicidal behavior in adolescent psychiatric inpatients." *Crisis, 27,* 66-71.

Imam, S.S. (2007) "Sherer et al., General Self-Efficacy Scale: Dimensionality, internal consistency, and temporal stability." *Proceedings of the Redesigning Pedagogy: Culture, Knowledge and Understanding Conference,* Singapore, May 2007.

Kalat, J.W. (2000) *Biological psychology: Introduction to behavioral neuroscience.* Pacific Grove, CA: Brooks/Cole.

Karen, R. (1994) *Becoming attached.* Oxford, CT: Oxford University Press.

Kenny, M.E. (1994) "Quality and correlates of parental attachment among late adolescents." *Journal of Counseling and Development, 72,* 399-403.

Kenny, M. E. & Gallagher, L.A. (2002) "Instrumental and social/relational correlates of perceived maternal and paternal attachment in adolescence." *Journal of Adolescence, 25,* 203-219.

Kenny, M.E., Lomax, R., Brabeck, M. & Fife, J. (1998). "Longitudinal pathways linking adolescent reports of maternal and paternal attachment to psychological well-being." *Journal of Early Adolescence, 18,* 221-243.

Kenny, M.E. & Sirin, S.R. (2006) "Parental attachment, self-worth, and depressive symptoms among emerging adults." *Journal of Counseling & Development, 84,* 61-71

Laible, J.J. & Carlo, G. (2004) "The differential relations of maternal and paternal support and control to adolescent social competence, self-worth, and sympathy." *Journal of Adolescent Research, 19,* 759-782.

Lamb, M.E. & Tamis-Lemonda, C. (2004) "The role of father." In
    M.E. Lamb (Ed.). *The role of the father in child development* (4th
    ed., pp. 1-31.) New York: Wiley.

LeCroy, C.W. (1988) "Parent-adolescent intimacy: Impact on adolescent
    functioning." *Adolescence, 23*, 137-147.

Lei, L. & Wu, Y. (2007) "Adolescents' paternal attachment and
    Internet use." *CyberPsychology & Behavior, 10*, 633-639.

Leondari, A. & Kiosseoglou, G. (2002) "Parental, psychological
    control and attachment in late adolescents and young adults."
    Psychological Reports, 90, 1015-1030.

Love, K.M., & Murdock, T.B. (2004) "Attachment to parents and
    psychological well-being: An examination of young adult college
    students in intact families and stepfamilies." *Journal of Family
    Psychology, 18*, 600-608.

Mackey, W.C. (2001) "Support for the existence of an independent
    man-to-child affiliative bond: Fatherhood as a biocultural
    invention." *Psychology of Men & Masculinity, 2*, 51-66.

Main, M. & Weston, D.R. (1981) "The quality of the toddler's
    relationship to mother and to father: Related to conflict behavior
    and the readiness to establish new relationships." *Child
    Development, 52*, 932-940.

Mallinckrodt, B., Cobel, H. & Ganti, D.L. (1995) "Working alliance,
    attachment memories, and social competencies of women in brief
    therapy." *Journal of Counseling Psychology, 42*, 79-84.

Markiewicz, D., Lawford, H., Boyle, A.B. & Haggart, N. (2006)
    "Developmental differences in adolescents and young adults'
    use of mothers, fathers, best friends, and romantic partners to
    fulfill attachment needs." *Journal of Youth and Adolescence, 35*,
    127-140.

McCormick, C.B., & Kennedy, J.H. (1994) "Parent-child
    attachment working models and self-esteem in adolescence."
    Journal of Youth and Adolescence, 23, 1-18.

McCormick, C.B., & Kennedy, J.H. (2000) "Father-child
    separation, retrospective and current views of attachment
    relationship with father, and self-esteem in late adolescence."
    Psychological Reports, 86, 827-834.

McWhorter, N., Doig, H.M., McHale, T., Dobroth, J.E., and Soper, H.V. (2006) "A Program for Reducing Recidivism in the Juvenile Justice System." *Abstracts of the 86th Annual Convention of the Western Psychological Association, 197.*

Noom, M.J., Dekovic, M. & Meeus, W.H.J. (1999) "Autonomy, attachment, and psychosocial adjustment during adolescence: A double-edged sword?" *Journal of Adolescence, 22,* 771-783.

Orth, U., Robins, R.W. & Roberts, B.W. (2008) "Low self-esteem prospectively predicts depression in adolescence and young adulthood." *Journal of Personality and Social Psychology, 95,* 695-708.

Overbeek, G., Vollebergh, W., Engels, R.C.M.E. & Meeus, W. (2003) "Parental attachment and romantic relationships: Associations with emotional disturbance during late adolescence." *Journal of Counseling Psychology, 50,* 28-39.

Paterson, J., Pryor, J. & Field, J. (1995). "Adolescent attachment to parents and friends in relation to aspects of self-esteem." *Journal of Youth and Adolescence, 24,* 365-377.

Pleck, J.H. (1997) "Paternal involvement: Level, sources, and consequences." In M.E. Lamb (Ed.), *The role of the father in child development* (3rd ed., pp. 66-103) New York: Wiley.

Pleck, J.H. (2007) "Why could father involvement benefit children? Theoretical perspectives." *Applied Development Science, 11,* 196-202.

Radin, N. & Russell, G. (1983) "Increased father participation and child development outcomes." In M. Lamb & A. Sagi (Ed.), *Fatherhood and social policy* (pp. 191-218). Hillsdale, NJ: Lawrence Erlbaum.

Rice, K.G. & Cummins, P.N. (1996) "Late adolescent and parent perceptions of attachment: An exploratory study of personal and social well-being." *Journal of Counseling & Development, 75,* 50-57.

Rohner, R.P. & Veneziano, R.A. (2001) "The importance of father love: History and contemporary evidence." *Review of General Psychology, 4,* 382-405.

Ronnlund, M. & Karlsson, L. (2006) "The relation between dimensions of attachment and internalizing and externalizing problems during adolescence." *Journal of Genetic Psychology, 167,* 47-63.

Rosenstein, D.S. & Horowitz, H.A. (1996) "Adolescent attachment and psychopathology." *Journal of Consulting and Clinical Psychology, 64*, 244-253.

Sarason, I.G. & Sarason, B.R. (2002) *Abnormal psychology: The problem of maladaptive behavior* (10th ed.). Upper Saddle River, NJ: Prentice Hall.

Shaw, S.K. & Dallos, R. (2005) "Attachment and adolescent depression: The impact of early attachment experiences." *Attachment & Human Development, 7*, 409-424.

Simons, K.J., Paternite, C.E. & Shore, C. (2001) "Quality of parent/adolescent attachment and aggression in young adolescents." *Journal of Early Adolescence, 21*, 182-199.

Spence, S.H., Sheffield, J.K., & Donovan, C.L. (2003) "Preventing adolescent depression: An evaluation of the problem solving for life program." *Journal of Consulting and Clinical Psychology, 71*, 3-13.

Stewart, S.D. (2003) "Nonresident parenting and adolescent adjustment: The quality of nonresident father-child interaction." *Journal of family issues, 24*, 217-244.

Stivers, C. (1988) "Parent-adolescent communication and its relationship to adolescent depression and suicide proneness." *Adolescence, 23*, 291-295.

Veneziano, R. (2000) "Perceived paternal and maternal warmth and African American and European American youths' psychological adjustment." *Journal of Marriage and the Family, 62*, 123-132.

Verschueren, K. & Marcoen, A. (1999) "Representation of self and socioemotional competence in kindergartners: Differential and combined effects of attachment to mother and father." *Child Development, 70*, 183-201.

Waters, E., Wippman, J. & Sroufe, L.A. (1979) "Attachment, positive affect, and competence in the peer group: Two studies in construct validation." *Child Development, 50*, 821-829.

Weinfield, N.A., Whaley, G.J.L. & Egeland, B. (2004) "Continuity, discontinuity, and coherence in attachment from infancy to late adolescence: Sequelae of organization and disorganization." *Attachment & Human Development, 6*, 73-97.

Willetts, M.C. & Maroules, N.G. (2004) "Does remarriage matter? The well-being of adolescents living with cohabitating versus remarried mothers." *Journal of Divorce and Remarriage, 41,* 115-133.

Williams, E. & Radin, N. (1999) "Effects of father participation in child rearing: Twenty-year follow-up." *American Journal of Orthopsychiatry, 69,* 328-336.

Dedication

This endeavor is dedicated to my Father in heaven, who watches over everything I have ever done and ever will do, in whom all things are possible. I thank my Lord Jesus Christ for providing me with a supportive and encouraging family as well as the opportunity, strength, and ability to accomplish this very important work.

Acknowledgements

I am very thankful and relieved to have come to a place in this project where I can take the opportunity to thank the many people who have made the completion of this work possible.

First and utmost, I would like to thank my wife and best friend, Carla, who has stood by my side and has given me love and endless support throughout this entire endeavor. Second, I would like to thank my children, all eight of whom have believed in, supported, and encouraged me to completion. Along with them, I thank the many people who helped me with my myriad of questions, technical support, and tutelage that was, and continues to be, life-changing.

Next, I would like to extend my thanks to psychiatrist and psychoanalyst Dr. Ronald Sager, who more than any other single person contributed to my understanding of human behavior and understanding of psychology and that things are not always as they appear.

Finally, this book would not have been possible if it were not for all the professors and researchers that have come before me. Without their contributions to the field of psychology, psychiatry, and the understanding of human behavior, this book would not have been possible.

INDEX

Tignor Publishing

Quick Order Form

Telephone Orders: 805-501-9429
Fax Orders: 805-624-7956 (Include this form.)
Email: orders@TignorPublishing.com
Web Order: http://www.JustBeADad.com

Mail Postal Orders to:
Tignor Publishing
1230-5 Madera Road #211, Simi Valley, CA 93065

To order additional copies of **Just Be a Dad: Things My Father Never Told Me**, complete the information below.

Ship to: (Please print clearly.)

Name_____

Address_____

City, State, Zip_____
—

Day Phone_____
___

_____ Copies of *Just Be a Dad* @ $28.00 each $_____
(Shipping and handling included in pricing.)
California residents add $8.25% tax ($2.31 per book) $_____

Total enclosed $_____

Method of payment: ☐Check / Credit Card: ☐MasterCard ☐Visa

Card Number:_____ Exp Date_____

CPC # (3 digit number on back of card): _____

Card-holders signature:_____

Make checks payable to: Tignor Publishing.

Tignor Publishing

Quick Order Form

Telephone Orders: 805-501-9429
Fax Orders: 805-624-7956 (Include this form.)
Email: orders@TignorPublishing.com
Web Orders: http://www.JustBeADad.com

Mail Postal Orders to:
Tignor Publishing
1230-5 Madera Road #211, Simi Valley, CA 93065

To order additional copies of *Just Be a Dad: Things My Father Never Told Me*, complete the information below.

Ship to: (Please print clearly.)

Name_____

Address_____

City, State, Zip_____

Day Phone_____

_____ Copies of *Just Be a Dad* @ $28.00 each $_____
(Shipping and handling included in pricing.)
California residents add $8.25% tax ($2.31 per book) $_____

Total enclosed $_____

Method of payment: ☐Check / Credit Card: ☐MasterCard ☐Visa

Card Number:_____Exp. Date_____

CPC # (3 digit number on back of card): _____

Card-holders signature:_____

Make checks payable to: Tignor Publishing

Just Be a Dad